# Public-Private Partnerships, Capital Infrastructure Project Investments and Infrastructure Finance

# Public-Private Partnerships, Capital Infrastructure Project Investments and Infrastructure Finance: Public Policy for the 21st Century

**JANE BECKETT-CAMARATA**

*Pennsylvania State University-Harrisburg, USA*

emerald
PUBLISHING

United Kingdom – North America – Japan – India – Malaysia – China

Emerald Publishing Limited
Howard House, Wagon Lane, Bingley BD16 1WA, UK

First edition 2020



**British Library Cataloguing in Publication Data**
A catalogue record for this book is available from the British Library

ISBN: 978-1-83909-655-6 (Print)
ISBN: 978-1-83909-654-9 (Online)
ISBN: 978-1-83909-656-3 (Epub)

Printed and bound by CPI Group (UK) Ltd, Croydon, CR0 4YY

ISOQAR
REGISTERED
Certificate Number 1985
ISO 14001

ISOQAR certified Management System, awarded to Emerald for adherence to Environmental standard ISO 14001:2004.

INVESTOR IN PEOPLE

# Table of Contents

## Part 4 Infrastructure Finance Policy Implementation Practices

# About the Author

Dr Beckett-Camarata teaches in the Penn State Harrisburg PhD and Master's program in public administration. Her finance teaching interests include public–private partnerships, government revenue systems, public financial management, budgeting, capital budgeting, infrastructure finance, cost accounting, and governmental accounting and managerial accounting. Dr Beckett-Camarata was a recipient of a Lilly Foundation Scholar Award for the advancement of teaching excellence. She has taught university courses in Russia and was a Fulbright Scholar at Kharhiv National University in Kharkiv, Ukraine, where she taught economic development finance. While at the University of North Wales, Bangor, Wales, she researched the impact of the European Union on bank regulation.

Dr Beckett-Camarata has authored many articles and book chapters. Her work has been published in the *Public Productivity and Management Review*, *Journal of Budgeting, Accounting and Financial Management*, *Municipal Finance Journal*, *International Journal of Public Administration*, *American Review of Public Administration*, *Journal of Business Research*, Handbook of Public Sector Economics and Handbook of Globalization, and Governance and Public Administration. She was the recipient of the Baruch College, CUNY distinguished Municipal Leadership and Finance Award, which funded her 2005 summer research on changes in New York City's pension fund infrastructure during fiscal crisis.

As a former chief financial officer in the Commonwealth of Virginia, Dr Beckett-Camarata managed operating and capital budgets, financial accounting and reporting, and revenue forecasting and public–private partnerships. She was instrumental in integrating the strategic plan into the budget and accounting system and establishing and integrating financial performance measures.

She serves as an expert reviewer for the Government Finance Officers Association and as an expert witness for the US Federal Court System in government budgeting. She also serves on the editorial board of several academic journals.

Dr Beckett-Camarata is active in professional organizations including the American Society for Public Administration, where she has served as cochair of the Finance Committee, Executive Council, and Audit Committee; Association for Budgeting and Financial Management, where she has served on the Board of Directors, the Program Committee, and the Curro Award Committee; National

Association of Schools of Public Affairs and Administration, where she has served on site visit teams and on the Commission on Peer Review and Accreditation; the Government Finance Officers Association; and numerous other organizations.

Dr Beckett-Camarata received a PhD in public policy and administration from Virginia Commonwealth University (1998); Master of Public Administration from the American University (1989); and Bachelor of Science degree with a concentration in Finance from Syracuse University (1983).

# Introduction

This book examines the use of Public–Private Partnerships (PPPs) in the context of capital infrastructure investment and infrastructure finance policy implementation. The decision to use PPPs should be framed and considered within the context of infrastructure finance policy, especially for Emerging Market Economies. In this regard, the use of PPPs can be seen more broadly as an efficient and effective public policy tool.

Governments worldwide are becoming increasingly more dependent on infrastructure finance policy to implement capital improvements planning. They typically identify one or more financing options in their infrastructure finance policy, including the use of PPPs and concomitant capital infrastructure investment. PPPs are a form of institutional arrangement between the public and private sectors (Hodge & Greve, 2016) for increased private sector involvement in the delivery of capital infrastructure. PPPs may be among the best option for delivering a completed capital infrastructure, especially with complex capital infrastructure involving more than basic construction and financing (Gross, 2018). Long-term Infrastructure Finance Policy should be the basis for capital infrastructure investment, capital improvements planning and financing and acquisition (Beckett-Camarata, 2019), and to achieve capital infrastructure finance policy goals. To date, there has been insufficient recognition of the importance of Infrastructure Finance Policy and capital improvement planning in identifying potential uses of PPPs (Beckett-Camarata, 2019). This lack of recognition is because the Infrastructure Finance Policy implementation phase includes a number of complex steps including comprehensive and strategic planning, capital needs assessment, project cost estimation, project priority ranking, and capital improvements planning (Bunch, 2013; Marlowe, Rivenbark, & Vogt, 2009; Millar, 1988; Srithongrung, 2018; Steiss, 2005; Vogt, 2004). Although much is written on various aspects of PPPs, this book is important because it integrates Infrastructure Finance Policy, the selection of PPPs to finance and deliver an infrastructure capital project as a policy option, and a unified and comprehensive Capital Management and Budgeting system to manage the PPP from a public policy planning and implementation perspective.

Thus, this book introduces a new lens to look at Infrastructure Finance Policy as a policy instrument with which to achieve long-term national and subnational finance policy objectives. It incorporates the identification, selection, implementation, and evaluation of PPPs within the framework of strategic infrastructure finance policy objectives and the capital improvements planning process. The book is unique in that it introduces the need to implement and evaluate the adoption of PPPs within the context of long-term capital investment and capital improvements planning and as a critical aspect of effective long-term infrastructure finance policy. With the incorporation of new market-oriented approaches to infrastructure finance policy decision-making in the public sector, there is a greater emphasis on economy and efficiency in order to deliver public services at the lowest cost (Osborne, 2002). However, additionally, there is a critical need to implement and evaluate the effectiveness of Infrastructure Finance Policy implementation. Governments may choose to finance some or all capital infrastructure investment and also use private sector expertise and efficiency (The World Bank, 2018a, 2018b) through PPPs to finance and deliver capital infrastructure.

# Part 1
# Overview of Public–Private Partnerships as Public Policy

The role of capital infrastructure as a positive contribution to government economic growth and quality of life is a well-known fact. For a long time, many governments were able to adequately finance capital infrastructure, although they were not able to meet total need and demand. Beginning in the 1970s, escalating during the 1990s energy crises, and even more pronounced in the 2008 global financial crisis, many countries, and especially emerging economies, were not able to sufficiently finance new capital infrastructure and/or repair or replace existing capital infrastructure. Increasing demographic changes and demands for new capital infrastructure exacerbated the existing imbalance between demand and supply, especially in developing countries. Also, government responses to growing fiscal crises led to budget cuts, deferral of capital infrastructure maintenance, and under-investment in new capital infrastructure. The decrease in quality of capital infrastructure such as roads and bridges, are evidence of inadequate funding for maintenance of existing capital infrastructure, building new or replacing existing capital infrastructure, resulting in the stunting of economic growth and the deterioration of the quality of life. Consequently, few countries can adequately finance ongoing capital infrastructure needs and demands without private sector involvement through some form of PPP, as an infrastructure finance policy option. On its own, the private sector will either under invest in capital infrastructure or fail to invest in capital infrastructure that are not socially optimal (Helm, Wardlaw, & Caldecott 2009) or a clear, low-risk profit partner.

As a result of this greater government need for private sector partnership in delivering certain capital infrastructure, governments increasingly must now work ever more closely with the private sector (Silvestre & Arujo, 2012). Consequently, many governments are becoming even more dependent on the private sector in the implementation of public policies (Wang et al., 2018) such as Infrastructure Finance Policy. This is especially critical for capital infrastructure investment since it is the foundation of a government's economic activity (Kumari & Sharma, 2016). The basic functions of a country are dependent on adequate capital infrastructure to provide essential services.

Chapter 1

# Overview of Public–Private Partnerships

Public–private partnerships (PPPs) are defined as a range of long-term, formal technical, operational, and financial contractual partnership arrangements between government and the private sector in which the private sector has more participation in capital asset delivery than traditional non-PPP Design-Bid-Build (DBB).

Traditional government capital infrastructure delivery involves the government contracting for and overseeing all aspects of design, construction, operation, and financing, with the private sector involved in a limited, defined manner. Traditional non-PPP government contracting approach to providing capital infrastructure such as highways is known as DBB. It is primarily a government capital asset delivery form, where the subnational government pays for the capital asset with some combination of its own funds, federal government funds, and financing (debt) that is ultimately repaid by revenue from taxes and/or user fees, such as toll revenue in the case of Concessions form of PPP (see page 4 for definition). When traditional capital infrastructure financing is available, a government entity either designs the capital infrastructure in-house or contracts with a private contractor to design it. If a private contractor is used, selection is normally based on the lowest-cost, private contractor bid. The private contractor then delivers the Design phase of the capital infrastructure project. A different private contractor is then secured in a separate bid to build the capital infrastructure such as a highway in the next phase, with the government delivering Operation and Maintenance or it may secure another contract for Operation and Maintenance. Under this type of DBB contract, private contractors have only a limited amount of risk. For example, they can pass-on to the government organization any increase in costs resulting from unforeseen changes in the contract scope. This characteristic of the traditional basic DBB contract increases probability that the private contractor will exceed the contract bid price since they can pass costs on to the government in the next phase of the infrastructure capital project. The government keeps a high degree of control over the capital infrastructure, such as the highway, during its useful life.

The use of a PPP form of capital infrastructure financing and delivery, such as a basic Design-Build (DB), provides for more private sector involvement in financing and delivering capital infrastructure and involves contract bid.

**Public-Private Partnerships, Capital Infrastructure Project Investments and Infrastructure Finance, 3–39**

**doi:10.1108/978-1-83909-654-920201001**

Generally, the private sector finances, designs, and builds the capital asset in one contract bid in the case of a new capital infrastructure delivery. If it involves an existing capital infrastructure that requires construction, the private sector bids for the Operation and Maintenance under one contract, with government financing.

The PPP contractual arrangement to deliver the capital infrastructure can take many forms and different levels of private sector involvement in financing and constructing government-owned capital infrastructure. The long-term PPP contractual relationships are between the government and the private sector, usually a private contractor, may be up to 25–30 years (Hodge, 2014; Hodge & Greve, 2016) or longer in the case of Concession form of PPP (see page 13 for definition). The long-term contractual relationship may also be between a government and a nonprofit entity such as in the case of some service Concession form of PPP agreements, but these are not considered PPPs.

There are many definitions of PPPs (Roehrich, Lewis, & Michael, 2014), and there is variation in the contractual relationship and in the implementation of PPP contracts. This variation in contractual relationship and execution of PPP contracts is especially true in forms of PPP involving separation of capital infrastructure ownership and in identification and separation of risk between the public and private contractors (Roehrich et al., 2014), and depends on the PPP form and partnership contractual relationship. PPPs are defined based on a public–private capital infrastructure financing and delivery continuum (as discussed on page 10), with either more government involvement in delivery or more private contractor involvement in the financing and delivery of capital infrastructure or service based on the location on the continuum. One of the most basic PPP forms is one where the private partner agrees to design and build capital infrastructure on behalf of the public partner to provide capital goods or services for which the public partner is ultimately accountable.

In a PPP contractual arrangement, the public partner enters into the PPP agreement to (1) finance and deliver a capital infrastructure project for which taxpayer resources may not be available in the capital improvement plan (CIP)/ current capital budget, (2) reduce construction or service costs through private sector efficiencies, (3) control the timing of capital expenditures, or (4) a combination of these purposes (DiNapoli, 2014).

## 1.1 Rationale for Public–Private Partnerships as Infrastructure Finance Policy Option

Government capital infrastructure is typically delivered within a standard government procurement process governed by law and regulation in all phases of capital infrastructure construction, such as design, construction, operation, and maintenance. In this standard procurement process, the government owns the infrastructure, but separately contracts for each phase of the capital project, often with different private contractors.

During a traditional capital infrastructure procurement process, government contracts with several private contractors: a private contractor to supply the infrastructure design, and then builds the infrastructure based on the design (which can come from a separate contractor), and then operates and maintains the infrastructure, or goes through a different government procurement process for the operation and maintenance phase. The unique characteristic of a capital infrastructure PPP is that the government enters into only one long-term contract with only one private contractor, as opposed to several different arrangements with multiple private contractors in a traditional non-PPP, government-financed capital infrastructure delivery. The partnership is more efficient for both the government and the private sector. The long-term nature of the PPP contractual relationship allows both partners to be able to plan, budget for, and commit long-term resources to deliver the capital infrastructure.

In a PPP contractual arrangement, the government normally retains ownership of the capital infrastructure. Still, the private contractor is given a much more significant role in capital infrastructure delivery and management, compared to the standard procurement process. In a PPP form of Build-Operate-Maintain, for example, the government contracts with one private contractor to build capital infrastructure and then to operate and maintain the infrastructure for a given number of years in exchange for a revenue stream during the life of the contract, using either user fees or availability payments. In the traditional capital procurement system, the government contracts with many different private contractors, whereas in the PPP, the government is directly contracting with one private contractor, who, in turn, is responsible for completing the capital project. Because the private contractor is fully responsible for delivering the capital infrastructure in PPP, including any cost overruns, the private contractor is more motivated to minimize costs than would the private contractor under the traditional procurement system (Vining & Boardman, 2008).

In addition to private contractor motivation to minimize costs, governments provide more varied core service activities than a private contractor. Governments may have less specialized capital infrastructure delivery expertise in the relevant capital infrastructure activity. The rationale for the government to use PPPs in capital infrastructure delivery is that the private contractor [depending on the private contractor, capital infrastructure delivery, and the financing arrangement] generally can deliver capital infrastructure more efficiently and at a lower cost (Vining & Boardman, 1999). Private contractors have more significant economies of scale and scope typically because the capital infrastructure construction activities private contractors perform are more narrowly focused than core general government activities, which are more complex and more extensive. Also, the private contractor may have more in-depth expertise in certain types of capital construction and operation than the government. The private partner, in some cases, maybe global in scope and thus able to deliver infrastructure internationally rather than only country specific. Governments can benefit by using the private partner's skills and thereby obtaining cost and efficiency gains by partnering with the private partner for the construction and/or management of capital infrastructure (OCED, 2015).

Private contractors, in general, and the PPP capital infrastructure private contractor–partner in particular, are more motivated to maximize profits, as noted above. The private contractor tends to have more efficient capital infrastructure operations and less bureaucratic rules and regulations in the process to deliver a capital infrastructure than the government, such as written, less complex procurement policies and highly skilled procurement expertise. The efficiencies are evident in such dynamic and fluid capital construction situations as there is greater flexibility in contract renegotiation (Vining & Boardman, 2005), for example. Also, the private contractor may have lower employee salary and benefit costs than the public sector (Dosi & Moretto, 2013). Large government capital infrastructure projects frequently cost more than originally budgeted because they are not able to duplicate private contractor efficiencies (Ansar, Flyvberg, Budzier, & Lunn, 2016).

The capital infrastructure cost difference is greater for small local governments [and for developing and emerging market economies], especially for design and construction (Vining & Boardman, 1992) forms of PPPs. As an example, in the case of developing and emerging market economies, such as Albania, securing increased capital infrastructure investment is critical to ensuring that economic growth is commensurate with social needs. The Organization for Economic Cooperation and Development (OECD) has estimated that total global capital infrastructure investment requirements will be 71 trillion USD or about 31.5% of annual world GDP from 2007 to 2030 (Klepsvik, Emery, Finn, & Bernhard, 2014). Governments in these developing and emerging economies cannot afford to finance the closing of these large and growing capital infrastructure gaps solely through tax revenues and grants (Klepsvik et al. 2014). Some mature economies also cannot afford to finance their significant capital infrastructure gaps as well, because of years of underinvestment and tight budgets. Long-term private participation in capital infrastructure provision can help reduce both short-term and long-term financial pressure on government operating and capital budgets.

Because of the need to fill large and growing capital infrastructure gaps, governments may choose to use PPPs for financing and delivery of new construction of physical and social capital infrastructure such as roads, bridges, tunnels, railways, harbors, airports, tramways, subways, irrigation networks, dams and canals, water pipelines, water purification and treatment plants, potable water supply, power lines, power plants, distribution networks, oil and gas pipelines, sanitation and sewage facilities, health and housing services, urban services, communications, and telecommunications networks. These large types of capital infrastructure typically require the involvement of some type of PPP contract arrangement. PPPs are also used by the government to modify, rehabilitate, or expand existing extensive government capital infrastructure or to monetize underperforming capital infrastructure and provide the government budget with additional capital. In that case, the revenue from the government's transferring its inherent right to operate a capital infrastructure (i.e., Concession) must be sufficient to justify the future loss of the infrastructure's ongoing user fee revenue (Uddin & Zack, 2016) to the contracting government.

The phases of a capital infrastructure project usually are comprised of large capital expenditures, often exceeding hundreds of millions of dollars (Newman & Perl, 2014), spread over several years. Depending on the form of PPP contractual arrangement, the government guarantees, either to pay for the capital infrastructure construction or at the other end of the continuum, to allow the private sector contractor to collect fees from users such as in a Concession partnership.

## 1.2 Role of Infrastructure Finance Policy in Infrastructure Delivery

As PPPs have become an increasingly important option in delivering capital infrastructure, and as governments have become more dependent on the private sector to finance capital infrastructure, the focus has become the government's Infrastructure Finance Policy. Infrastructure Finance Policy focuses the decision to either finance a capital infrastructure through the traditional government-financing (using tax exempt bonds, for example) as a policy option or to deliver a capital infrastructure through a PPP (Huge & Jones, 2015).

The Infrastructure Finance Policy choice of a PPP option is (1) to have a more efficient and effective overall capital planning, management, and budgeting program, (2) to provide capital improvements on time and within capital budget, (3) to more effectively manage the use of long-term debt, provide for more enhanced public value, and (4) to provide a better balance between traditional means of funding government capital improvements (long-term debt, equity financing, and capital reserves).

While there are capital infrastructure private partnership investment opportunities available on a global level, private investors in government capital infrastructure often do not fully take advantage of these opportunities, usually because of weak government Infrastructure Finance Policy (Klepsvik et al. 2014). Capital infrastructure investment can pose specific risks to private investors, even under normal circumstances. The choice of using of one single private partner through a PPP arrangement with government under an Infrastructure Finance Policy is a relatively recent basis for capital infrastructure financing and delivery in many countries, Some countries do not have either the necessary basic capital infrastructure in-house contacting expertise for choosing a PPP or experience and capacity to manage the inherent risks involved in complex PPPs. In that case, they need to include training in PPP contract negotiation and implementation as part of their PPP policy. A well-developed Infrastructure Finance Policy can provide a basis to increase the quality and quantity of private investment in infrastructure (Klepsvik et al., 2014) because it spells out the government policy priorities.

At both the national and subnational levels, the link between public Infrastructure Finance Policy and regulatory and institutional frameworks is a basis for mitigating risk and attracting and maintaining private investment in public capital infrastructure. This connection between policy and its institutional frameworks is making public capital infrastructure financing and delivery more attractive for both PPPs and private investment based on the government policy goals of improving government service delivery through both efficiency and effectiveness, facilitating investor access to government land, and setting a level-playing field between government capital infrastructure financing and delivery, private contractors, and private investors. Infrastructure finance policy is implemented through well-developed capital infrastructure plans such as National Infrastructure Plans (such as Mauritius National Plan) or Master Plans at the subnational level. These plans articulate investor protections, formal institutional systems for contract dispute resolution, and clarity concerning circumstances under which contracts are renegotiated (Klepsvik et al., 2014).

## 1.3 Public–Private Partnership Relationships and Public Policy

PPPs involve a combination of both public and private control of rights over property, such as infrastructure or financial residuals, depending on the form of partnership. This combination of public–private control over property rights can significantly increase the complexity of the public–private partner relationship (Weimer & Vining, 2017) throughout the life of the contract. The more widely dispersed the ownership control of a given capital infrastructure, the higher the transaction costs of government effectively monitoring the agents who manage the PPP (Baker, 2016; Weimer & Vining, 2017). The higher transaction cost is especially true regarding the advanced PPP Concession form, which tends to be extraordinarily complex. The division of ownership of property rights in certain more advanced forms of PPPs such as Concessions is more pronounced and complexity increases in part because of the long contract period. This is the case because ownership rights are differentiated, with the government owning the capital infrastructure, but the private partner owning shares of the revenue that the capital infrastructure generates in Concession PPPs.

Clarity of ownership of property control is essential in the context of PPP contract negotiating and monitoring. The clarity of ownership is necessary because of potential capital infrastructure contract problems due to the ambiguity public–private partner ownership rights in some partnerships such as Concessions, and the resulting complexity in those public–private contractual relationships. The contract complexity stemming from ambiguity in ownership rights further opens the door and provides the opportunity for one of the partners to take advantage of the lack of clarity, and shifts risk and benefits more to their position. PPP ownership control are likely to be even more ambiguous because of risks of unanticipated events such as natural disasters that may result in damage to capital infrastructure, inconsistent economic circumstances that change the number of revenue streams or unforeseen technological transformations that reduces costs or renders certain capital infrastructure obsolete (Weimer & Vining, 2017). The need to identify potential PPP contract uncertainties that may also arise in PPP contracting is critical because such lack of clarity can invite opportunistic behavior, especially on the part of the private partner (Weimer & Vining, 2017). This split ownership of infrastructure and division of property rights can create principal–principal problems and principal–agent relationship complexities in the PPP contract relationship.

These principal–principal and principal–agency relationship complexities are compounded because governments work through public agencies to provide public goods that are underserved in the market (market failure). Governments use labor and other input factors to produce outputs, but do not have to create a market test to exist. The extent to which the government agency contributes to efficiency depends on its policies, such as its Infrastructure Finance Policy. The level of monitoring and motivation of those principal representatives who determine agency budgets and lead their organizations is also important. This principal–agent problem, discussed in Chapter 2, stems from the fact that employers and employees do not necessarily have the same interests, and it is costly to monitor the behavior of employees. Government employers operate in an environment of information asymmetry (Epstein & O'Halloran, 1999). The agent is in a better position to know the minimum transaction cost of producing a given level of output than either the public or their representatives (principals) who determine the agency budget (Weimer & Vining, 2017).

In the market, a transaction between two parties is mediated by price, and competition provides a basis for an equitable exchange transaction. A transaction cost is the cost of any activity engaged in to satisfy each party to an exchange transaction. As a result, the perceived value is given and received in agreement with the exchange parties' expectations (Pongsiri, 2001), such as a PPP contract. Transaction costs, discussed more fully in Chapter 2, are the result of the imperfections in the exchange environment in which information is incomplete or where one party may seek to promote its interests at the expense of others by engaging in opportunistic behavior (Williamson, 1981). The demand for equity is the basis of transaction cost, and equity is one of the essential elements in determining the nature of organizational activities (Ouchi, 1980).

Transaction Cost Theory helps inform understanding of the factors that make it more efficient to enter into either traditional capital contracts or nontraditional contractual partnership relationships (such as PPPs) (Joskow, 1991), and is the case with New York State PPP contracting. The basis of Transaction Cost Theory is the identification of the sources of transaction costs, which may make the transaction, such as PPP transactions, more expensive. Transaction costs include precontracting, contracting, and negotiating costs, as well as after-contract costs such as monitoring, renegotiating, and project close-out costs. These costs can be borne by the public partner, the private partner, or both. Regardless of who bears the cost, they are costs that must be taken into consideration in determining the total transaction cost of the PPP contract (Vining & Boardman, 2005). Infrastructure Finance Policy is the strategic basis for guiding the decision on the most efficient and effective option for capital infrastructure delivery.

## 1.4 Infrastructure Delivery Forms of Contractual Arrangement

There are many forms and variations of private sector involvement on the capital project financing and delivery continuum between government provision and private sector provision (OCED, 2008, 2009), as noted in the Introduction. The private sector arrangement for capital infrastructure building and operation can include a basic PPP Design and Build form of arrangement at one end of the continuum, such as New York State, or a more complex PPP Concession form of agreement at the other end of the PPP continuum, such as Indiana Toll Road or Tirana International Airport. The private partner may build new capital infrastructure, and financing responsibility is shifted in whole or in part from the government to the private sector, whether it is for construction or operation and maintenance. The capital infrastructure financing details are negotiated and spelled out in the PPP contract.

Each national and subnational government has its policies, laws, and regulations governing PPP forms. The following are 13 typical forms of PPPs used, depending on the type of contractual partnership relationship needed for the project. Following the descriptions of the typical forms, examples of selected forms more recently used by national and subnational governments are provided.

### *1.4.1 Traditional Infrastructure Funding and Delivery Form of Contractual Arrangement*

**Design-Bid-Build (DBB).** The traditional government capital infrastructure delivery. The government uses separate bids for design and construction. A private contractor designs under one contract (or the government may provide the design) and under another contract, a different private contractor constructs the infrastructure for a fixed price not to exceed or guaranteed maximum price. This arrangement is to meet the performance specifications and requirements of the government contract. The government finances the capital infrastructure. The government owns the infrastructure and is solely responsible for O&M. It can either perform such services in-house or contract out the O&M services to another contractor.

The typical contractual structure for this arrangement is a Consultancy Contract, and public funds are used.

### *1.4.2 PPP Infrastructure Financing and Delivery Forms of Contractual Arrangement Continuum*

**Design-Build (DB).** This form is the basic PPP arrangement. The government bundles the bids for the phases of the construction into one bid. The private partner designs and builds the capital infrastructure under one contract. The government owns the capital infrastructure and finances the capital infrastructure. DB is the most common form of PPP and has the least risk transfer.

The typical contractual structure for this arrangement is a Service Contract or Management Contract and Private Activity Bonds are typically used. The private partner is paid through milestone payments.

**Design-Build-Operate (DBO).** The government bundles the bids for the phases of the project construction into one bid. The private partner performs all the functions of the DB type but also operates the constructed infrastructure for the length of the PPP contract. The public partner is responsible for financing design and construction and the operation and maintenance of the infrastructure.

The typical contractual structure for this arrangement is a Service Contract or Management Contract. Private Activity Bonds are typically used, and the private partner is paid through availability payments.

**Design-Build-Maintain (DBM).** The private partner designs and builds the infrastructure. The government operates the constructed infrastructure, while the private partner performs the maintenance or repairs on the project for the duration of the PPP contract, meeting the availability or infrastructure usability requirements of the contract.

The typical contractual structure for this arrangement is a Service Contract or Management Contract. Private Activity Bonds are typically used, and the contractor is paid through availability payments.

**Design-Build-Operate-Maintain (DBOM).** The private partner is responsible for the design, build, operation, and maintenance of the contract. The private partner is paid from the revenue that comes from the operation of the constructed infrastructure.

The typical contractual structure for this arrangement is a Service Contract or Management Contract. Private Activity Bonds are typically used, and the private partner is paid through availability payments.

**Design-Build-Finance-Operate (DBFO).** The private partner finances the infrastructure with their funds. The private partner is paid over the life of the infrastructure from revenue that comes from the constructed capital infrastructure.

The typical contractual structure for this arrangement is a Design-Build-Finance Contract. The financing is through private equity, and the private partner is paid through availability payments.

**Design-Build-Finance-Operate-Maintain (DBFOM).** The private partner designs, builds, finances, operates, and maintains the capital infrastructure. The private partner performs all four functions and provides financing for the capital infrastructure using private financing. The government owns the completed capital infrastructure, but the private partner is paid over the life of the infrastructure from the revenue that comes from the completed capital infrastructure.

The typical contractual structure for this arrangement is a Design-Build-Finance Contract. The financing is through private equity, and the private partner is paid through availability payments.

**Design-Build-Finance-Operate-Maintain-Transfer (DBFOM).** The private partner performs all the functions of the infrastructure, including financing. The private partner is paid through the revenue generated by the operation of the completed capital infrastructure. The private partner owns the completed infrastructure for the term of the PPP contract. After the contract, the private partner transfers ownership of the infrastructure, including all O&M responsibilities, to the public owner, and the contractor is paid through availability payments.

The typical contractual structure for this arrangement is a Design-Build-Finance Contract. The financing is through private equity.

**Build-Operate-Transfer (BOT).** A government grants a private partner the right to construct and operate a capital facility for a specified amount of time. The government is involved in the project design or provides the project design to the private partner, but the government remains liable for any design errors or omissions.

The government owns the constructed capital facility and pays the contractor either from public funds or from revenue that comes from the completed capital infrastructure. The private partner may or may not contribute some of the infrastructure financing. The private partner transfers operations to the government when the contract ends.

The typical contractual structure for this arrangement is a Build-Operate-Transfer Contract. The financing is through private equity.

**Build-Transfer-Operate (BTO).** After infrastructure construction, the government and the private partner enter into a separate contractual agreement in which the private partner operates the completed capital infrastructure and performs the O& M for a specified period. The advantage to the Private Contractor is operating income and transfer consideration.

The typical contractual structure for this arrangement is a Build-Transfer-Operate Contract. The financing is through private equity.

**Build-Own-Operate-Transfer (BOOT).** The PPP private partner has ownership of the infrastructure for the life of the contract. The private partner may provide some or all the project financing. The advantages to the Private Contractor: Operating Income, government subsidies, transfer considerations.

The typical contractual structure for this arrangement is a Build-Own-Operate-Transfer Contract. The financing is through private equity.

**Build-Own-Operate (BOO).** The private partner constructs, operates, and maintains the capital infrastructure for the life of the infrastructure. The government pays for the use of the infrastructure. At the end of the contract, the government may or may not purchase the infrastructure from the private contractor. The private partner pays for the contract. The advantage to the Private Partner: operating income.

The typical contractual structure for this arrangement is a Build-Own-Operate Contract. The financing is through private equity.

**Lease-Develop-and-Operate (LDO).** The private partner leases the facility from the government and uses its financing to modernize or expand the capital facility and operates and maintains the facility under contract with the government. The government pays the private partner for the government's use of the capital facility.

The advantages to the private partner are leasing income and transfer consideration.

The typical contractual structure for this arrangement is a Lease. The financing is through Bank Debt, and the payment mechanism is through shadow user fees.

**Concession.** The government sells the right to operate and maintain an existing capital infrastructure to a private contractor. The length of the concession is for many years, sometimes 99 years (Uddin & Zack, 2016). This form of PPP has more risk transfer than other PPP forms.

The typical contractual structure for this arrangement is a Full-Concession/ Development Rights Contract. Financing is through private equity, and the payment mechanism is through user fees.

## 1.5 Summary

These PPPs forms shape the relationship between the public partner and the private partner in the financing and delivery of the capital infrastructure. The choice of the option to use a PPP to finance and deliver a capital infrastructure is guided by the Infrastructure Finance Policy and implemented through infrastructure finance polices. Examples that can highlight and explain these forms follow.

The following are a series of PPP examples ranging from DB to Concession, arranged according to their economic type. The examples are used throughout succeeding chapters, so having an explanation of each at this point will prepare the reader.

## 1.6 Examples of Public–Private Partnership Forms of Contractual Arrangements

The following are examples of PPP contracting arrangements:

### *1.6.1 Bridge PPP Design-build Contract in a Mature Economy*

The United States, New York State Mario Cuomo Bridge PPP **Design-Build**

Governor Mario M. Cuomo Bridge replaced the existing Tappan Zee Bridge in New York State. The new Governor Mario M. Cuomo Bridge processes 140,000 vehicles every day, which is more than the original bridge capital design capacity. A DB PPP was used by New York State to replace the original Tappan Zee bridge to improve operations and safety. HDR was the lead designer and a subcontractor for Tappan Zee Constructors, LLC, a consortium that included Fluor Enterprises, American Bridge Company, Granite Construction Northeast, and Traylor Bros. The Governor supported legislation to authorize the use of PPP DB form in New York City on a project-by-project basis (Khoury, 2019).

### *1.6.2 Airport PPP Concession Contract in a Developing Economy*

Tirana Albania International Airport PPP **Concession**

The Concession Agreement Form of PPP chosen for the airport was signed in October 2004 by the Albanian government and Tirana Airport Private Partners. The PPP Concession contract involved Construction, Operation, and Maintenance of the airport. The Concession contract required the private partner Concessionaire to design, finance, install, build, maintain, operate, and manage the airport terminal construction. UK planning and construction performance standards were adopted. The contract included the construction of 7 km of access roads, which shortened the distance from the capital city of Tirana, a new air cargo terminal; renovation and construction of the airport infrastructure; a new car parking area, and a wastewater treatment plant (Ramboutsous, 2019).

Tirana, Albania International Airport PPP **Concession Contract Refinancing**

Refinancing is a change or replacement of the existing lenders or terms on which debt obligations have been agreed between a project company and its lenders. Changed market conditions and/or advancement of a project can lead to a situation where more favorable financing terms become available such as a lowering of interest rates.

In the case of Tirana Albania Airport PPP, by supporting the first refinancing of a PPP in Albania, the European Bank for Reconstruction and Development (EBRD) allowed Tirana International Airport to be able to refinance its Concession operations under a PPP form and on terms comparable with those available for PPP capital infrastructure in mature PPP market economies. This refinancing is a clear and positive message to the markets about the improvements in the development of the commercial, political, and legal environment for PPPs in Albania. It also enhances the likelihood of a wider range of competitive bidders for future PPPs in the broader sector in the country. Some of the more conservative equity investors view this first Albanian PPP airport refinancing transaction to enhance equity returns. They then reassess the attractiveness of Albania as a capital investment option (EBRD, 2019).

### *1.6.3 Toll Road PPP Concession Contract-mature Economy*

State of Indiana, United States Toll Road PPP **Concession**

The Indiana Roll Road is between the Ohio Turnpike and the Chicago Skyway. The Indiana Toll Road was a good candidate because it was used primarily for truck and interstate commerce travel and any negative impact from the lease would not be borne only by local users (Holzrichter, 2019). The Indiana Toll Road Lease is an example of a PPP lease/concession agreement established to operate and maintain the Indiana Toll Road. In 2006, ITR Company Concession (now owned by IFM Investors) paid Indiana $3.8 billion for operating rights to the Indiana Toll Road (Weeklysift.com, 09/14) and the Concessionaire pledged to make an immediate $200 million in capital improvements and another $4.4 billion over the life of the lease (Holzrichter, 2019; Weeklysift.com, 09/14). The Concessionaire pledged to maintain and operate the toll road in exchange for the revenue generated by the infrastructure. The lease agreement with the State of Indiana runs for 75 years, through 2081 (INDOT, 2016). Tolls were stipulated in the contract for 5 years and then indexed. The State dedicated the proceeds mainly to a 10-year capital improvement program that financed capital infrastructure, repaid across the State (Holzrichter, 2019).

### *1.6.4 Wind Farm Energy PPP Build-own-operate Contract-transitioning Economy*

Mauritius Utility-Scale Wind Farm **Build-Own-Operate** PPP

The Cure pipe Point Wind Farm is in the municipality of Cure pipe Point in the Republic of Mauritius. The Wind Farm is an example of a Build-Own-Operate PPP contract. The partners in the PPP are Suzlon Group and PAD Green/Valum Holding Consortium as PPP private partners. The private partners in this PPP formed a Special Purpose Vehicle. The Central Electricity Board, Mauritius, is the Public Partner (Mauritius Ministry of Renewable Energy and Public Utilities, 2012; WindpowerEngineering.com, 2014).

## 1.7 Infrastructure Finance Policy and Funding Sources

This section identifies and defines government infrastructure finance policy and sources and describes capital infrastructure funding sources. A government may provide indirect support through the transfer of capital infrastructure that support the partnership (Asian Development Bank, 2019), or direct support for a PPP project through tax revenue, debt, guarantees, grants, tax expenditures, and other public investments.

Sufficient, timely, and appropriate government investment in capital infrastructure is critical to success (Grimsey & Lewis, 2002) of its capital improvement program. Large amounts of government financing over long periods are needed to pay for capital infrastructure planning, design, construction, operation, and maintenance. Given the sizable government capital infrastructure needs, private investment in capital infrastructure is also needed, sometimes in partnership with the government, to support the delivery of the considerable government capital infrastructure needs. The efficient and effective delivery of a capital infrastructure must be based on Infrastructure Finance Policy. Adequate capital infrastructure financing and delivery, environmental protection, and economic development, improved standards of living, and increased employment opportunities (Kumari & Sharma, 2018) are the outcome of sound Infrastructure Finance Policy.

## 1.8 Infrastructure Finance Policy

As noted previously in the discussion of the role of Infrastructure Finance Policy, the policy focuses the decision to either finance a capital infrastructure through traditional government-financing (i.e., tax-exempt bonds) as a policy option or to deliver a capital infrastructure through a PPP.

Infrastructure Finance Policy is defined previously as the formal system that guides capital improvement planning in identifying potential financing sources such as PPPs (Beckett-Camarata, 2019). Infrastructure Finance Policy implementation is the basis for sound capital improvements planning, capital needs analysis, capital infrastructure cost estimation, capital infrastructure priority ranking, and capital infrastructure financing through the capital budget. Capital infrastructure financing, based on Infrastructure Finance Policy, can be implemented through government financial support policies, either (1) direct or (2) indirect, which encourage private financing in PPPs (Wang, Chen, Xiong, & Guangdong, 2018).

### *1.8.1 Infrastructure Finance Direct Support Policies*

Formal government infrastructure finance policies provide support for an infrastructure investment choice. Examples of public infrastructure finance indirect support policies (described below) include guarantees such as (1) exchange rate policy, (2) tax revenue policy, (3) debt management policy, (4) tax expenditures policy, and other similar infrastructure finance policy support (The World Bank Legal Resource Center, 2018).

#### 1.8.1.1 Exchange-rate Policy

The exchange rate is the amount of a country's currency that can be exchanged for foreign currency. Exchange rate policy is the level of the exchange rate as a choice between two policy goals. The first goal is stimulating local trade items' producers and the second goal is raising local purchasing power (Frieden, 2014).

#### 1.8.1.2 Tax Revenue Policy

Tax revenue policy is the written laws and regulations governing the raising and collecting of tax revenue. The United States relies significantly more on individual income taxes and property taxes compared to the OECD average. On average, 23.9% of total tax revenue from individual income taxes were raised by OCED countries (Tax Foundation, 2019). The share in the United States was 38.6%, a difference of almost 15% (Tax Foundation, 2019). This difference is, in part, because more than 50% of US business income is reported on individual tax returns. OECD countries averaged 5.7% of total tax revenue from property taxes, compared to 15.4% in the United States (Tax Foundation, 2019). Taxes on goods and services were only 15.9% of total tax revenue in the United States, compared to 32.4% in the OECD (Tax Foundation, 2019). All OECD countries (except the United States), levy value-added taxes (VAT) at relatively high rates. Subnational sales tax rates in the United States are relatively low by comparison (Tax Foundation, 2019).

#### 1.8.1.3 Debt Management Policy

Debt Management Policy is the written guidelines, allowances, and restrictions that guide the debt issuance practices of subnational governments, including the issuance process, management of a debt portfolio, and adherence to various laws and regulations. The policies reflect state and national laws and regulations. A formal written debt management policy should improve the quality of capital financing decisions, provide clear debt policy, provide guidelines for the structure of debt issuance, and demonstrate a commitment to long-term capital and financial planning (GFOA Board, 2019). The use of a written Debt Management Policy is an indication to rating agencies and capital markets that a government is well-managed, and therefore is likely to meet its debt obligations promptly. Debt management policies should be developed with attention to the issuer's specific financial situation and available financing options and be implemented through operating procedures. Debt management policies should be approved by the governing body to provide transparency and to ensure a common understanding regarding the issuer's approach to debt financing (GFOA Board, 2019).

### *1.8.2 Infrastructure Finance Direct Support Funding Sources*

Infrastructure financing is identified in the CIP by title and by type such as the construction of a new capital infrastructure or the repair or replacement of an existing capital infrastructure, for example. Financing the infrastructure capital infrastructure is approved in the capital budget for the construction or repair or replacement of the capital infrastructure. Once financing is secured and appropriated in the budget, the capital infrastructure depending on the type of capital improvement is then broken down into projects, and the funds are then broken down according to the project. The overall capital infrastructure financing is based on infrastructure type. Capital infrastructure financing is generally through a combination of equity and debt.

The following are sources of government financing for capital project: Tax Revenue and Fund Balance, Government Debt, Sovereign Wealth Financing, Multilateral Development PPP Quasi-Governmental Financing.

#### 1.8.2.1 Tax Revenue and Fund Balance

Some governments may use annual revenues and fund balances as sources for pay-as-you-go capital financing. Pay-as-you-go financing is the funding of capital infrastructure, especially infrastructure capital infrastructure, from revenue sources other than long-term debt. Those funding sources include current revenues; revenues raised in prior years and held as capital reserves; current or prior years charges to property, such as special assessment and impact fees; and revenue and grant revenues from the federal, state, or other governments. Other governments may use earmarked current revenues, such as special revenues, to finance specific types of infrastructure, for example, road maintenance and repair. Some governments use multiyear capital management and planning reserve funds for capital needs and requirements and earmark other recurring revenue sources to use in combination with fund balances. The funding decision should be based on a sound Infrastructure Finance Policy. An example of part of such a subnational policy may be one that specifies that any Governmental Fund balance that exceeds a certain percentage of Expenditures is available to be used to finance part of needed capital improvements (Marlowe, Rivenbark, & Vogt, 2009).

#### 1.8.2.2 Government Debt

Pay-as-you-go capital financing is not usually a viable government option for capital infrastructure because they are too large, complex, and the funding and expenses too uneven to be financed solely from the operating budget. The government is usually not able to accumulate enough funds in capital reserves to finance a capital infrastructure entirely from capital reserves. In governments that use a CIP, which is a multiyear (6 years) plan for delivering capital needs, a government has adequate time to build a capital reserve to put toward a capital infrastructure and reduce the amount of borrowing.

Most governments use some combination of both pay-as-you-go capital financing sources and debt sources to pay for capital infrastructure. A government that finances all or most of its capital infrastructure with pay-as-you-go may experience delayed capital infrastructure delivery or not be able to start the capital infrastructure construction and will result in increasing capital infrastructure deficiencies. The following are major government debt financing options for significant capital infrastructure:

*1.8.2.2.1 General Obligation Debt Financing.* Governments that issue debt usually need the support of their citizens when they are planning to issue debt for capital projects. Bonds are the best way to finance capital infrastructure requirements because the decision to issue bonds is determined and approved either directly by the citizens, through bond referenda, or by their elected representatives, directly or by appointed boards (Gross, 2018). This support is needed because the debt to be issued is backed by the full faith and credit or general fund tax revenue. The government must also follow federal laws and regulations at the time of the debt issuance in addition to zoning, environmental, licensure, and other regulatory requirements.

Interest received by tax-exempt bondholders is free from national income tax and may also be exempt from subnational income tax. As a result, private investors accept a lower interest rate payment on these investments in return for a reduced tax burden. The lower interest rate reduces borrowing costs for subnational governments, which is a direct benefit to taxpayers (Gross, 2018).

*1.8.2.2.2 Revenue Bond Debt Financing.* Revenue bonds are issued for a specific capital infrastructure such as water, sewer, and are paid for from revenues received when the project is completed. The typical security for revenue bonds is revenue from fees or charges generated by the capital project financed with the revenue bonds. One category of revenue bonds is qualified private activity bonds. These bonds finance a specified list of public-purpose projects where repayment comes from nongovernment sources such as privately owned airlines at airports, rent payments from low-income housing, and tuition from colleges and insurers of patients at hospitals.

Issuers of tax-exempt debt can issue two types of taxable bonds: (1) tax credit bonds (tax credit bonds were only issued from 2010 to 2012). Tax Credit Bonds are a type of bond that offers the holder a federal tax credit instead of interest, and (2) direct subsidy bonds. With direct subsidy bonds, the issuing organization receives a payment from the national government for part of the interest costs.

*1.8.2.2.3 Lease or Lease-purchase Debt Financing.* Lease or Lease-Purchase debt is secured by the government property financed with the debt, and also sometimes by other property or by payments (lease revenue) made by the government serving as the lessor. The security for some lease debt includes both property and lease revenues.

A capital lease transfers the title of the leased property to the local government lessee. The lease covers a large part of the property's useful life. Lease payments have a present value (PV) equal to all or nearly all the leased property's value at the lease inception and contain a nominal purchase option.

*1.8.2.2.4 Special Obligation Debt Financing.* Special obligation debt refers to special or limited tax, nonproperty tax or nonlocal tax, and special assessment, tax increment, and moral obligation debt. Special obligation debt includes (1) limited obligation debt, (2) special assessment debt, (3) nonproperty tax debt, and (4) moral obligation debt.

**Limited obligation debt.** This debt is secured by and paid from a special or limited tax or revenue source. Subnational governments use this debt for specific capital purposes such as street improvement, downtown revitalization, or solid-waste management. One example is highway bonds, which are backed by gasoline taxes or other revenue related to motor vehicle use of streets or highways (Marlowe et al., 2009). Because limited obligation debt is payable from specific and fixed revenue sources, the bonds include covenants to increase their attractiveness to private investors.

**Special assessment debt.** This debt is issued to finance public improvements that benefit adjacent or nearby property. The bonds are secured by assessments against the benefitting property and levied by the local government undertaking the capital construction. Investors look for coverage to compensate for possible nonpayment of assessments by property owners or a decrease in payment of the special assessment in an economic downturn (Marlowe et al., 2009). By issuing special assessment bonds secured by revenue from different assessment projects rather than one project, a subnational government can broaden the security for the bonds, keep interest costs down, and improve attractiveness to potential investors (Marlowe et al., 2009).

**Nonproperty tax debt.** This debt is secured by all legally available revenue, except local property tax and all locally levied taxes. Enterprise revenue is unavailable to the extent that it is already committed to secure and meet coverage requirements for debt service bonds. When a subnational government issues nonproperty or nonlocal tax debt, it may have to identify one or more specific revenue sources to pay debt service. If the sources are significant and dependable, it will improve the credit quality of the bonds (Marlowe et al., 2009).

**Moral obligation debt.** This type of debt is not secured by the local government and as a result carries a higher risk of default, but a higher rate of return for the investor. It also comes with a moral pledge of repayment by the government in the event of default.

### *1.8.3 Sovereign Wealth*

Many countries use sovereign wealth funds to make investments because their economies are reliant on one source of income, for example, oil revenues (World Economic Forum, 2017). Sovereign wealth funds allow countries with high savings rates to export their capital and are significant sources of financing for PPP capital infrastructure. Sovereign wealth funds are country-owned investment funds made up of stocks, bonds, precious metals, or other financing instruments. Sovereign wealth funds are usually created when a government has years of surpluses and little debt.

### *1.8.4 Multilateral Development Banks*

Multilateral development banks are financial institutions that provide support for economic and social activities in developing countries. Multilateral development banks include the following three sources:

(1) **World Bank**. The World Bank provides loans to developing countries to reduce poverty and inequality. The World Bank borrows on the international capital market and lends to developing countries. The World Bank receives its financing from the 188 member countries that it, in turn, lends to developing countries. Because the World Bank can borrow at low-interest rates, it can lend to developing countries at low-interest rates (The World Bank, 2019).

(2) **African Development Bank** (AfDB). The Bank's financial resources are a small source of Africa's capital infrastructure financing requirements. Current fiscal constraints in donor countries suggest that official development assistance could well be mostly stagnant in the coming years. With the changing global economic environment, AfDB is exploring options for attracting additional investment from emerging economies and new finance sources and donors, including sovereign wealth and pension funds. The Bank's focus is on developing new ways of ensuring that funds invested by the Bank are leveraged to attract more from other investors, such as broader use of financing PPPs through new investors (African Development Bank, 2019).

(3) **Asian Development Bank** (ADB). The Asian Development Bank provides loans, grants, and technical assistance to developing member countries, to the private sector, and through PPPs. The purpose is to support the building and maintenance of capital infrastructure. Most of its activity is in water, energy, transport, urban development, and information and communications technology. ADB is increasing its operations by 50% from $14 billion in 2014 to more than $20 billion in 2020. Seventy percent of this amount is going toward capital infrastructure (Asian Development Bank, 2019).

### *1.8.5 Quasi-governmental Export Credit Agency*

Export credit agencies are private or quasi-governmental agencies that act as intermediaries between governments and exporters to issue export financing. Financing may be in the form of credits or credit insurance and guarantees or both. Export credit agencies also invest in capital infrastructure and are found in many developing countries. Export Credit Agencies utilize three main types of financial support: (1) Direct lending, (2) Financial Intermediary Loans, and (3) Interest rate equalization assessment.

**Direct Lending.** This form of lending is usually to fill in gaps in financing from other lenders. An example of this is the UK Export Finance Agency, which assists private contractors with work capital loans.

**Financial Intermediary Loans.** A financial intermediary facilities loans between a lender and a contractor. An example is an insurance company that provides insurance to reduce default.

**Interest rate equalization assessment.** An interest rate equalization assessment involves lending at below-market rates. It receives compensation for the difference between the below-market-rate and the actual market rate from the Export Credit Agency, such as the UK Export Finance Agency.

Direct government financial support in PPP financing can also involve an up-front, short-term cash outlay to defray initial construction costs, to purchase land, to cover bid costs, or for initial maintenance. Direct support financing is used in cases where the project is subject to the risk that private investors or lenders are not able to adequately cover. It can involve waiving fees that the private contractor may not be able to cover or providing short-term loans or viability gap financing. Most PPPs require some type of direct short-term and/or long-term government financial support, so it is essential to have policies in place to provide strategic direction. Efficient PPP financing involves some level of government financial support for some projects to ensure that government capital infrastructure financing bears the risk that it can manage, and to supplement projects which are economically but not financially viable.

## 1.9 Infrastructure Finance Indirect Support Funding Sources

### *1.9.1 Indirect Support Funding Policies*

#### 1.9.1.1 Tax Expenditure Policy

Tax expenditure policy is the written laws and regulations governing tax expenditures. These tax expenditures decrease the tax households or corporations owe. To benefit from a tax expenditure, a taxpayer must take specific actions or meet certain criteria. For example, some households that have childcare expenses can reduce their taxes by claiming a tax deduction for their spending on day care, and corporations can receive a tax subsidy for investing in machinery (Center on Budget and Policy Priorities, 2019).

#### 1.9.1.2 Land Policy

Land policy is the written laws and regulations governing the establishment of rights and title over land is key to capital infrastructure projects where a private partner is investing in infrastructure attached to the land. In most PPP projects, primarily where the private partner is investing in existing or new capital infrastructure, the private partner will require confirmation that it has rights to the property in the country. Thus, private lenders look for security over those infrastructure. PPP may require the transfer of rights in public capital infrastructure to the private sector operator. The government may want to transfer rights over, or ownership of, project infrastructure to the project company or operator. Also, there may be a requirement for the project company to transfer ownership of capital infrastructure to the awarding authority after construction or at the end of the project period (The World Bank PPPLRC, 2018a).

A government may provide indirect support through the transfer of capital infrastructure that supports the partnership (Asian Development Bank, 2019) or direct support for a PPP project through tax revenue, debt, guarantees, grants, tax expenditures, and other public investments.

### *1.9.2 Indirect Support Funding Sources*

#### 1.9.2.1 Tax Expenditures

Tax expenditures are preferential tax treatments by the government to achieve social or economic goals, such as reducing poverty. Tax expenditures may, in some cases, distort economic incentives toward investment, such as investment in capital infrastructure. A tax expenditure is equivalent to having the taxpayer pay the tax that would be owed without the special tax provision and simultaneously receive a government grant equal to the amount of tax in that provision (Mikesell, 2014). Tax expenditures encourage selected economic activities such as investment, housing, municipal borrowing, and/or reduce taxpayers' liability in certain circumstances such as casualty loss reduction. The use of tax expenditures to foster private participation in capital infrastructure investment, if used appropriately, can be a feasible approach to fostering private participation in capital infrastructure investment.

#### 1.9.2.2 Land

The government may choose to provide in-kind funding mechanisms, i.e., where the government is not providing direct funding but is instead providing indirect capital project support. For example, providing land for capital infrastructure development such as the building of a highway, road, or other capital infrastructure. The decision to provide in-kind funding such as infrastructure transfer should be based on a feasibility study that analyzes public interest, environmental impact and protection, and national and sector strategic objectives.

## 1.10 Private Infrastructure Financing Sources

This section describes the function of the private sector in capital infrastructure finance and sources of private sector financing. In PPPs, private organizations may also invest in public capital infrastructure. Governments may also use private capital to finance public infrastructure that cannot be funded from current tax revenue. Infrastructure Finance policy, in the context of PPPs, includes the use of private capital through PPPs to finance capital infrastructure.

Infrastructure finance policy provides the opportunity to choose PPPs among various alternative infrastructure finance policy options. Most PPP capital infrastructure projects are financed with some combination of government tax revenue and borrowing and private financing, depending on the size of the infrastructure. When borrowing is required to provide financing through government bonds, the investors will accept a relatively lower rate of return because the bonds are backed by the full faith and credit of the government. The government can also use private financing for capital infrastructure through PPP, but the source of repayment remains taxes or user fees such as tolls.

Khmel and Zhao (2015) describe the private sector choice of capital infrastructure financing through equity, debt, and senior debt from the perspective of the level of risk and of the expected outcome of the capital infrastructure financing. Private providers of financing of capital infrastructure such as banks, banking syndicates, international financial institutions, a counterparty of the private contractor, and governments may be sources of private sector financing depending on the type of capital infrastructure, the degree of risk, and the ability of the private contractor to raise capital.

Private partner financing in capital infrastructure delivery through a PPP is different from the traditional private contractor investment. Having the government as a partner in capital infrastructure construction and financing for the most part determines the success of the project completion and delivery (Khmel & Zhao, 2015). Governments provide financing (depending on the type of PPP), provide the institutional structure for the capital infrastructure project design and implementation, and assess capital infrastructure project risk.

Typically, a government advertises for bidders for construction or replacement of a capital infrastructure, and interested private contractors bid on the capital infrastructure proposal. A private contractor who is awarded the contract puts together the financing structure for constructing the capital infrastructure, usually a combination of equity and debt. Private contractors tend to borrow [use debt] through PPP financing arrangements in highway infrastructure, for example (Khmel & Zhao, 2015).

Risk profiles and expected return on investment (ROI) based on the specific characteristics of the capital infrastructure and the government institutional characteristics impact the cost of capital. There are inherent risks in certain types of capital infrastructure construction that make the project more costly for investors, such as a high level of ecological and technical risk during the construction phase. The environmental and technical review processes can increase project costs and cause significant delays and a high level of initial capital expenditure. Usually, highway infrastructure projects require a high initial investment. Full return of the investments is expected only after a long period. The most favorable social rate rarely provides the maximum level of income, considering the necessary costs (Huizinga, Laeven, & Nicodeme, 2006).

The depreciation period is likely to be significantly longer than the loan maturity period which, for indirect reasons, sometimes may prevent. The project [capital infrastructure] generates income after some time. The initial risk is unlikely to match the financing requirements during the first time of implementation of the project immediately following the close of the final phase of the project (Khmel & Zhao, 2015).

The characteristics and nature of capital infrastructure can impact private investor decisions on whether to enter into a PPP capital infrastructure financing arrangement. More extended period to maturity, fixed and low (but favorable) real ROI, long sunk costs, high-risk portfolios inherent in some PPP forms, high number of capital outlays, steep capital infrastructure valuations because of tax treatment, and pricing rules can deter some private investors from entering into a capital infrastructure delivery arrangement using a PPP (Kumari & Sharma, 2017).

## 1.11 Commercial Market Private Sector Financing Sources

### *1.11.1 Development Finance Institutions*

Development finance organizations are bilateral, multilateral, or regional institutions that are supported by countries with developed economies. Development financing institutions usually provide financing to the private sector to promote capital infrastructure development. The purpose is to ensure commercial market investments that would otherwise not be made. Development finance institutions help private companies access financing in countries where access to foreign capital markets and provide risk-mitigation products that allow investors to proceed with PPP projects they might not otherwise be able to pursue. Development finance institutions provide loans with longer maturities than other financial products. Examples of capital infrastructure development finance institutions are (1) European Bank for Reconstruction and Development, (2) the European Investment Bank, (3) Interamerican Bank Development Group (IBD), and (4) IUK CDC group.

**European Bank for Reconstruction and Development (EBRC).** EBRD private sector loans for projects usually start from a minimum of €3 million up to €250 million. The average amount is €25 million (European Bank for Reconstruction and Development, 2019). The loans are structured with a high degree of flexibility to provide loan profiles that match private client and capital project needs. The individualized approach determines each loan currency and interest rate formula. The basis for an ERDB loan is the expected cash flow of the capital project and the ability of the client to repay the loan over the agreed period. The credit risk can be taken by the bank or may be partly syndicated to the market (European Bank for Reconstruction and Development, 2019). A borrower's capital infrastructure may be used to secure a loan, or it may be converted into shares or be equity-linked. Loan details are negotiated with the client on a case-by-case basis (European Bank for Reconstruction and Development, 2019).

**European Investment Bank (EIB).** The European Investment Bank lends to both the public and private sectors. It supports small companies through local banks and lends money to innovative start-ups. Mid-cap companies (those with a market capitalization between 1 billion and 5 billion USD) can receive direct support for research and development investments (Franklin Templeton, 2019). The bank does not lend more than half of the cost of a project because it wants loans to crowd-in financing from private investors and other public financial institutions. EIB offers a range of financial products at favorable terms. For specific projects that support innovation and skills in Europe, the bank accepts more risk than a commercial bank. The bank also offers technical assistance to help prepare and implement capital projects (European Investment Bank, 2019).

**Interamerican Bank Development Group (IBD).** IBD provides loans to promote capital infrastructure that is aimed at access to electricity, water, and sanitation in urban and rural areas that have a direct impact on poverty reduction. IBD recognizes the need to foster financing instruments that leverage private sector participation in capital infrastructure and the need to strengthen regulatory capacity to be able to expand private participation in capital infrastructure (Interamerican Development Bank Group, 2019).

**UKCDC Group.** UK CD group provides investment loans to companies that are aimed at environmental and social responsibility and that are aligned with the group's standards (CDCgroup.uk, 2019).

### *1.11.2 Private Equity Financing*

Private equity financing is also an essential component of PPP infrastructure financing, although it involves more risk than government financing (The World Bank PPPLRC, 2018a, 2018b). Private equity financing is a collective investment arrangement involving investment in equities. Such collective investment methods, in the context of PPPs, benefit from investing as part of a group and sharing in the risk and rewards of the collective PPP equity investment.

Private equity sponsors are investors in the private partner that will be providing capital project expertise and some of the services to the private contractor, such as construction or operations services. Equity financing is generally through equity contributions in the private partner through share capital and other shareholder financing. Equity is the lowest priority of financing contributions in a capital project. The other contributors, such as lenders, have priority rights to project infrastructure and revenues before the equity contributors realize an ROI, or on termination or insolvency on any repayment. Equity contributors bear the highest risk and can potentially receive the potentially the highest ROI (World Bank PPPLRC, 2018a, 2018b). Lenders prefer front-ended or pro-rata equity investment to maintain their cushion ratios on debt drawdown.

Private equity financing sources such as commercial banks may require a bank or third-party payment guarantee on equity payments to be made as the capital infrastructure project moves forward so that they will be available at the agreed-upon time (The World Bank PPPLRC, 2018a, 2018b).

### *1.11.3 Commercial Banks*

Commercial banks are significant investors in PPP capital infrastructure projects through senior loans and guarantee financing (performance guarantees and letters of credit) (The World Bank, 2018a, 2018b). The multiphased, complex, large-scale nature of and duration of PPP capital financed projects means that many banks, especially in developing countries, do not have the technical capacity or adequate capital to invest in PPP capital infrastructure. In many instances, if commercial banks invest, they invest as part of a banking syndicate.

## 1.12 Infrastructure Finance Policy Design and Implementation

This section describes Infrastructure Finance Policy design as the choice to use PPPs among infrastructure financing policy options, and the balance between private capital to finance infrastructure and the use of government infrastructure financing. It describes how PPPs may be financed, depending on the contract terms, in whole, or in part at various phases of the Capital Project. PPPs can play an essential role in capital infrastructure planning and management by basing the type and use of PPPs in the financing decisions on the government's infrastructure finance policy. This is important in achieving a balance between public and private (market) financing and maintaining legal long-term debt limits.

Infrastructure Finance Policy, the formal strategic policy that guides the capital infrastructure financing phase of capital improvement planning and financing and identifying financing sources, is the policy implementation starting point. Governments determine the funds needed to finance capital infrastructure and how to allocate financing between the public and private sectors, in part, based on their debt policy, past use of debt (debt affordability), their ability to finance new capital projects with debt, as well as their ability to fund a project through use short-term and long-term tax revenue. During the government's Capital Improvements Planning process, capital infrastructure projects are identified. Private investors will be interested in the government's master plan, its CIP, its capital infrastructure finance policy, and the government's history of involving the private sector in delivering capital projects. Political commitment is particularly crucial for assuring potential private investors that their investments will be sound and that institutional and regulatory transaction cost requirements will be cost-effective. Investors expect that there will be consistency in PPP institutional capability and capacity, legal, and regulatory requirements.

Governments determine the funds needed to finance capital infrastructure and how to allocate financing between the public and private sectors, in part, based on their debt policy, past use of debt (debt affordability), their ability to finance new capital projects with debt, as well as their ability to fund a project through use short-term and long-term tax revenue. During the government's Capital Improvements Planning process, capital projects are identified. Private investors will be interested in the government's master plan, its CIP, its Infrastructure Finance Policy, and the government's history of involving the private sector in delivering capital projects. Political commitment is particularly crucial for assuring potential private investors that their investments will be sound and that institutional and regulatory transaction cost requirements will be cost-effective. Investors expect that there will be consistency in PPP institutional capability and capacity, legal, and policy requirements.

One of the challenges that governments face in designing and implementing Infrastructure Finance Policy is to balance short-term funding needs and long-term infrastructure finance policy options. This is especially true in choosing between the traditional method of financing of a capital infrastructure project with government tax-exempt bonds (debt) and financing and delivery using a PPP. How bond rating agencies analyze PPPs impacts bond ratings (Huge & Jones, 2015). Often the private partner supplies their financing analyses because the associated government costs are not as quickly determined as it would be in the government bond structure under the traditional tax-exempt financing method.

### *1.12.1 Capital Market Infrastructure Debt Financing*

Once the decision is made to use PPP to finance a capital project, capital market debt financing is well-suited to some PPP project financing because it has a more extended financing period than commercial bank loans. Most long-term debt that state and local governments issue for capital project financing and other purposes is tax-exempt debt. With tax-exempt debt, the interest paid to the holder of the tax-exempt debt is not subject to federal income taxes (GFOA, 2019). A taxable rate of return for tax-exempt municipal debt is the rate that an investor would have to earn on a taxable security to produce after-tax income that is equal to the tax-exempt interest on the municipal debt (Marlowe et al., 2009). Additionally, in the United States, many states that have an income tax will exempt the interest income earned by state residents on debt issued by the state or local government. The tax-exempt nature of the most state and local government debt continues to define the municipal debt market.

When financing a PPP capital project using a Concession contract becomes part of the Concessioner's responsibility, the effect of the private partner/Concessioner's rating on the government's bond rating is considered. If the private partner's credit is not healthy, the PPP private partners may earn a bond rating that is well below what would be typical if using traditional government tax-exempt bond financing (Huge & Jones, 2015). The government's current bond rating also becomes part of the bond rating process for any related capital project debt issuance, and the benchmark rating usually serves as the ceiling for any related PPP debt. The government's bond rating usually is higher than the final bond rating assigned to a PPP. This is because many risks such as completion risk, cost risk, debt structure, and securitization are borne by the private partner/concessionaire. When combined, these additional risks may ultimately put the bond rating into Baa/BBB to Ba/BB category. These rating differences may make a big difference in PPP capital project financing costs, but that should not lead to the government's decision to use traditional tax-exempt financing. Each PPP capital project financing arrangement is considered on its own merits (Huge & Jones, 2015).

PPPs can play an important role in capital management and budgeting by basing the type and use of PPPs and the financing decisions on the government's Infrastructure Finance Policy. The role of infrastructure finance policy is vital in achieving a balance between public and private financing and maintaining legal long-term debt limits.

### *1.12.2 Debt Financing and Long-term Debt Capacity*

Determining how much long-term debt a government is currently able to afford is a critical part of capital management and planning in choosing whether to use a PPP and the form of PPP. Government finance officials must assess the government's financial resources that are available to pay the long-term debt, debt service, and long-term lease obligations. Many governments have formal long-term debt policies. Long-term debt policies (discussed in Chapter 4) are written guidelines and legal restrictions that guide debt issuance practices of subnational governments. Such policies include the debt issuance process, management of debt, and adherence to laws and regulations governing long-term debt.

Part of a long-term debt capacity assessment (discussed in Chapter 4) is the analyses of current financial conditions, forecasted future resources, and use of key debt ratios. The most frequently used measures of long-term debt capacity are (1) net debt per capita, (2) net debt as a percent of assessed valuation (for local governments), and (3) annual debt service on net debt, which is typically general fund revenue (Marlowe et al., 2009). General Obligation Bonds are included in net debt unless they are issued to finance improvements for a self-supporting government enterprise fund, and the revenues from that enterprise fund cover debt service on the bonds.

Revenue Bonds and other debt are issued to finance capital improvements for such capital projects as water, sewer or electricity, or other capital infrastructure. Debt capacity depends on the ability of the enterprise such as water, sewer, or electricity, or other capital infrastructure to produce enough revenue to pay ongoing operating and maintenance expenses and debt service. The ratio of annual net income (gross income less capital operation and maintenance expenses) to annual debt service is used to evaluate capacity. A positive coverage ratio of greater than 1.0 is required when a government has outstanding revenue bonds and is planning to issue new revenue debt. A self-supporting government enterprise will depend on the enterprise's ability to set fees high enough to cover all expenses, and capital outlays, including debt service (Marlowe et al., 2009). The role of bond rating agencies is essential in determining the use of debt financing to finance a PPP.

## 1.13 The Role of Bond Rating Agencies in Infrastructure Debt Financing

A bond rating evaluates a debt issuers strength or weakness based on factors based on the issuer's ability and willingness to make principal and interest payments on the debt when due and to comply with other obligations that the issuer assumes under the debt contract (Guzman & Moldogaziev, 2012).

Bond ratings have a significant impact on the cost of and use of long-term government debt. There are three major bond rating agencies: Fitch, Moody's, and Standard and Poor's (S&P). A bond rating is a current rating agency opinion on the creditworthiness of an issuer regarding a debt, or a financing program of the issuer. Subnational governments obtain nationally recognized bond ratings to make their debt more attractive to investors (Marlowe et al., 2009).

### *1.13.1 Bond Rating Agencies*

#### 1.13.1.1 Fitch Rating Agency

When assigning a bond rating to a PPP project, Fitch compares any proposed PPP-related debt to the amount that a government would have issued if it had chosen to finance the capital project using traditional government tax-exempt bond borrowing. Fitch adds the amount of any outstanding capital project debt to existing debt levels the government has already assumed.

Outstanding capital project debt includes federal loans, private activity bonds, bank debt, or other forms of financing a private concessionaire may have gotten. This calculation does not consider any scheduled project milestone payments unless the debt was issued to meet such obligations (Huge & Jones, 2015). Operations, maintenance, or life cycle costs are not calculated as debt because these costs would have occurred regardless of financing type. Fitch does not consider whether a revenue source can be used to offset a debt-financed liability until the issuer can demonstrate 3 years of revenues that cover the cost of any availability payments. (Availability payments are made by the government at regular intervals to the private concessionaire after the project is completed and ready to be used and are not based solely on the receipt of specific revenue sources such as a toll.) Up to this point, the debt incurred is recognized as net tax-supported General Obligation debt. Fitch analyzes if this scenario holds for the capital project life cycle. After obligations are met during the 3-year measurement period, Fitch may classify the amount of any remaining debt as a contingent liability.

#### 1.13.1.2 Moody's Investors Rating Agency

When assigning a rating to a PPP project, Moody's calculates the amount of debt to be added to a government's long-term debt as the higher of the liabilities reported on the public entity's financial statement or the termination payment the government would need to make if the private partner were to default (Huge &

Jones, 2015). For example, in the State of Indiana's Ohio River Bridges PPP, the amount owed under a default by the private partner equated to 80% of the outstanding amount owed on the bonds (Huge & Jones, 2015).

In order to be self-supporting and not considered in the debt calculation, a government must demonstrate that the capital project revenue will offset any availability payments in the case of a concession contract, including operations, maintenance, and life cycle costs for the life of the capital project. The Moody's self-supporting requirement test can be met by documenting several years of continuous debt coverage and showing how debt coverage will continue. The government must commit available project revenues to meet all outstanding long-term debt obligations during the life of the capital project or until retirement, whichever occurs first (Huge & Jones, 2015).

#### 1.13.1.3 Standard and Poor's Bond Rating Agency

When assigning a rating to a PPP project, S&P evaluates a government's PPP obligation to establish whether the government the obligation is debt-like, and to identify whether pledged revenues are fully or partially backed by tax revenue. These factors are considered in the agency's decision to count the PPP payment obligations as debt, a contingent liability, or something else when calculating a government's nontax-secured debt. If a PPP obligation is determined to be secured solely by nontax private investor–backed revenue, the payments will not be included as part of the government's debt (Huge & Jones, 2015).

For tax-based revenue (general obligation, appropriations, or special tax), S&P evaluates government payment obligations depending on whether they are periodic milestone payments or availability payments. If periodic milestone payments are written into the PPP contract, they will be added to a government's debt obligations, even if the debt obligations are met using appropriations, as opposed to a debt instrument. The reason is that the commitment and revenue used to fulfill the obligation are the same as paying the outstanding debt. S&P views milestone payments as contractual payment commitments made by the government PPP partner (Huge & Jones, 2015).

When the amount of tax-backed revenues is determined (before including any PPP financing obligations into the debt analysis), the rating agency will calculate the net present value (NPV) of future milestone payments and the capital part of availability payments made by the government entity to the concessionaire. The discount rate is tied to what the borrower forecasts as the cost of financing it would have incurred if it had issued its debt for the project. It also includes what the agency considers to be additional factors (such as an entity's bond rating and duration of the subject PPP agreement). In turn, this NPV calculation becomes the basis for PPP debt that is represented by both milestone and availability payments. Milestone payments are then incorporated into S&P's debt analysis at financial close. Availability payments are considered contingent liabilities during infrastructure construction and added to the government's long-term debt obligations when the availability payments begin. Availability payments considered as contingent liabilities would usually occur when the capital project construction is well underway. How PPPs may be financed at various project phases depends on the Capital Project contract terms. It may be more feasible to build certain types of infrastructure capital projects in phases that parallel costs incurred with any changes in demographic shifts with the capital project being constructed.

## 1.14 Infrastructure Finance Policy as a Guide to Capital Management and Budgeting

Infrastructure Finance Policy guides CIP financing decisions and is the basis for implementing Infrastructure Finance Policy through to the Capital Budget. Using private partners in capital infrastructure financing and delivery requires an articulated and stable government investment environment. The foundation for that milieu is the Infrastructure Finance Policy. It provides the basis for the government to approach financing its long-term capital budget infrastructure needs and priorities, the gaps in government funds, and the alternative sources of financing to fill the identified capital infrastructure project funding variances.

A CIP, articulated through the capital infrastructure planning, management, and budgeting process, is based on an Infrastructure Finance Policy design which form the basis for a systematic method of long-term capital infrastructure project selection, as well as the type and use of PPPs in the financing and delivery decision. Capital infrastructure planning is essential in achieving a balance between public and private financing and maintaining legal long-term government debt limits.

Infrastructure Finance Policy, which describes the strategic priorities for allocating resources to capital infrastructure, will receive scrutiny from potential investors. They will pay attention to the government's articulated intention to promote private participation (Klepsvik et al., 2014). This intention can be through formal written plans to increase specific short-term capital infrastructure maintenance projects such as road and bridge repair or formal Infrastructure Finance Policy to promote private participation in capital infrastructure financing and delivery through long-term partnerships such as PPPs. The stability of political leadership and commitment to PPP is also crucial in supporting the government's Infrastructure Finance Policy. Such a guarantee assures potential investors that their investments in government infrastructure are supported by the highest levels of government (Klepsvik et al., 2014) and will transcend changes in political leadership.

In the Mauritius government example, Infrastructure Finance Policy, articulated in their National Development Program, provides the basis for multiyear capital investment plans. The Plan provides policy guidance in that it asserts the need for the public sector to be significantly involved in the implementation of public services (Mauritius NDP, 2018, p. 33). One of the objectives that flow from the Government's Infrastructure Finance Policy is that at least 10% of financing for major public infrastructure between 2012 and 2015 should come from Foreign Direct Investment Inflows (Klepsvik et al., 2014; Mauritius NDP, 2018). In countries where there is no written, clear coherence between national and subnational government infrastructure investment policies, capital projects may experience an increased need for PPP contract renegotiation. Stability in private investment in government infrastructure (stemming in part from government use of an Infrastructure Finance Policy and multiyear capital infrastructure investment plans) is especially critical in cases where a national or subnational government infrastructure investment planning involves large-scale capital infrastructure projects requiring more substantial than typical infrastructure investment. In the context of PPP, it is especially important if PPPs are used to reiterate the government's commitment to PPPs (OCED, 2015) as articulated in a written Infrastructure Finance Policy. It is also vital that PPP laws are clearly defined, transparent, and enforced to ensure private investment stability and that government institutions are in alignment with the laws. Such laws include investor protection; contract design and renegotiation; capital infrastructure procurement, including competitive bidding; regulation, and pricing of capital infrastructure markets (OCED, 2015). The complexity and high degree of difficulty of the typically 1,000–2,000 pages of a PPP contract and the additional accompanying design specifications require adequate, competent, and knowledgeable government expertise and adequate lead time to assess the capital project, the project design, and the PPP contract specifications (Gross, 2018).

Governments commonly identify more than one option to finance and deliver a Capital infrastructure over a period of years in developing their CIP. A PPP is one capital project financing and delivery option among many options identified in the CIP. PPPs are especially appropriate where the capital infrastructure are more involved than basic capital infrastructure construction and financing. For example, PPPs may be especially appropriate for (1) complex capital infrastructure that involve land acquisition, particularly those complex situations where land acquisitions are integrated with private development activities; (2) high-risk capital infrastructure with large long-term revenue streams that are challenging for a government to manage; issues with government capital construction workforces; (3) governmental restrictions; (4) ongoing operation, and maintenance issues; political considerations; (5) contract delivery timing or risk constraints; and (6) the need for financing upfront or other financing limitations (Gross, 2018).

### *1.14.1 Taxable Debt Financing and PPP Financing*

Because some PPP forms often involve some use of taxable debt financing (such as bank loans, private placement, capital markets, and taxable equity), they may have higher financing costs than tax-exempt government financing (tax-exempt bonds) if the taxable debt is used. However, from time to time, PPPs may use tax-exempt financing, and there may be factors that offset higher intrinsic interest rate and equity return costs for PPPs (Gross, 2018). In current markets, proceeds from a typical government borrowing during construction can have a high negative arbitrage that significantly increases costs. In such instances, PPP private financing may help reduce negative arbitrage more efficiently than conventional tax-exempt government financing. Also, it may help resolve challenges such as up-front land acquisition costs and control over a revenue stream that a typical government-financed project faces. Although a PPP project may have higher financing costs, depending on the financing sources, the PPP, as a means of capital infrastructure project delivery, may be more beneficial to the government than not delivering the capital infrastructure (Gross, 2018).

The total cost of capital for financing a capital infrastructure project tends to be similar, whether it is obtained through public or private sector financing using PPP when all relevant costs are considered (CBO, 2012). The perception of risk of losses drives the overall rate of ROI. Large, complex capital construction carries inherent financial risk even when government guarantees repayment of any debts incurred to finance the capital infrastructure construction (CBO, 2012). Some form of equity investment, whether implicit or explicit, is required to absorb potential cost overruns or revenue shortfalls (CBO, 2012). For highway capital infrastructure projects financed by government borrowing, taxpayers play the role of equity investors, bearing the risk that revenues might be less (or more) than the payments that have been promised (CBO, 2012).

## 1.15 PPP Infrastructure Financing and Delivery Risk Classifications

Infrastructure financing delivery risk can be classified into four main categories:

(1) **Financial Risk** is related to increased financing costs, including equity risk, accounting, and economic risk, liquidity risk, bankruptcy risk, counterparty risk, refinancing risk, fluctuations in exchange rates, and currency devaluation risk.
(2) **Commercial Risk** in project completion because of problems with project construction, operation, and maintenance and includes technical risk, construction risk, operational risk, performance risk, demand risk, and effort risk.
(3) **Country Institutional Risk** resulting from political pressure, the inadequacy of policies, rules, regulations, laws governing contracting, and the use of PPPs; force majeure risk such as from natural disaster or war. There are other risks, such as theft or residual value risk (Kumari & Sharma, 2017).
(4) **Cyber Risk** (operational risk management) resulting from growing physical and cyber risk to countries (such as the United States) (Voltaic, 2019). The cybersecurity risk is challenging to analyze because most existing frameworks and approaches are designed for the infrastructure-level or

> organization-level risk assessment and management (Voltaic, 2019). However, most risk involves different levels of government and private sector, and a bottom-up approach involving both sectors is required to integrate an operational and adaptable cyber risk management system (Voltaic, 2019). Having a government's cyber crisis management plan sufficiently integrated with its crisis management planning, including public, private, and PPPs during a cybersecurity crisis are essential for clarity in potential cybersecurity risk. Following 9/11, there was an influx of funding to support counterterrorism and other capabilities, but there has not been similar resource support for potential cybersecurity crises (Voltaic, 2019).

The private sector, which also faces cybersecurity risk, has the incentive to partner with the public sector to inform, develop, and provide solutions to mitigate the risk. The public sector should better integrate the private sector in critical capital infrastructure (especially telecommunications, water, and transportation) project delivery, regardless of financing source, because of the nature of the risk. PPPs should not be limited to service agreements but should be a basis for cultural change by building trust relationships, sharing information, and close collaboration.

Depending on the PPP form of arrangement, some risks may be transferred from the public partner to the private partner. The government should factor in the cost involved for any risk transfer away from the government to the private partner when negotiating the contract. An example of a Commercial risk is a toll road where bondholders and equity investors assume most of the risk (financing, construction, maintenance, traffic flow). As part of the contract, the bondholders and equity investors also control the toll rates. Risk transfer goes in both the direction of the public partner and the private partner. Private partners are typically experienced with PPP risk but need to be compensated by the government for any risk that they assume. The government should identify this risk and balance risk and cost between the government and the private partner in contract negotiations.

Such private sharing of risks is an essential factor in promoting efficiency gains from PPPs. The private partner in a PPP may bear a significant portion of the capital project risk in the operation and management phase of a more advanced form of a complex capital project. Project construction delays and cost overruns can hamper the ability of the private partner to collect Concession payments from either the government or the public for delivering capital infrastructure or services. Successfully mitigating risks, such as project delay, cost overruns, or demand risk that are inherent in some toll road capital project Concession operations and management, are a significant source of efficiency gains from PPPs.

The most critical types of risks that can be experienced in PPPs and which may be borne by the government are (1) Financial risk (increased financing costs); (2) Commercial risk ((a) Project Delay and Cost Overrun; (b) Infrastructure demand shortfalls, and (c) Unforeseen Structural Deficiency) (OCED, 2009).

### *1.15.1 Financial Risk (Unforeseen Increased Financing Costs)*

There is also financial risk from unforeseen increases in financing costs. An example of a PPP risk that a government may take is the risk related to the possible future failure of a capital project by private partner that was set up as a limited liability corporation (LLC) or SPV to enter the PPP project (Gross, 2018). The LLC or SPV will typically have few capital investment other than the original equity and debt proceeds that they raise for the capita project. If there is a problem, for example, with capital project cost overruns or operating issues such as revenue shortfalls, with the project, and the government has no capital infrastructure to use to address the problem, the government experiences risk. During the development, structuring, and negotiation of a PPP contract, the government needs to proactively develop strategies to mitigate risk by determining what kinds of risk and how much risk they are willing and able to accept. Some government decision-makers may accept the high risk because they will not be in office in the future when the impact of the risk may be experienced. Thus, it is critical to have a clearly articulated Infrastructure Finance Policy, which provides the basis for the government to strategically select capital infrastructure financing and delivery option decisions based on risk tolerance.

### *1.15.2 Commercial Risk (Project Delay and Cost Overrun Risk)*

One significant risk is the construction risk from capital project delays and overruns. Capital project delays and cost overruns can occur when initial cost estimates are not correct. First, the design team is selected; the project limitations are established, the project budgets and project plans are developed. However, project construction bids can be significantly higher than the project budget, and the project can incur cost overruns before construction begins.

### *1.15.3 Commercial Risk Infrastructure Demand Shortfalls Risk*

Another risk is demand risk from potential demand shortfalls in the use of the capital infrastructure by the public. An example of demand risk from potential shortfalls in use of the capital infrastructure is the Indiana Toll Road. The most important source of financial uncertainty is demand risk (Buckberg, Kearney, & Stolleman, 2015). This uncertainty is especially true for the construction of new capital infrastructure where the private partner's compensation is dependent on user volume, and no history exists of prior user volume (Buckberg et al., 2015) Force majeure are those risks such as from natural or man-made disasters and war such as floods, hurricanes, or tornados. There are specific incentive structures that can be used by the government to attract investors. These incentive structures allow them to share the risk with the government in return for some protection from the downsides of demand risk, discussed in Chapter 3.

### *1.15.4 Commercial Unforeseen Structural Deficiency Risk*

Another risk is unforeseen structural deficiencies in the original capital infrastructure. For example, Denver, Colorado's Airport terminal remodeling PPP is facing long delays because of deficiencies in the original structure of the Airport building (MSRB, 2019).

Accurately assessing and allocating potential risk is critical in analyzing potential efficiency gains of using a PPP versus traditional government financing. The nature and degree of risks born by the private sector is a significant reason for government officials in determining whether to participate in a PPP and how to price contracts to compensate private partners for potential increased risk (OCED, 2009). A successful PPP requires requisite government contracting expertise as well as a significant investment in time from various government staff at all levels, working together to evaluate, allocate, and monitor a capital project over a relatively long time. The substantial investment of time is needed at top levels of government, as well as at the contract execution and monitoring levels. Table 1.1 is provided to better illustrate just how risk allocations are structured

Table 1.1. Mauritius Cure Pipe Wind Farm PPP Risk Allocation by Nature and Party Bearing Risk.

| **Risk** | **Nature** | **Party Bearing the Risk** |
|---|---|---|
| *Preconstruction phase risk* | | |
| Commercial risk | | |
| Finalization of project structure | Many project development partnerships EPC Contract, O&M Contract. Final multientity project structure may take more than budgeted time | Private contractor |
| Finalization of contractual framework of bid process | Seller would have to enter ESPA with CEB. Delay in execution of contract is risk for each party | Both CEB and seller |
| Approvals and clearances | Seller needs to obtain all approvals and clearances pertaining to the project which may take more than budgeted time | Seller with CEB |
| Financial closure | Any delay risks cost overruns | Seller |
| Site risk | | Seller |

Table 1.1. *(Continued)*

| Risk | Nature | Party Bearing the Risk |
|---|---|---|
| | Unavailability or inability of the project land to be used at the required time or manner adversely affects the service delivery | |
| *Design, construction, and commissioning phase risk* | | |
| Commercial risk | | |
| Project completion | Seller would have to construct the wind farm within a period of 730 days from date of signing of the ESPA | Seller |
| Project cost overruns | The project cost overrun includes cost escalations due to delays in project commissioning | Seller |
| Design deficiency or technology risk | Risk pertaining to inability of the project to handle the required demands or expected output specifications | Seller |
| *Risk sharing in the operation phase* | | |
| Commercial risk | | |
| Operations and maintenance cost | O&M costs exceeding the estimates used for establishment of financial viability by the bidders | Seller |
| Latent defect | Seller incurring major corrective maintenance costs due to force majeure events or due to equipment defects | Seller |
| Wind speed risk | Any decrease in the wind speed would result in decrease in the generation of electrical energy | Seller |
| Performance loss and supply shortfall | Difference in actual performance of the project | Seller |

Table 1.1. *(Continued)*

| Risk | Nature | Party Bearing the Risk |
|---|---|---|
| | vis-à-vis the envisaged or planned performance at the time of bidding | |
| *Risk sharing principles during project life cycle* | | |
| Financial risk | | |
| Exchange rate | Bidder would be quoting 80% of the tariff in USD and the balance in MUR. The CEB would be making payments converted to MUR exchange rate risk arises in this arrangement | CEB |
| Interest rate | Uncertainty over the macroeconomic determinants of benchmark interest rates | Seller |
| Inflation | It will affect the project at the construction phase as well as operational phase | Seller |
| Force majeure | Nonpolitical events such as epidemics earthquakes, flooding, and cyclones, impacting construction and/or operation | Both CEB and seller |
| CDM market | Pertains to risk in variation of additional revenue achieved by selling Carbon Emission Reduction Certificates under CED framework | Seller |

*Source:* Republic of Mauritius Ministry of Renewable Energy and Public Utilities (2012).

and assessed in each phase of Mauritius Cure Pipe Farm Wind Farm construction.

## 1.16 Summary

This section summarizes the role of Infrastructure Finance as Public Policy and discusses the need to understand the use of PPPs in the context of infrastructure finance policy.

In order for PPPs to be successful, their selection must be within an overall Infrastructure Finance Policy framework, which spells out the criteria for using a PPP as a policy option. The government's Infrastructure Finance Policy framework should provide PPP as an option, and provide a basis for selecting the form of financing, factoring in government institutional constraints, Infrastructure Finance Policy goals of the government, the legal and regulatory constraints, commercial, financial, and financing requirements and constraints, interest of the market, and unique requirements of the sector based on characteristics of the system or population.

Infrastructure Finance Policy guides the capital infrastructure project financing phase of capital improvements planning and financing and identifying financing sources. It is the starting point for policy implementation and evaluation. The funds needed to finance capital infrastructure and how to allocate financing between the public and private sectors, in part, are based on the debt policy, past use of debt (debt affordability), ability to finance new capital projects with debt, as well as their ability to fund a project through use short-term and long-term tax revenue. Private investors pay close attention to the government's policy and planning framework, including Infrastructure Finance Policy, and the government's prior involvement of the private sector in delivering capital projects. Political commitment is also essential for assuring potential private investors that their investments are made within a stable environment and that institutional and regulatory transaction cost requirements will be cost-effective. Investors look for consistency in PPP institutional capability and capacity, and the government's legal, regulatory, and policy environment.

Chapter 2

# Infrastructure Finance Policy Design and Implementation

This section describes public–private partnerships (PPPs) as an Infrastructure Finance Policy design and implementation as an evaluation tool. It describes how the efficient and effective use of scarce public resources is a critical challenge for governments and one in which many governments fall far short of infrastructure finance policy design goals. It describes how PPPs often use taxable financing, including taxable debt (bank loans, private placement, capital markets) and taxable equity. It also describes why PPPs may have higher financing costs than some tax-exempt government financing but are used because they may have more benefits than costs.

## 2.1 Infrastructure Finance Policy as a Basis for Efficient and Effective Use of Scarce Public Resources

Infrastructure Finance Policy is a policy tool designed to achieve long-term national and subnational infrastructure finance policy objectives. Public policies, such as Infrastructure Finance Policy, are the foundation for a government institution to efficiently and effectively deliver a needed capital infrastructure or service. Such policies are critical even when the service is intangible or when the government organization only ensures that another organization, such as a private partner, provides the infrastructure or service (Weimer & Vining, 2017). Once the Infrastructure Finance Policy is in place, there is a range of institutional arrangements available for implementing the policy and delivering needed government goods and services. These arrangements include the direct provision by the government to private sector organizations providing a form of government provision of goods and services (Weimer & Vining, 2017) from which the government can choose. To be successful, government policy decisions on the nature of capital infrastructure financing and delivery, such as Infrastructure Finance Policy decisions, involve the clear delineation of organizational boundaries. Analysis of the most efficient and effective form of public goods and service financing and delivery in specific circumstances requires the attention to the rules of the game that govern the organizational boundaries for transactions

**Public-Private Partnerships, Capital Infrastructure Project Investments and Infrastructure Finance, 41–71**

**doi:10.1108/978-1-83909-654-920201002**

(Weimer & Vining, 2017) such as capital infrastructure financing and delivery through PPPs.

One delineating boundary characteristic in analyzing options from which to choose the most efficient and effective form of financing and delivering public goods and services is that in public organizations, public managers, on an individual basis, cannot legally retain revenue over expenditures as profit (Bilodeau, Laurin, & Vining, 2007) because public organizations have a balanced budget requirement, as opposed to a profit motive. A significant purpose of clearly establishing and, as needed, redrawing organizational boundaries, as in the case of PPPs, is to improve the efficiency with which the government services are delivered (Weimer & Vining, 2017). Without a profit motive, the government must consider other efficiency factors in deciding whether a government capital infrastructure project should be financed and delivered through traditional sole government provision or use of a PPP. The challenge is to identify the costs and benefits in the PPP policy option, with efficiency in the use of scarce public resources as one policy priority decision criterion.

Infrastructure Finance Policy is a strategic government policy instrument that establishes the role of private partners as an option in efficiently and effectively delivering capital projects. It introduces a new lens to look at PPPs as a policy instrument to achieve long-term national and subnational finance policy objectives. It integrates the identification, selection, implementation, and evaluation of PPPs within capital infrastructure projects financing options, the capital improvements planning process, and long-term Infrastructure Finance Policy objectives.

## 2.2 The Role of Infrastructure Financing by Private Institutions in Efficient and Effective Delivery of Capital Infrastructure

PPPs allow government to deliver a needed capital infrastructure without the immediate need to increase current taxes and/or incur additional long-term debt and to maintain a balanced budget. The private financing strategy that the private partner selects to raise capital fulfills a vital role in both the private partner and financial institution's contribution toward the financing of the PPP capital infrastructure project. The private financing strategy, if private financing is used, is based on the decision by the sponsoring private institution. The strategy determines the capital structure of the project, the amount needed through equity financing, and how much should be borrowed through debt financing (Akintoye & Beck, 2009). Private investors of the capital project, such as banks, a consortium of banks, international finance institutions, subcontractors to the private partner, and government budgets, can be sources of financing. Governments set the rules of the game through their institutions.

## 2.3 How Financing Can Affect Partnership Incentives

Depending on the incentives associated with private financing on a PPP, incentives may encourage the private partners to reduce and control project costs because they increase their profit margin and will receive a payment only if the cash flows are sufficient to cover costs (CBO, 2012). Governments can also use incentive payments or penalties that are contingent on the private partner meeting specific milestones pertaining to project costs or project progress or completion (CBO, 2012).

## 2.4 Institutional Constraints to Efficient and Effective Use of Scarce Public Resources in the Delivery of Infrastructure

Institutions, especially government institutions, provide the rules of the game in a society (North, 1990), as well as the basis for shared values and beliefs of government managers concerning other players' choices and intentions (Aoki, 2001, 2007). The shared beliefs are especially true of other players' choices and intentions under the rules of the game for carrying out public policy, such as their role in implementing Infrastructure Finance Policy. Players base their negotiating and decision-making strategies on these collectively recognized rules of the game (Stiller & Meirjerink, 2016) such as Infrastructure Finance Policy as a basis for shared beliefs regarding decision-making in financing and delivering capital infrastructure. Some coordinating institutional factors constrain the efficient and effective use of scarce resources in capital infrastructure financing and delivery. Such factors include transaction costs associated with coordinating institutional relationships and policy exchange transactions such as market exchange, free-rider problems, distributional issues, bounded rationality in understanding policy alternatives, and asymmetric information. Transaction costs may hinder coordination of rules of the game, especially new or changed rules of the game (Grief & Laitin, 2004), primarily associated with complex capital infrastructure financing, as related to the use of PPPs.

Also, institutional factor constraints involve interactions between political, legal, economic, and organization actors. The institutional policy arena establishes the rules of the game for economic policy exchange transactions to take place. The economic policy sphere is where economic transactions are carried out between the government and private agents/private partners. The political sphere is where the exchange between government principals and private agents takes place. In the political sphere, the political exchange does not include private agents; instead, the government can provide public goods to a private agent in exchange for the issuance of money. The private agent may respond by refusing to accept the government's exchange offer. Policy actors in these different policy arenas are identifiable, and rules of the game can be enforced in each area with social customs backed by the threat of ostracism (Aoki, 2007) in addition to laws and regulations, subject to institutional constraints.

The institutional constraints in evaluating (1) efficiency and (2) effectiveness as options for the use of scarce resources start with an understanding of concepts of scarcity and competition in the market. The notion of scarcity as it pertains to scarce resources in this context means that a government's decision to deliver a capital infrastructure through a PPP, based on the government's Infrastructure

Finance Policy options, is subject to constraints from the rules of the game. The concept of scarcity uses price theory as an essential part of the analysis of efficiency as a criterion for assessing institutional quality, and it sees changes in relative prices as a major force inducing institutional change. Institutional change, however, does not necessarily lead to more efficient institutions and economic growth (Eggertsson, 2005). Incomplete information (information asymmetry) and limited mental capacity are some of the factors that determine the cost of transactions in institutions, both private and public, and impacts both their economic and operational efficiency. Institutions are not only created to be socially efficient but also to serve the interests of those with the most bargaining power (North, 1990). Thus, institutional capacity and capability structure is an essential component of the efficient use of scarce resources. An administratively weak institutional framework affects the operational efficiency of the organizational arrangement for any given PPP contract (Brousseau & Glachant, 2002). An ineffective institutional framework would weaken the policy option to use PPPs because the interests of the private partner against unexpected events are not protected, while a strong effective institutional framework encourages institutional contractual arrangements in despite the uncertainty of the exchange environment (Baker, 2016).

### *2.4.1 Institutional Constraints to Efficient and Effective Infrastructure Delivery*

#### 2.4.1.1 Rules of the Game as Constraints

Democratic societies such as the United States allow for degrees of freedom in market exchange transaction boundaries when operating within the rules of the game. The problem with bureaucracies in democratic societies is that the exchange transaction boundaries are not clearly and carefully structured. Sometimes they are too narrow in scope; at other times, too broad in scope, blocking their ability to efficiently and effectively set and enforce the rules of the game, for example, when choosing PPPs as an Infrastructure Finance Policy option, negotiating the contract and in implementing PPPs. Adherence to the rules of the game and possessing the capacity and capability to follow those rules will control the degree of freedom and efficiency and effectiveness. The capability to follow the rules depends in part on government choice of the partnership in the form that best allows both partners to benefit from the relationship and, at the same time, provides for optimum social value.

The economic growth and development of a government cannot be measured by its efficiency alone in providing capital infrastructure, but also its effectiveness in providing social infrastructure which improves the overall quality of life (Prud'homme & Bocajero, 2005). Capital infrastructure plays an essential role in improving the well-being and quality of life of citizens (Kumari & Sharma, 2017; Prud'homme & Bocajero, 2005). Examples of capital infrastructure are roads, transportation, energy, and telecommunications, housing, education, and healthcare.

When a government decides to enter into a basic PPP contract such as Design-Build, for example, it can more readily identify the degrees of freedom in operating within the capital procurement rules of the game. In that case, the government can more narrowly specify the private partner performance requirements, relative to other more advanced types of PPP contracts. An example is the Cuomo Bridge Design-Build PPP form. This form allows the private partner to more easily determine the risks and investments required to deliver the capital project successfully.

Understanding the challenges of negotiating and managing complex contracts where the rules of the game on which the contract is based are not always clear (such as a PPP), on the other hand, can be better understood through the Brown, Potoski, and Van Slyke (2018) contracting framework. This framework is like traditional, non-PPP, contracting for complex goods and services. In this traditional, non-PPP exchange, the government wants to procure a product that helps achieve its mission objectives for a price within its budget (Brown et al., 2018). The private contractor, on the other hand, wants adequate compensation to cover costs and to earn a profit. In this scenario, the exchange is win-win if it delivers positive value to both the buyer (government) and the seller (private contractor). The Brown et al. (2018) basic contracting framework can also be used as a foundation for understanding highly complex and detailed contracts. Such contracts are entered into within a market economy operating in a democratic society, versus one that operates in an emerging market economy, and where a government establishes and articulates the conditions for the rules of the game. The framework provides the conditions for a successful contracting outcome, such as a PPP contract. Public managers whose agencies depend on simple products obtained through contract to achieve their mission can have faith in a well-functioning process and professional procurement to secure a positive [contracting] outcome (Brown et al., 2018). Complex capital infrastructure project contracts, such as PPP Concession contracts, on the other hand, are a challenge to procure, negotiate, and monitor to ensure that the rules of the game are adhered to because the many and varied large capital project requirements which are negotiated and spelled out in the contract make an all-encompassing, rules of the game.

Once a decision to finance and deliver a capital infrastructure using a PPP is made, the rules of the game in terms of government contracting, including PPP contracting, begin with the broader set of institutional policies that guide public sector purchasing regulations, public laws. The overarching legal, economic, political, and social institutional framework that governs the PPP capital contract is the formal and informal, but still important, policies and procedures that delineate the obligations of the two parties (Brown et al., 2018). Given the complexity of more advanced PPP forms, these rules of the game are more straightforward to enforce by public administrators when using basic PPP forms such as Design-Build. However, for advanced, PPP complex contract forms such as Concessions, information asymmetry in project requirements, and contract specifications make writing an all-encompassing initial PPP contract almost impossible. Specifically, contracts for more complicated PPP capital projects include more advanced, complex rules of the game such as government PPP contract rules, exchange rules such as how the private partner is compensated, and who bears the risk such as for cost overruns, and capital project authority rules. PPP contracts, especially the more advanced PPP contract types, such as Concessions, bind the partners to the exchange transaction in ways that make it difficult to pull out of the PPP contract. Consequently, successful completion of the PPP depends even more heavily on the capability and capacity of the institutional, economic, political, and legal policy actors, individually and in combination. The dependence on the policy actor's capability and capacity is because the rules of the game set the limits on contract deviation and what changes are negotiable/renegotiable and nonnegotiable/nonrenegotiable.

Partnership relationships in a PPP are generally between government and one private contractor. However, complex contractual partnership relationships, such as advanced PPP form, also require some basic level of cooperative institutional contractual agreement. A win-win contractual relationship outcome, such as a successful PPP contractual outcome, is more probable when the contract exchange rules of the game promote institutional cooperation (Brown et al., 2018). A win-win contractual relationship is undermined when one partner (unknown to the other partner) reduces the benefits that the other partner expects to receive and takes advantage of a cooperative institutional framework in order to secure its benefit. In that case, one partner engages in opportunism or the pursuit of self-interest (Williamson, 1975).

Cooperative institutional frameworks require a thorough and understanding by the government of the complex elements of the PPP contract and expertise in writing the long-term contract within a set of rules of the game that promote partnership cooperation. A successful, win-win, PPP contract outcome is based on strong institutional, political, economic, legal, organization. A complex, advanced form of PPPs can only be successful where the institutional quality, capacity, and capability of the government in managing the rules of the game is stable and determined by economic discipline that focuses on efficiency and the search for optimum social welfare (Baker, 2016) and social value. More specifically, the institutional dimensions, e.g., the political, economic, judicial, and institutional, must be taken into consideration and incorporated into a cohesive whole, especially considering the magnitude of the additional coordination costs they generate (Baker, 2016). Creating and maintaining the quality, capability, and capacity of leadership of these public institutional elements is key to institutional governance efficiency and a control on transaction costs (Baker, 2016). Institutional quality impacts private investment in PPP (Wang, Liu, Xiong, & Zhou, 2018) and effects PPP transaction cost.

### *2.4.2 Transaction Cost as a Constraint to Economic Efficiency*

Another way to evaluate the efficiency of the outcome of the use of PPP to deliver a capital infrastructure is to use Transaction Cost Theory (TCT) to explain why some economic activities such as government-initiated PPP contract transactions are organized as market transactions. In contrast, others are organized as government economic activities. In evaluating government economic activities in the context of Infrastructure Finance Policy and capital financing policy alternatives, transaction costs, and public value, must be considered, since they are components of institutional quality.

## 2.5 The Relationship between PPP, Transaction Cost, and Organizational Characteristics

### *2.5.1 PPP Transaction Cost and Economic Efficiency*

TCT describes the optimal governance structure to complete efficient transactions. Transaction cost recognizes the efficiency of different organizational forms in explaining why some economic activities are organized as markets, and others are organized as hierarchical units (Weimer & Vining, 2017) such as government agencies. TCT accepts that production costs are only part of the cost of an institutional decision on how best to supply a good or service, and such production costs are associated with making, executing, monitoring, and renegotiating of contracts among institutional entities which are involved in the production.

The theory of transaction cost was developed by Ronald Coase (1937), who defined transaction costs as those of carrying out an exchange transaction on the open market. Williamson (1975, 1987, 1999) built upon the original Coase theory. Transaction costs are the economic equivalent to costs due to friction in physical systems, as distinguished from production costs (Williamson, 1987). Transaction costs are efficient to the extent that there are no other alternative governance institutions that can be used with net gains over and above the chosen institution (United States Department of Transportation, 2019). TCT merges ex-ante and ex-post problems that stem from asymmetric information, property rights, and the incompleteness of contracts caused by systemic, bureaucratic institutional delays and inefficiencies. It puts together transaction characteristics, such as infrastructure contract specificity and risk uncertainty, with institutional structures to decide as to the optimal choice of preferred (most efficient) management form for a given transaction. TCT is different from other contractual theories of the firm by its comprehensiveness in approaching transaction cost problems and the rigor of its conclusions (Baker, 2016).

Subsequent TCT authors have built on the work of Coase and Williamson. Crocker and Masten (1996), for example, established the importance of transaction costs in organizational structure choice and design decisions in the public utility sector. Baker (2016) built on the Crocker and Masten (1996) construct for choosing an appropriate institutional structure for the provision of public services as applied to efficiency in public utility transaction costs. TCT can be used to interpret the impact of institutional characteristics on the amount of transaction cost (Baker, 2016).

Transaction costs in the context of PPPs refers to the institutional characteristics and costs of establishing and maintaining a partnership; more specifically, it refers to the legal, financial, and technical advisory costs incurred by both public and private sectors, especially in the procurement, contracting, and operational phases of a project (Dudkin & Valila, 2005) as well as political and social costs. Costs for organizing the bidding process; participating in it; negotiating the contract between the public sector and the winning private bidder; monitoring the private sector partner's compliance with the contract; and renegotiating the contract during its lifecycle are all included as determining transaction costs.

When identifying potential transaction costs in a PPP, one of the issues is the capability and capacity of the contracting partners. Understanding the political, economic, legal, and organization capacity and capability elements of a PPP and how they affect transaction efficiency and how they are bounded by "man as he is, acting within the constraints imposed by real institutions" (Coase, 1937, p. 231) is also central to understanding government contracting capability and capacity. PPPs have a higher chance of success (efficiency) if the government can foster substantial competition among private firms for partnership contracts (CBO, 2012) when choosing the private partner. The challenge that TCT suggests is that the contract planning, writing, negotiating, renegotiating, and monitoring is complicated, and the threat of opportunistic behavior is more prevalent when the PPP project is more advanced since

- the costs of writing the contracts are connected to the required expertise for drafting specifications that assure public service quality,
- because of technical specifications, government attract few responders, which limits competition and strengthens the negotiating power of private contractors,
- infrastructure [asset] specificity creates a mutual dependency situation between partners and increases the risk of opportunism,
- the complexity of PPP contract negotiations, the frequency of renegotiations in some cases, and the contract cancellation risk increase costs, which are then reflected in the price that users must pay for the service, and
- the risk of uncertainty associated with unforeseen exogenous events also increases the frequency of contract renegotiations and complicates the management of certain capital projects (Baker, 2016; Williamson, 1975, 1987, 1999).

### *2.5.2 Typical PPP Contracting Stages as Potential Sources of PPP Transaction Cost and Inefficiency in Contract Negotiation Stages*

The stages in the contract bidder selection and contract tender process involve a degree of transaction cost and information asymmetry. Each stage in the contract negotiation process is thus prone to the substantial transaction cost. The following are typical PPP Contracting Stages:

*Stage 1: PPP Contract Negotiation: Form PPP Procurement Team*

The traditional capital project procurement team is supplemented with legal and financial expertise pertinent to the specific PPPs.

*Stage 2: PPP Contract Negotiation: Internal Decision Meeting*
The type of bid proposal is determined based on the PPP legal framework, how many negotiating meetings are needed, type of bid, and if negotiated bid, the process through the negotiation meetings, and when to request a final proposal.
*Stage 3: PPP Contract Negotiation: Information meeting for Potential Bidders*
The official announcement of the proposed capital project and call for bids. An informational meeting with a presentation of the proposed project to attract potential bidders can be scheduled. A contract notice is also published online.
*Stage 4: PPP Contract Negotiation: Prequalification of Bidders*
Interested private contractors submit a series of predefined criteria and documentation, including the private contractor's potential strengths and prior experience with similar projects.
*Stage 5: PPP Contract Negotiation: Selection of Shortlists*
A shortlist is drawn up based on the criteria.
*Stage 6: PPP Contract Negotiation: Invitation to Participate*
Due to tender process cost, the invitation may be issued to between three to five bidders, depending on the number judged as meeting the criteria relevant to the project. The invitation specifies the service required in output terms, proposed contract terms, and terms and conditions for the submission of bids and evaluation criteria.
*Stage 7: PPP Contract Negotiation: Presentation and Negotiation Meetings*
Several meetings are held individually with each of the bidders, typically three, where the bidders present all parts of their offer. To clarify ambiguities, negotiate issues, and give the bidders opportunities to adjust their proposal before the final submission of bids, their offer is reviewed.
*Stage 8: PPP Contract Negotiation: Receipt and Evaluation of Final Bids*
When final bids are received, they are evaluated by prespecified criteria and points. These points include price, design, and qualities, in addition to an overall understanding of the project. The proposals received a weighted score based on the project criteria.
*Stage 9: PPP Contract Negotiation: Selection of the preferred bidder and final evaluation*
Adapted from Thomassen, Vassbo, Solheim-Kile, and Lohne (2016).

Once the bidder is selected, the contract documents are then prepared. Capital Project documents include

PPP Contract Documents
Overall PPP contract that incorporates all public partner and private partner agreements
Capital Project Agreement regulating the design and construction phase
Capital Project hiring agreement
Capital Project Operating Agreement
Lease of Land (if appropriate)
Physical Inventory Agreement

In number 9 above, the final stage, the preferred bidder is selected, based on weighted scores, and the contract is negotiated. Before a PPP contract is signed, however, senior government management approval of the preferred bidder is required. As stated above, because the stages in the contract bidder selection and contract tender process involve a degree of information asymmetry, especially as it pertains to risk, each stage in the capital contract negotiation process is prone to substantial transaction costs.

New York State's PPP Design-Build procurement process is an example of an alternative to the traditional forms of capital infrastructure procurement that is efficient because it reduces transaction costs. In the traditional method of capital infrastructure procurement, a public institution, such as the Department of Transportation, uses a two-step bidding process. One is for an initial design proposal, and the other is for the construction of the winning design, called design-build, if a PPP is used. In the PPP Design-Build form, the process eliminates the middle step, and bids are solicited for both design and construction in one step. This form is an example of efficiency in both time and [transaction] cost (DiNapoli, 2014).

### *2.5.3 PPP Contract Uncertainty and Risk*

Issues regarding capital infrastructure contract uncertainty and risk and their impact on transaction costs are often harder to identify upfront in the PPP, since one of the partners in the PPP can influence the exchange environment through its power to define the rules of the game, or to redefine and renegotiate PPP project property and contractual rights after an unforeseen event (Baker, 2016) such as a flood, tornado, or other natural disaster. Governmental institutions can also influence the courts on contract dispute settlements wherever judicial integrity and independence are weak (Baker, 2016). Transitionally, this currently appears to be the case in Albania, for example, and as such, increases both a high degree of uncertainty and risk, thus increasing transaction costs (Beckett-Camarata, 2019).

When the government rules of the game are clearly defined and enforced, contract negotiation, finalization, and implementation of capital project contracts such as PPP contracts are less expensive. This cost reduction is because the risk of opportunistic behavior decreases (Baker, 2016). In countries where institutions are efficient, such as the United States, contract uncertainty and risk are minimized, and PPP transaction costs are lowered. Consequently, investors are generally willing to accept lower rates of return (depending on the government's bond rating, for example) considering the lower transaction costs related to Infrastructure Finance Policy, decision-making process, and management and implementation of contracts (Bergstahler, Hail, & Leuz, 2006). The cost of capital is also lower where institutional governance and the rule of and respect for the law are strong (Baker, 2016; Bergstahler et al., 2006).

An example of contract uncertainty and risk in Mauritius is the Cure Pipe Wind Farm contract establishing bid parameters and transparent criteria for evaluation because of lack of wind data availability. The Transaction Advisors evaluated options such as capital cost as bidding criteria, but the capital cost did not include the technological advancement and performance levels of the turbines. Also, wind data were not available for 2–3 years, the recommended time for estimating a reasonable level of generation from the wind park. The decision was made to use tariff-based bidding based on a normative wind speed with adjustment formula vis-à-vis change in the wind speed. After 2 years, the tariff was adjusted based on the average recorded wind speed of 2 years. The solution was innovative and helped balance the risk of wind speed perceived by potential investors and deployment of best wind technology that can yield maximum generation in the site for the procurer (Mauritius Wind Farm Report, 2012, p. 16). Again, the PPP was flexible enough to allow mutual modification of the contract and maintain a win-win partnership balance.

### *2.5.4 Infrastructure Finance Policy Implementation and Creating Public Value*

The role of public value needs to be considered as a factor in evaluating the use of PPP as an Infrastructure Finance Policy option. Creating public value is defined as constructing something that is valued by the public, or is good for the public, assessed against public value criteria (Alford & Hughes, 2008; Alford & O'Flynn, 2009; Benington & Moore, 2011; Bryson, Crosby, & Bloomberg, 2014). In creating public value, the government's creation of the rules of the game should be based on the full range of democratic and constitutional values. Recognizing that both policymakers and public managers should choose among the range of policy alternatives for financing capital infrastructure provides not only for efficiency but also creates public value. In that respect, public administrators should help create and guide policy networks (such as networks of capital project delivery) that help maintain and enhance overall effectiveness, capacity, and accountability of the system (Bryson et al., 2014, p. 448) such as the system for financing and delivering capital infrastructure. Formally identifying a public value enables policy debates about shared values, institutions, systems, processes, and people. Public value also is the public policy connection to policy design, implementation, analysis, organization, economics, and politics (Smith, 2004). In identifying and creating public value, government institutions can be a convener, catalyst, and collaborator, sometimes steering, sometimes rowing, and sometimes partnering (Bryson et al., 2014) as in the case of PPPs.

The criterion for government decision-making should be the effective, expected change in social welfare (Boardman & Vining, 2012) and public value brought about by the decision to finance a capital infrastructure delivery through the use of a PPP. In government decision-making regarding the choice to use PPPs to finance capital infrastructure, the options are based in part on (1): whether the capital infrastructure is needed and planned for, (2) the priority of the capital infrastructure, and (3) the preferred method to finance the capital project, e.g., through traditional financing or some form of PPP, in the context of Infrastructure Finance Policy.

In the initial analysis of funding options, the starting point should be identifying the strengths and weaknesses of funding options for proposed capital infrastructure before inclusion in the Capital Improvement Plan (Fishbein & Morrell, 2009) as described in Table 2.1.

The expected change in social welfare and public value can be more challenging to analyze in advanced PPP forms, given the long-term nature of the contract. In an advanced PPP form such as a Concession, as noted in Chapter 1, the government normally transfers the right to operate and maintain an existing capital infrastructure to a private partner, such as the case with the Indiana Toll Road Concession. The length of a Concession is usually for many years, sometimes 99 years. In other PPP forms, the government grants a private partner the right to build and operate a capital facility for a specified amount of time. In some PPP forms, the public partner owns the constructed capital facility and pays the private partner either from public financing (tax revenue or debt, or

Table 2.1. Infrastructure Funding Option Analysis.

**Example of a subnational government sewer installation and road resurfacing government funding option analysis:**

| **Option** | **Effect** | **Justification** |
|---|---|---|
| Raise $9 million property tax levy by 4% annually over 5 years | The portion of the property tax bill that goes to the entity would increase ~$24 a year | Levy has been raised only once in 10 years but citizens face other tax increases |
| Take $7 million from the $35 million permanent fund | The fund has previously used $8 million from this fund for road and sewer work | The funds are available but the more money the entity uses, the less interests the permanent fund earns |
| Increase Home Rule Law Sales Tax from 0.5% to 0.75% | The entity would raise about $2.5 million for the capital improvements | With an increase, the entity's Home Rule Law Sales Tax would be the same or less than most other governments. That have the tax but may drive customers elsewhere |
| Initiate a new $10,000 tax on any demolished building | Would raise $300,000–$500,000 per year | Could discourage private development |
| Initiate a Real Estate Transfer Tax on buyers | Could raise $2–$3 million per year | Requires a voter approval |

*Source:* Adapted from Fishbein and Morrell (2009).

both) or from revenue that comes from the completed capital project (user fees). The private partner may or may not contribute some of the capital infrastructure financing, depending on the PPP form. At the end of the PPP contract period, the private partner transfers operations to the government (The World Bank, 2019). In some PPP forms, the government is involved in the capital project design or provides the capital infrastructure project design to the private partner, but the government remains liable for any design errors or omissions. In those cases, the government partner will be credited with delivering the capital project but put current minimal financing into the PPP at the outset and pay the most significant part of the capital infrastructure cost at a later budget period. This financing arrangement may contribute toward financial efficiency by balancing the current operating and capital budgets and can be monitored by periodically comparing to preestablished performance benchmarks. Governments pay for the capital infrastructure project (payment timing depends on the PPP form) but may defer a large portion of the PPP contract payments to later fiscal year budgets.

## 2.6 Incomplete Information and Bounded Rationality in PPP Contract

### *2.6.1 Incomplete Information in PPP Contracts*

When information is incomplete, and there is limited mental capacity (often referred to as bounded rationality), partners are limited in processing large amounts of complex information (Simon, 1979), especially as that information pertains to PPP contracts. Individuals within different institutions use different mental models to understand the world around them. They consequently often arrive at different understandings of the way the world works and driven by their world perspective and understanding of their available options for financing a capital project such as PPPs. This difference in understanding leads to information asymmetry. Information asymmetry in PPPs can occur for several reasons. Sharing information that could reduce or eliminate asymmetry takes time and increases cost (Hart 2003; Xiong, Zhao, & Wang, 2018). Additionally, the private contractor usually is not willing to reveal proprietary information that may be pertinent to contract negotiation (Reynaers & Grimmelikhuijsen, 2015; Xiong et al., 2018). Many contracts do not articulate under what specific circumstances a contract can be renegotiated (Xiong et al., 2018), which adds to information asymmetry.

Incomplete information, or information asymmetry, as it pertains to PPP contract negotiation/renegotiation is defined as the first time when the public and private partners can begin to plan their negotiation strategy when one partner has information that other partner does not have (Xiong et al., 2018). In the case of some PPP Concession contracts, the reasons for the contract renegotiation is not specified, and the public partner does not have complete information on the actual risk of the private partner (Xiong et al., 2018).

The more advanced and complex Concession form of PPP agreement provides an example of how information asymmetry may impact the partnership contract. PPP contracts are multifaceted and typically create complex partnership relationships, especially the more advanced forms on the PPP continuum. The more advanced forms can involve a high degree of unforeseen events/risks in contract negotiation and renegotiation. Information asymmetry can occur especially during initial contract negotiations in the more advanced form of PPPs, because of (1) inherent complexities in the long-term contractual nature of the more advanced PPP contract itself, (2) the large-scale investment arrangements, and (3) the high degree of potential risk. It is especially not possible to identify or consider all possible risks in Concession contracts (the most advanced PPP form, for example, during the bidding period and renegotiation is typically used to arrive at information symmetry in order to renegotiate risk) (Guasch, 2004; Xiong et al., 2018). Either the public partner or the private partner can initiate contract renegotiation.

In government-initiated contract renegotiations, the government can make certain contract adjustments to maximize public value, for example, speeding up payments to the private partner, increasing investment based on its infrastructure finance policies, and/or amending the contract performance requirements.

In private partner–initiated contract renegotiations, the private partner renegotiates any increased risk through different types of public partner, for example, debt guarantee or concession contract extension (Crus & Marques, 2013; Guasch, 2004; Xiong et al., 2018). Private partner–initiated renegotiations can be especially challenging in terms of information asymmetry. Information asymmetry can occur from the private partner because of initial misestimation in the capital project design phase and the resulting underestimation of the amount of the work involved and additional cost or possible over-forecasting revenue of the revenue (Xiong et al., 2018). Private partner–led PPP contract renegotiation can potentially reduce project social value because the private partner does not typically identify the social value as a significant factor in its negotiation and because social value costs and benefits are not always readily identified and quantified by the public partner. Thus, the presence of such information asymmetry provides an opportunity for opportunistic behavior on the part of the private partner (Xiong et al., 2018).

### *2.6.2 Bounded Rationality in PPP Contracts*

Bounded rationality is the idea that humans are rational, but his rationality is limited (Simon, 1982). Public administrators may have limited experience in formulating and solving complex issues and problems and in processing complex information such as with advanced forms of PPPs. The behavioral assumptions of bounded rationality and the issue of opportunism in PPP contracts in the context of uncertainty and the number of participants in the contract transaction are analogous to friction in a machine in that, taken together, they prevent a transaction from being completed efficiently (Boyle, 2009).

In the Infrastructure Finance Policy implementation process, the decision to finance a capital project using a basic PPP, and how to structure the PPP contract is relatively straightforward and the boundedly rationality issue moot. In more complex policy decision-making, the decision to deliver a capital infrastructure using a PPP, in what form, and structuring the PPP contract is usually more complicated, especially in the case of the use of more advanced PPP forms and contracts, such as Concessions. This complexity is because of the unusually long length of time for the contract, for example, up to 99 years in some cases. The decision to use a PPP to finance a capital infrastructure shifts the balance between the government and private contractor in the capital infrastructure financing and delivery.

## 2.7 Infrastructure Finance and Delivery Balance Shift in Public and Private Partnerships

One Infrastructure Finance Policy design goal in using PPPs is to deliver a public good or service, such as capital infrastructure more efficiently and effectively than other capital infrastructure financing options. Market incentives, such as the use of competitive bidding in selecting a private contractor, are used at each phase of the capital project in traditional procurement of capital infrastructure delivery. With the use of a PPP, the balance in financing and delivering a capital infrastructure is shifted from the traditional method of public sector solely delivering the capital infrastructure through traditional procurement with several bids and several contracts. With a PPP, the shift is to a partnership, with the private partner (depending on the form of partnership) having a more significant role in financing and delivering the capital infrastructure more efficiently and effectively than public sector delivery alone through one contract. The change from sole government financing and delivery to a partnership in the financing and delivery shifts the role of the government from sole provider to government as a partner with the private sector and manager of the contract for the delivery of the capital infrastructure. The focus then shifts to the assessment of public administrators' role in capital infrastructure delivery to effectiveness as well as efficiency, in addition to their role in responsiveness to public needs (as is the case when sole public sector delivery is used) as well as on public/social value. The focus in assessing the Infrastructure Finance Policy shifts from solely the most efficient use of financing capital infrastructure delivery to include evaluating the use of appropriate incentives to attract private contractors to balance public capital infrastructure financing and delivery needs.

The criteria for assessing the effectiveness of the Infrastructure Finance Policy, as it relates to the choice to use PPP to deliver a capital infrastructure project, are (1) whether the infrastructure finance policy encourages increased private sector involvement and (2) whether government incentives are effective in doing so. Such incentives will only work if the private contractor believes that the PPP contract is profitable. Financial incentives do not make financially unattractive capital projects attractive but rather make financially attractive projects more attractive (Eckerd & Heidelberg, 2015).

One effective way for the government to provide incentives to private PPP partners to minimize capital project costs is to use of performance quality standards to incentivize cost-cutting. The use of contract performance quality standards in the PPP contract is to avoid the possibility of private partners' low quality of capital infrastructure construction (Buckberg, Kearney, & Stolleman, 2015) because of cost-cutting. The use of quality contract performance input and output standards written into a contract is viable if the specified quality level can be clearly identified in the contract and readily tested by both the public and the private partners (Buckberg et al., 2015). It is important then for the government to negotiate and write a PPP contract that specifies the level of private partner performance quality, that private partner agrees to, and which can be monitored and enforced by the government in order to be able to ensure partnership efficiency gains (Buckberg et al., 2015).

Since a well-developed PPP inherently incentivizes private partner cost-cutting, some partners may lower wages of those working on the capital infrastructure project to reduce contract costs. While this may reduce contract costs for the private actor, it may reduce the quality of the work on the project. One quality standard which should be considered is the use of private partner labor quality standards in a PPP contract (Buckberg et al., 2015).

The government can provide incentives to lower the PPP contract cost by arranging meaningful and accepted incentives to minimize cost at specific project stages and requiring standards of quality in the PPP contract. The government can, in effect, provide incentives to lower the total contract cost, while ensuring the quality of the capital infrastructure, reducing time to completion of the capital contract and the same time, insure that the capital project is operational. The mutually beneficial incentives in the more advanced PPP contract can hold the private partner responsible for paying future costs (part of the contract phase completion) of completing various capital project phases while giving the private partner full decision-making power and control of the infrastructure in the completion of each phase (Buckberg et al., 2015). The public partner must accurately identify and transfer risk, as well as adequately compensate for that risk, in order to more fully achieve efficiency gains.

The primary method for transferring risk requires government identification of the known and potential risks in capital infrastructure delivery and mutually assurance that the risk transfer is jointly negotiated in the PPP contract. In traditional capital infrastructure procurement, risk assessment is clear and transparent to partners. Taxpayers bear most of the risk, except for performance risk (Buckberg et al., 2015).

### *2.7.1 Risk Transfer in PPP Contracts*

What is essential in risk transfer is whether a specific PPP contract will mitigate risk or minimize the consequences of unforeseen risk (Boardman & Vining,

2012). There are risks inherent in any capital project contract. Regardless of whether or not a PPP is chosen, the use of a PPP, depending on the PPP form, has the potential of the private partner to bear some types of risk transfer better than the traditional government capital project financing and delivery (Boardman & Vining, 2012). The risks should be identified, the amount should be included in the production (transaction) cost, and the private partner compensated for the risk. If a private contract partner in a PPP becomes bankrupt, the government usually steps in to complete the project (Adarkwa, Smadi, & Alhasan, 2017), whether through traditional government delivery or by securing a new private partner to complete the project. PPP private partners usually are not willing to accept a significant transfer of demand and revenue risk in a Concession, for example, which depends on both demand and price. Governments, especially governments in emerging economies that do not have prior experience with PPPs, do not have experience with advanced forms of PPPs or do not have adequate political, economic, organizational, and legal, capacity, and capability and usually do not transfer revenue risk. As a result, the private partner profits are guaranteed in the PPP contract (depending on the PPP form) (Boardman & Vining, 2012).

As discussed previously, the amount of capital infrastructure project transaction cost depends on capital infrastructure complexity, risk, contractor market competitiveness, and institutional capacity and capability. More complex PPP projects such as Concessions inherently have higher amounts of transaction costs due to higher demand and revenue risk, low competitiveness, and limited competition. Transaction cost is compounded where the public partner's capability and capacity are limited, and the private partner seeks to take advantage of the capability and capacity limits in the form of opportunism (Boardman & Vining, 2012).

Transaction cost ultimately impacts the cost of financing and delivery of the capital infrastructure. Government financing for capital infrastructure, if financed traditionally through debt from issuing bonds (General Obligation Bonds backed by the full faith and credit of the government), will have a favorable borrowing cost (depending on the bond rating of the government) because it has a relatively low risk of default. However, the bonds are backed by tax revenue, and taxes come at the expense of reduced consumption, which then reduces potential investment. Because consumption tax rates of interest are relatively low, the cost of long-term government borrowing for capital projects is relatively lower than private sector borrowing for the same purpose. This situation depends on the capability and capacity of the PPP partners and the level of risk and complexity of the advanced PPP.

The cost of the government's contract and project monitoring a private partner in a PPP will generally be higher than traditional government delivered project monitoring. The high transaction cost is inherent in the complexity of the bundling of the private contract bidding, private partner selection, contract negotiation, implementation of the PPP contract, and the long length of time. Most of the transaction cost is in the procurement of the private partner, but contract monitoring and renegotiation are also sources of the transaction cost. Opportunistic bidding behavior by the private contractor can occur during capital project procurement. Such behavior typically involves the bidders, in their bid proposals, intentionally understating possible risk involved or understating the project cost in order to outperform other bidders (Ho, 2006).

If contract renegotiation is anticipated in a government procurement process, building a mechanism to renegotiate the contract into the bidding process may be limited because both partners may come to assume renegotiation as a given (Hart & Moore, 1994). Typically, PPP contracts undergo a standard negotiation process during capital infrastructure contract procurement, as discussed previously. Financial renegotiation is the change in terms of the financial arrangement after the contract is signed when the terms and conditions which formed the basis of the partnership financial agreement change significantly (Ho, 2006). In a PPP, financial renegotiation can take place when project cost, market demand, or other market conditions become unfavorable to either party to the contract.

As discussed in Chapter 1, capital infrastructure delivery, whether it is government-financed through traditional financing such as the use of General Obligation Debt or a PPP and private partner financing (depending on the PPP form), relies on particular debt or equity financing or some combination for financing. In the case of capital infrastructure, financing of capital projects ultimately depends on debt, user fees, tax revenues, or a combination. The use of PPPs provides for private financing, depending on the PPP form. Given the use of these financing sources, and the fact that capital infrastructure are long-lived, political, and citizen support is essential.

Countries such as Australia, United Kingdom, and Canada primarily use equity financing through PPPs for financing capital projects. In contrast, the United States primarily uses debt financing as the principal source of financing capital projects, and delivering capital infrastructure using equity financing through PPPs is still growing. In order to attract more equity financing in the United States for capital projects, the use of private placement and/or equity financing will have to be viewed as more efficient and effective than debt financing.

While a PPP is one financing option for delivering a capital infrastructure, it is not always the most efficient delivery method, depending on the contracting expertise of the government, the credit rating of the government, the nature of the capital infrastructure itself, the expertise of the private partner, and the degree of interest of private investors. Capital infrastructure delivery should be evaluated using such policy implementation and evaluation tools as risk analysis and cost–benefit analysis (within the context of Infrastructure Finance Policy) to determine whether a capital infrastructure is more efficiently delivered by a government using GO bonds for funding as compared to using a basic Design-Bid-Build PPP approach. In addition to the cost–benefit analysis, a risk analysis study should also be conducted, which would identify risk and include risk analysis. The more advanced the form of PPP, the higher the risk (design risk, demand, risk, revenue risk) involved. The risk should be balanced between the public partner and the private partner and be negotiated through the contract via the use of user fees such as tolls and availability payments, and more recently, through revenue sharing. In a PPP user fee financing arrangement such as a Concession, the private partner collects and retains all fees from users of the service such as bridge tolls and bears all the risk of uncertain demand for the service. In an availability payments partnership arrangement, the government partner collects revenue from the users and makes fixed, recurring payments to the private partner, if the private partner meets contract performance standards.

In a PPP arrangement, a revenue-sharing contract can directly align government and private investor benefits. If the capital project exceeds or falls short of negotiated threshold rates of return, the partners can either share the excess return or absorb the shortfall in contractually defined proportions. This type of contract flexibility is appealing to private investors who may be more willing to enter into an agreement where they are required to share the projects potential benefits with the government if the government, in turn, provides some protection from demand risk on the downside (Buckberg et al., 2015).

## 2.8 Public Sector Efficiency Issues in Infrastructure Finance and Delivery

This section discusses issues impacting public sector efficiency in capital infrastructure financing and delivery. It explains how the public sector typically has few or no incentives for efficiency built into its capital project planning, capital project investments, and Infrastructure Finance Policy implementation organizations and processes. Thus, the organization and its processes may be poorly positioned to efficiently support the building and operating of capital infrastructure in many countries (government failure). Injecting such incentives into a bureaucracy can be difficult, though not impossible, as demonstrated by individual countries developing a government-wide culture dedicated to efficiency, one that also implements high-quality systems to deliver critical public services effectively.

### *2.8.1 Principal–Principal Relationship Efficiency Issues in PPPs*

Principal–principal and principal–agency relationship complexities, introduced in Chapter 1, are compounded because governments need to work through public agencies to provide public goods to citizens who would be underserved otherwise by the market. The public sector uses labor and other input factors to produce outputs but does not have to operate in a competitive market to exist. The extent to which the government agency contributes to efficiency depends on the level of expertise, capacity, motivation, and monitoring of those principal representatives who determine agency budgets and lead their organizations.

The principal–agent problem, discussed earlier, stems from the fact that public sector employers and employees do not necessarily have the same interests, and it is costly to monitor the behavior of employees. Government employers operate in an environment of information asymmetry (Epstein & O'Halloran, 1999). The agent is in a better position to know the minimum cost of producing a specific output level than either the public or their representatives (principals) who determine the agency budget (Weimer & Vining, 2017).

Public sector managers (agents) operate in an environment of information asymmetry not only in contracting with private contractors, as discussed previously, but also in their relationship to the public at large, as well as other government managers and employees. However, the managers are usually better equipped to identify representatives (principals) who determine their agency's budgets (Weimer & Vining, 2017). Because of the limited time that principals must review the agency's budget, an in-depth evaluation of the ways the agency's resources (Weimer & Vining, 2017) and the way those resources are ultimately allocated is not always equitable. Government managers must manage their resources within their budget appropriation and are required to balance their budget. It is economically more efficient for a government manager to produce output at minimum cost (where revenue exceeds expenditures) so that they can keep their Fund Balance. However, doing so may lead to the perception that taxes are too high or that revenue estimates were inaccurate, or some combination. Such uncertain perceptions can lead to a lower budget appropriation in the next budget cycle. Because budgets in the public sector are not only management tools for managing resources, but political and legal tools to manage resources within budgets, managers have little budgetary discretion.

Economic efficiency in public sector capital project planning, management, and implementation is dependent on an institution's capacity and capability, such as its PPP contract expertise. As a result, some PPPs do not have lower costs (Boardman & Vining, 2012), again, depending on the PPP form. In the United Kingdom, the Highways Agency paid a 25% premium on construction cost on its first four PPP road projects to ensure they were built 'on time and to budget' (Boardman & Vining, 2012). Construction prices of European road PPP projects were 24% higher than for traditionally procured PSA projects (Blanc-Brude, Goldsmith, & Valila, 2009). Governments in some countries may not be positioned to efficiently deliver significant capital infrastructure needs through PPPs, especially in particular emerging economies, due to need for procurement staff who are capable and well-trained in more complex PPP procurement. So trained, they will be able to efficiently and effectively evaluate, negotiate, renegotiate, and monitor complex PPP capital contracts.

#### 2.8.1.1 Evaluating Economic Efficiency of Infrastructure Finance Policy Options

One way that economic efficiency can be evaluated is by determining the costs and benefits of capital infrastructure. Cost–benefit analysis is one method that can be used to analyze and evaluate the efficiency of large capital projects. Such analysis can be especially useful in determining potential financing options. It is the process of identifying and assessing all current and future costs and benefits. If the present value of the expenditure exceeds the present value of the costs, the capital infrastructure is recommended for inclusion in the capital budget (Marlowe, Rivenbark, & Vogt, 2009). Cost–benefit analysis provides a decision rule that focuses on choosing a policy alternative that provides the most significant net benefits (Weimer & Vining, 2017). Because efficiency is one goal for deciding on a policy alternative, the cost–benefit analysis can provide a quantitative technique for assessing efficiency (Weimer & Vining, 2017).

A cost–benefit analysis should begin with defining the service-level objectives of the capital infrastructure is crucial because it provides decision-makers with additional data when benefits are difficult to quantify. It helps decision-makers with additional context when benefits are challenging to quantify. It helps decision-makers understand how service-level objectives may be affected if the proposed project is approved, rejected, or postponed. The steps involved are as follows:

- *Identify alternatives* for delivering the capital project. If there are alternatives, the cost–benefit analysis can be used to identify the option with the highest economic value.
- *Identify all costs and benefits* associated with each policy alternative that can be valued in monetary terms. Intangible costs are essential to identify based on their social value rather than the economic value, which is often the case for government support services with public goods characteristics.
- *Forecast future streams of costs and benefits.* After direct and indirect costs have been identified and given a monetary value, all direct and indirect costs and benefits are forecast for the expected useful life of the capital infrastructure or for some other appropriate time frame. A discount rate is then selected and used to calculate the net present value (NPV). NPV is the difference between present value (PV) of benefits and the present value (PV) of costs.
- *Choose the proposed project* with the benefit in comparison with the cost. The subnational government usually chooses the project with the highest NPV, ceteris paribus (Marlowe et al., 2009) (See Table 2.2).

Since capital infrastructure require a large part of the capital budget, governments need to have a clear understanding of the sources of capital project financing and their overall fit (Fishbein & Morrell, 2009) within their Infrastructure Finance Policy goals. The government should review all potential and current capital financing sources, especially those tied to or strongly influenced by the economy. If one-time revenue sources are used, they should be understood in that context, and revenue sources that are elastic, such as sales taxes, will decrease when the economy slows down. Thus, if the option is to use a PPP, it must fit with overall Infrastructure Finance Policy goals and their overall compatibility with economic policy goals. In a situation where revenue sources are constrained, and budgets must be balanced, governments need to analyze their expenditures versus revenues and be conservative in their revenue estimates, especially those tied to the economy.

Table 2.2. Wind Farm Feasibility Study Cost–Benefit Analysis Wind Farm Capacity: 20 MW with 1.5 MW Turbines.

| | |
|---|---|
| *Initial investment* | |
| ESPH investment | $16,650,00 |
| 15 year loan | $38,850,000 (@0.0325 interest) |
| *Initial cost* | |
| Construction | |
| Wind turbine cost | 54,600,000 |
| Legal fees | |
| Transmission line | 900,000 |
| *Cost over time* | |
| Operation and maintenance | 0.01 $/kWh |
| Labor cost | 10% of revenue |
| Loan payment | 3,313,461 |
| Rate of inflation | 2% of revenue |
| *Revenue* | |
| Expected rate of electricity | Varies by year |
| Estimated production of proposed site | 102,000 MWh |
| Expected rate of inflation | 10% |

**Cost-Benefit Analysis and Payback Period Wind Farm Capacity: 20 MW with 800 kW Turbines**

| **Year** | **1** | **2** | **3** | **4** | **5** |
|---|---|---|---|---|---|
| **Production (MWh)** | 84,000 | 84,000 | 84,000 | 84,000 | 84,000 |
| **Revenue** | | | | | |
| Price of electricity (per kWh) | 0.100 | 0.103 | 0.105 | 0.108 | 0.110 |
| **Total revenue** | 8,400,000 | 8,610,000 | 8,825,250 | 9,045,881 | 9,272,028 |
| **Costs** | | | | | |
| O&M | 840,000 | 840,000 | 840,000 | 840,000 | 840,000 |
| Labor | 840,000 | 861,000 | 882,525 | 904,588 | 927,203 |
| Loan payment | 3,397,044 | 3,397,044 | 3,397,044 | 3,397,044 | 3,397,044 |

Table 2.2. *(Continued)*

| | | | | | |
|---|---|---|---|---|---|
| Rent | 168,000 | 172,200 | 176,505 | 180,918 | 185,441 |
| **Total Cost** | **5,245,044** | **5,270,244** | **5,296,074** | **5,322,550** | **5,349,688** |
| **Cash flow** | 3,154,956 | 3,339,756 | 3,529,176 | 3,723,331 | 3,922,341 |
| **Discounted cash flow** | 2,868,142 | 2,760,129 | 2,651,522 | 2,543,085 | 2,435,465 |
| Initial investment payback $17,070,000 | 14,201,858 | 11,441,729 | 8,790,207 | 6,247,122 | 3,811,657 |

*Source:* Balasubramanian, Jovanovic, and Kirk (2010).

## 2.9 The Role of Institutional Dimensions in Infrastructure Finance Policy Design and Implementation

### *2.9.1 The Role of the Institutional Dimensions in the Use of PPPs and Infrastructure Finance Policy*

This section describes how the institutional dimensions (political, economic, legal, and organization) are critical to successful Infrastructure Finance Policy implementation.

## 2.10 Political Dimension

The political dimension can play a role in impacting the use of PPPs because of political stability through the implementation of government changes such as constitutional changes, coup d'état, or social unrest (Alesina & Perotti, 1996). The political dimension influences legal and bureaucratic capability and capacity, since the division of powers defines the degree of judicial independence (Hayo & Voigt, 2007), as can be seen in the case of Albania. This situation, in turn, impacts the reliability of public managers and, ultimately, the appropriate use of PPPs (Baker, 2016). Thus, politics, and more generally, the institutional dimension, must be considered in evaluating transaction costs because of the extent of the coordination and boundary costs it produces (Baker, 2016; Dumez & Jeunemaitre, 2010) and its impact on PPP costs.

Government political ideology can influence PPP adoption. A PPP policy option also aligns with market-based reforms (Warner & Hefetz, 2012). The political dimension impacting PPP is critical because politics, more generally, and the impact on the institutional dimension, must be considered in evaluating transaction costs because of the extent of the coordination costs it produces (Baker, 2016; Dumez & Jeunemaitre, 2010).

### *2.10.1 Political Dimension in Albania*

In emerging economies such as Albania, civil society is still growing. There is still limited government organizational capacity and capability and judicial independence and, as a result of the imbalance, undue political influence (unicef.org, 2017). Labor unions are powerless; both the authorities and private companies are typically hostile to organizing and collective bargaining efforts. Civil society outside Tirana is especially underdeveloped and is identified as a critical piece needing to be addressed in the European Union in the integration process, which is still ongoing. The Albanian government has acknowledged the need to establish more inclusive policymaking (United Nations and Government of Albania, 2017).

### *2.10.2 Political Dimension in New York State*

The New York State Legislature passed and signed into law an Executive Budget Bill that included provisions created the Infrastructure Investment Act (Part F, Chapter 56 of the Laws of 2011 as part of the 2011 budget language bill). The Act authorized certain state agencies (such as the Thruway Authority, the Department of Transportation, the Office of Parks, Recreation and Historic Preservation, the Department of Environmental Conservation, and the New York State Bridge Authority) to use PPP Design-Build form in procurement of construction, replacement, or repair of highways, bridges, dams, flood control projects, canals, and parks, or to correct health and safety defects or comply with federal and state laws (Mujica, 2019). The Governor, in the Executive Budget, authorized a Design-Bid-Build form of PPP for use in the Mario Cuomo Bridge. The Port Authority of New York and New Jersey also have PPP authorization.

### *2.10.3 Political Dimension in Indiana*

In Indiana, the Governor in 2005 needed several million dollars to his 10-year plan for new highway construction and maintenance throughout the state. To that end, the state solicited bids for the 157-mile Indiana Toll Road connecting Chicago Skyway to the Ohio Turnpike. Because the toll road extends the length of the state, over several years, has involved both state and local governments and different Governors, the political dimension has impacted the use of PPPs.

### *2.10.4 Political Dimension in Mauritius*

Mauritius has been politically stable since it won independence from the United Kingdom in 1968. The government is a stable, multiparty, parliamentary democracy with shifting coalitions that are a feature of its politics. The president is head of state, and the prime minister has full executive powers and heads the government (Indiapost.com, 2019). The Alliance Lepep won legislative elections held in December 2014, a coalition comprising the Militant Socialist Movement (MSM), the Mauritian Social Democrat Party (PMSD), and the Liberation Movement. The coalition secured a comfortable parliamentary majority, with 53 out of 69 seats (Indiapost, 2019).

## 2.11 Economic Dimension

Economic factors can influence PPP adoption, such as outstanding debt and real per capita gross domestic product (GDP) (Boyer & Scheller, 2018). PPPs can create the possibility for efficiencies in capital infrastructure because of greater private partner involvement and market pressures Market economies and emerging market economies, such as Albania, are in different places in terms of their economic system's ability to successfully use PPPs as an Infrastructure Finance Policy option to address their capital infrastructure needs.

### *2.11.1 Economic Dimension in Albania*

The Albanian government's economic system, for example, is evolving from a Centrally Planned economy to a Market Economy. As a result, public governance is no longer seen as a coercive process with the state responsible for delivering public goods and services but is now being defined in terms of interactions between government, markets, and civil society (Baker, 2016; Wettenhall, 2003). To deliver market-oriented goods and services, including public goods and services, Albania is attempting to be more responsive to its constituents' capital infrastructure needs through new forms of service delivery (Beckett-Camarata, 2018, 2019). One alternative form of capital infrastructure financing and delivery that the Albanian government has adopted is the use of PPPs to deliver capital infrastructure such as airports and roads.

### *2.11.2 Economic Dimension in New York State*

New York State's GDP is the value of products originating from all industries in the state, as defined by the US Bureau of Economic Analysis. In 2017, New York State's GDP was over $1.5 trillion, 8% of the US total. The State ranked 34th in the nation for economic growth, with real GDP growth of 1.1% from 2016, less than half the national increase. The financial activities sector comprised just over 29% of the State's real GDP. The second and third top industries, professional and business services and transportation, trade, and utilities, together make up 27.2% (DiNapoli, 2018).

### *2.11.3 Economic Dimension in State of Indiana*

Indiana's economy is stable. The State of Indiana's experience with the Indiana Toll Road PPP was that the state entered into a Concession form of PPP. In exchange for building, operating, and managing the toll road, the PPP partners receive the tolls paid by motorists, and the state owns the road. However, due to the timing of the 2006 partnership and the Great Recession of 2008, the economic dimensions of this PPP were problematic from its inception. The economic dimensions of this project have had a significant impact on the success of the PPP.

### *2.11.4 Economic Dimension in Mauritius*

The economy is stable, with a GDP of $27.5 billion (The World Bank, 2019). Mauritius' economy is based on robust economic policies and sound banking practices (The World Bank, 2019). The Government of Mauritius has experience with PPP, and the government entered into a Build-Own-Operate PPP. The World Bank ranks its economy as 25th in the world, with a fiscal health score of 73.6 (The World Bank, 2019).

Real GDP growth in Mauritius reached 4% in 2017. The main drivers of growth were the services sector, especially finance, and the trade and accommodation services. The latter benefited from a buoyant tourism sector; a vital sector supported by the recent acceleration in the global economy. Tourist arrivals increased by 5.2% in 2017 to reach 1.34 million, a number equivalent to the island's entire resident population (The World Bank, 2019).

The inflation rate picked up to 6.9% in February 2018, compared to 1.3% a year earlier. The principal price increases affected vegetable products as local supply was hit by bad weather. However, the central bank's core inflation measure, excluding more volatile items (such as food), remained under control at 2.9% in January 2018 (The World Bank, 2019).

Fiscal policy has been stable with an overall budget balance of −3.2% of GDP planned for the current fiscal year, which ends in June. If achieved, this would be a small reduction from the 3.5% of GDP budget deficit outturn of FY 2017/18 (Indiapost, 2019). Public sector debt levels are substantial, at approximately 56% of GDP (by the domestic statutory definition) (The World Bank, 2019).

## 2.12 Legal Dimension

Respect for the government institutions that govern relations between the citizens and the government involves the Rule of Law (Contract Management) is an essential foundation for the success of PPPs. The rule of law is operationally defined as the degree to which agents have confidence and in and abide by the rules and norms of society, and, the quality of contract enforcement and the courts (The World Bank, 2013). The rule of law is especially crucial for PPPs in emerging market economies.

### *2.12.1 Legal Dimension in Albania*

Albania is an emerging economy and, as such, has experienced issues with Rule of Law. The Tirana International Airport was built under a general law authorizing activities and sectors of the economy, Law 9663, enacted December 18, 2006, as amended (The World Bank, 2011).

For example, Albania ranks 53 out of 102 countries in the 2015 WJP Rule of Law Index (United Nations and Government of Albania, 2017). The lack of consistent coordination between ministries and departments, limited technical capacity, high staff turnover, and fragmented methods of providing services, all negatively impact the pace of legislation and regulation implementation (United Nations and Government of Albania, 2017). While Albania has made strides in dealing with these issues, which were needed for Albania to be admitted for membership in the European Union, the particular rule of law problems dealing with legal, jurisdictional, and contract enforcement remain and continue to impact PPP transaction cost in that country (Beckett-Camarata, 2018).

The Albanian government reform agenda to depoliticize the government organizations, the legal system, and electoral processes must be accompanied by improvements in those institutions capacity and capability (United Nations and Government of Albania, 2017). Strengthening institutional effectiveness, transparency, accountability, and service delivery is the basis for building a strong institutional foundation for strengthening the rule of law in Albania (United Nations and Government of Albania, 2017). Albania, however, needs to make further progress concerning other rule of law dimensions, such as the adherence by public administrators to rules of law and implementation of promulgated regulations (Beckett-Camarata, 2018; The World Bank, 2013).

The judicial system in Albania has limited accountability, poor interinstitutional cooperation, a backlog of cases, and widespread corruption. Access to justice through the legal system is impeded by procedural obstacles such as low court capacity, high court fees, and long length of judicial procedures (Beckett-Camarata, 2018). There are inconsistent application and uneven enforcement of laws, which still present significant challenges to the quality of and adherence to the rule of law. Though judges' training and career management have improved, assessment of the judicial system reveals corruption, undue interference by the executive branch, limited transparency, and a growing backlog of cases.

### *2.12.2 Legal Dimension in New York State*

The Mario Cuomo Bridge was built under the New York State law authorizing Design-Build PPP form. While more private sector control is available under the law, New York State chose to keep full public control over the Design-Build project, and only five state agencies are authorized to use Design-Build under the Infrastructure Investment Act. This control was seen in the case with the Mario Cuomo Bridge (formerly known as the Tappan Zee Bridge) (DiNapoli, 2014).

### 2.12.3 Legal Dimension in State of Indiana

The Indiana Toll Road was built under Indiana PPP statutes for transportation projects, Indiana Code 15.5 (IFA Projects), and Indiana Code 8-15.7 (INDOT Projects). These laws define which projects must be procured using the INDO vs IFA law. Both PPP statutes are similar in procurement and contracting requirements.

Any PPP that involves tolls, long-term contracts greater than 2 years, financing, or projects on Interstate 69 must be procured under the IFA code (INDOT, 2016). The contract is between the IFA and the private contractor, and INDOT provides technical expertise and oversees contract implementation and monitoring. The contract is financed through INDOT appropriations. INDOT transfer funds to IFA and IFA pays the expenses under the PPP contract using those appropriated funds.

### 2.12.4 Legal Dimension in Mauritius

Mauritius has an efficient and transparent legal environment that supports economic development, and the country has property rights based on the rule of law, but enforcement is relatively weak (The World Bank, 2019). The system of property transfers has been made more efficient. The judiciary is independent, and the government does prosecute corruption, but its enforcement is not consistent (The World Bank, 2019).

The Wind Farm was built under the Mauritius law for PPP in 2004. The law, which was amended in 2008, provides for the implementation of PPP. The law defines the terms and conditions for the use of a PPP and very clearly spells out the responsibilities for the Mauritius Ministry of Finance Public-Private Partnership Unit and the private contractor. It clearly articulates responsibilities in each step of the contracting process. The Law established a PPP Unit within the Procurement Office, which is responsible for managing PPPs.

## 2.13 Organization Dimension

The public sector administrators' ability to implement policies relevant to PPPs, such as Infrastructure Finance Policy and procurement management, is critical to the effectiveness of PPP contracts law. Public sector procurement management involves the acquisition of goods and services through contracting, purchasing, renting, and long-term leasing (Thai, 2001). Government organization effectiveness is operationally defined as the quality of public services, the quality of the civil service, and the degree of independence from political pressures, the quality of policy formulation and implementation, and the credibility of the government's commitment to such policies (Asongu & Kodila-Tedika, 2016).

### *2.13.1 Organization Dimension in Albania*

Improving government effectiveness in emerging economies such as Albania has centered on a coherent strategic and budgetary planning system (The World Bank, 2011). It is, however, still in need of a well-developed process for translating government objectives into precise commitments and measurable targets (The World Bank, 2018a, 2018b), especially regarding PPP.

While improvements in government effectiveness in Albania have been noted by external evaluators such as the World Bank, such improvements in government effectiveness have been limited and even undermined by continuing weaknesses in the quality and integrity of public procurement processes and regulations and the inadequate use of merit-based hiring of qualified public administrators (Beckett-Camarata, 2018). This weakness, in turn, has impacted the efficient use of PPPs in Albania.

The Tirana International Airport PPP was a Concession agreement that was signed in 2004 by the Albanian Government and Tirana Airport Partners for the construction, operation, and maintenance of the International Airport of Tirana (Mother Theresa). The Airport PPP was guided by the Albanian Ministry of Transport, which is responsible for public transport operations in the country. The Minister of Finance convened a Committee and subcommittee working group to review bids submitted by private contractors. The Concessionaire was given exclusivity rights under which the government will not license, authorize, or operate any other airport with commercial cargo and passenger flights in the Republic of Albania, except for emergency landings.

### *2.13.2 Organization Dimension in New York State*

The Mario Cuomo Bridge, which replaced the Tappan Zee Bridge in New York State, was procured under State Design-Build PPP procurement law. The PPP Design-Build Bridge used state government employee procurement expertise with experience in significant capital infrastructure traditional procurement from across state agencies, supplemented using private independent consultants and advisers hired by the state (DiNapoli, 2014). New York State has one statute governing PPP. The New York State government has limited experience with private financing of large capital infrastructure, and even basic capital contracts can be more complicated than the state typically enters.

### *2.13.3 Organization Dimension in Indiana*

The Indiana Toll Road is a Lease/Concession PPP contract agreement to operate and maintain the Indiana Toll Road. INDOT and/or the Indiana Finance Authority (IFA) may contract with a private contractor to manage all or part of the transportation capital infrastructure. The state traditionally uses a Design-Low Bid-Build form for capital infrastructure delivery. PPPs that involve tolls, long-term contracts higher than 2 years, financing, or construction on Interstate 69 fall under the IFA statute.

### *2.13.4 Organization Dimension in Mauritius*

Mauritius received independence from the United Kingdom in 1968 and has undergone economic change from a low-income, agricultural economy to a diversified, upper-middle-income country. The change to a diversified, upper-middle-income country has attracted a large amount of foreign investment. As a result, the country has one of the highest GDP per capita in the African region (The World Bank, 2019).

The government has entered into a total of 200 PPPs (The World Bank, 2019). The Mauritius Ministry of Finance and Economic Development, through the PPP Unit, assesses the potential PPP project based on three guiding principles for evaluating a potential PPP: (1) affordability, (2) value for the money, and (3) appropriate risk transfer. The PPP Unit advises the government on the formulation of PPP and on the development of best practice guidelines and procurement relative to PPP projects (Mauritius Ministry of Finance and Economic Development, 2019).

## 2.14 Summary

This section summarizes the combined impact of the political, economic, legal, and government organization dimensions on public sector focus in Infrastructure Finance Policy and capital management and budgeting, the need to include knowledge of those dimensions' effectiveness in evaluating the use of PPPs in Infrastructure Finance Policy and capital infrastructure planning, and introduces the different goal foci of the public and private sectors.

Taken together, the political, economic, legal, and organization framework impacts capital planning and management, either positively or negatively, depending on the capacity and capability in each dimension.

In Albania, for example, as it transitions to a market economy, there is also a need for greater institutional capacity and capability in both the executive and legislative institutions to establish and *systematically* monitor the implementation of government policies, including Infrastructure Finance Policy, and consistently track progress toward government objectives (SIGMA, 2001), including capital planning and management.

There is a lack of coherent system of Albanian PPP policies, which translate PPP laws into a unified capital budget financing system. Until the national government has such a unified system in place, government effectiveness can be assessed using broadly defined objectives and outcomes in various sectors of government PPP activity, such as periodic external evaluations, using benchmarks (Beckett-Camarata, 2018).

In the case of Mauritius PPPs, there is strong cohesive political, economic, legal, and government organization framework, especially executive and legislative institutions, to systematically monitor government infrastructure finance policies, including its Infrastructure Finance policy. Mauritius has an efficient and transparent legal environment which supports economic development and PPPs, but its legal enforcement is not consistent (The World Bank, 2019).

In New York State, there is a strong political, economic, legal, and government organization (though fragmented) base to continue to establish and implement a coherent system of PPP policies which can then be translated under a cohesive infrastructure finance system.

In the case of the State of Indiana, there is a relatively strong political, economic, legal, and government organization base to continue to establish and implement a system of PPP policies.

Chapter 3 provides a more detailed discussion of the legal framework governing PPPs.

Chapter 3

# Legal Framework Governing PPPs

## 3.1 Laws Governing PPPs

This section examines selected existing laws that govern the Public–Private Partnership (PPP) project phases in the chosen cases. It discusses how PPP laws are conditioned on the legal tradition of an individual national or subnational government. The section differentiates between PPP laws in countries with civil law systems versus common law systems and their respective effects on PPP contract execution. It describes how the legal framework is critical to the success of the PPP form, contractor selection, and project implementation. The legal framework is essential because it provides the conditions necessary to attract capital infrastructure financing (Vissier, Martin-Sisteron, & Seniuta, 2015).

Laws, in concert with collaborative governance, are part of a political system and are the basis for formal collaborative contract relationships (Rosenbloom, 2013). The legal framework shapes a set of decision rules, such as the use of PPPs, while management and politics provide and shape the decision-making arrangements (Amsler & O'Leary, 2017).

As introduced in Chapter 1, PPP laws must be clearly defined, transparent, and enforced to ensure private investment stability and that government institution are in alignment with the laws. Such a legal system forms the basis for investor protection, contract design, renegotiation, and capital infrastructure procurement, including competitive bidding, regulation, and pricing of capital markets (OCED, 2015).

### *3.1.1 Albanian Laws Governing PPPs*

Under Albania PPP Law of 2013, Concession is a form of a PPP Agreement between the Contracting Authority and the economic operator. Three types of Concession are defined in the PPP Law of 2013: (1) Public Works Concession, (2) Public Service Concession, and (3) Mixed Concession (Article 3) (The World Bank, 2018).

#### 3.1.1.1 Definition of PPP

See Albanian Law above.

**Public-Private Partnerships, Capital Infrastructure Project Investments and Infrastructure Finance, 73–99**

**doi:10.1108/978-1-83909-654-920201003**

#### 3.1.1.2 Scope of Albanian PPP Law No. 125/2013

The Contracting Authority considers potential projects for Concessions/PPPs proposed by the Prime Minister's Office, other Contracting Authorities from the same level, local and international financial/development/scientific institutions and organizations, and unsolicited proposals (Law 125, Article 17).

The Commission for Concessions/PPP set up by the Contracting Authority and Unit for Concessions/PPP is responsible for identifying solicited or unsolicited projects and draft feasibility studies (Law 125, Article 18).

For Concession with a value of less than 300 million Albanian leks (approximately USD 2.43 million), the Contracting Authority may only prepare a summarized Concession award analysis instead of a full feasibility study (Law 125, Article 19.4).

A project requiring financial support requires prior approval by the Albanian Ministry of Finance regarding fiscal affordability, sustainability, and feasibility (Law 125, Article 42).

*3.1.1.2.1 Rights and Obligations of the Public Partner under the Law.* The right to conclude security agreements relating to the project with prior notification to the Albanian Ministry of Finance (Law 125, Article 27.4).

Obligation to keep and ensure the validity of the guarantee and security instruments (Law 125, Article 28).

Right to award Concessionaire additional works/services which were not included in the basic contract without conducting a new award procedure under certain circumstances (Law 125, Article 33).

The right to require the Concessionaire to subcontract a minimum of 30% of the total value of the Concession contract to third parties (Law 125, Article 34).

The right to terminate the Concession contract if the Concessionaire fails to perform the obligations because of insolvency, serious breach, or failure to finance the project within a specified period (Law 125, Article 36).

Obligation to resolve any unsolved property relations in a manner conducive to the unhindered performance of the project if the government is the owner of the immovable property/public goods involved in the Concession (Law 125, Article 37).

Contracting Authority provides binding assurances relative to a change in the law in favor of the Concessionaire. The Council shall approve such binding commitment of Ministers upon the Contracting Authority's request (Law 125, Article 41).

*3.1.1.2.2 Rights and Obligations of the Private Partner under the Law.* Obligation to establish a special purpose vehicle as Concession Company (Law 125, Article 26).

Obligation to deposit performance guarantees and/or security instruments to the Contracting Authority before signing or entry into force of the Concession contract (Law 125, Article 28.1).

Obligation to pay a Concession fee under certain circumstances (Law 125, Article 29).

Right to transfer, upon prior written consent by the Contracting Authority, the Concession contract to a suitable third person. For those Concession contracts that impact or create a risk to the government budget, prior approval from the

Albanian Ministry of Finance shall be requested by the Contracting Authority (Law 125, Article 32).

The obligation for the Concessionaire to follow specific rules to subcontract the Concession contract to third parties (Law 125, Article 35).

Facilities constructed under a Concession contract, including additions and improvements, unless otherwise provided for in the contract, shall be owned by the Contracting Authority. The Concessionaire is obliged to transfer the ownership of the facilities following the termination of the contract (Law 125, Article 38).

The right to create security over any payments received or receivable by it under or in connection with a Concession contract (Law 125, Article 40).

The right to appeal the decision of the Contracting Authority, which is deemed to be unjustified during a competitive procedure, to the Public Procurement Commission (Law 125, Article 43).

*3.1.1.2.3 Rights and Obligations of Both Public and Private Partners under the Law.* The right to modify the Concession contract in cases of endangering the national security, environment, nature and human health, force majeure, change of legal framework, and other factual or legal changes (Law 125, Article 31).

The right to terminate the Concession contract when either party is unable to perform the obligation or serious breach by the other party without timely property rectification or upon mutual consent (Law 125, Article 36) (The World Bank PPPLRC, 2018a).

#### 3.1.1.3 Guiding Principles for Albania PPPs

The basic principles in awarding Concession PPPs are based on transparency, nondiscrimination, proportionality, efficiency, equal treatment, mutual recognition, and legal certainty (Article 9).

#### 3.1.1.4 Albanian Procurement and Contract Law

The Public Procurement Agency (PPA) under the Council of Ministers is the unit responsible for PPPs in Albania. The Contracting Authority may use competitive bidding, limited bidding, or direct negotiation procedure for the selection of a private partner, under procurement law (Article 22.3). The most economically viable offer will be awarded (Article 23.1). The interested parties in the competitive bidding are entitled to request the change or correction of the standard documents in the tender documents (Article 24.3). The Contracting Authority is authorized to review and accept unsolicited proposals, but the original proponent shall participate in bidding without any preferential treatment. If it is not the winning bidder, the original proponent will be reimbursed for its costs for the unsolicited proposal (Article 25) (The World Bank, 2019).

### *3.1.2 Mauritius Laws Governing PPPs*

The PPP Act, 2004 (PPPA): This act defines PPPs and describes oversight of PPPs through the PPPA of 2004, as amended in 2008. The Public Procurement Act of

2006 and the Public Procurement Act of 2008 are consulted if an issue is not covered.

The Build-Operate-Transfer (BOT) Projects Bill, 2016 (BOTPB) (applies in cases of PPP that involve construction).

In its first Budget in 2015, the new elected Mauritian Government articulated plans for a Smart City Program. The large-scale capital infrastructure program has several objectives: (1) creation of smart cities across Mauritius, (2) mixed-use development projects in general commercial; leisure and residential; industrial; educational; medical; and tourism clusters, and (3) technology and innovation clusters (Mauritius Budget, 2015). The guiding principles are innovation, sustainability, efficiency, and quality of life in urban development and a regeneration program covering existing towns, including improvement of capital infrastructure and enhancing the appearance of sites and buildings across the country.

Following the enactment of the Budget, amendments were made to the Investment Promotion Act, 2000 to introduce the concept of Smart Cities. Smart City Program Investment Promotion Regulations were passed in 2015, with detailed requirements for ventures seeking to develop a capital infrastructure under the Smart City Program.

Mauritius identified greenfield sites, which are expected to be new centers for business, finance, and administration. The projected cost of these 13 smart cities is about MUR 23.5 billion (approximately $660 million). The financing requirement is extensive, requiring PPPs in the form of local and international lending institutions, private equity entrepreneurs, and government funds. The Smart City legal, regulatory, and financing structure, the BOT Act, was announced on April 5, 2016, to provide the legal and regulatory framework to secure PPPs' financing to meet the financing needs of the Smart City Infrastructure Program (Mauritius Budget, 2015).

#### 3.1.2.1 Mauritius Definition of PPP

A PPP Agreement is between a Contracting Authority and a private party in which (1) the private partner performs a Contracting Authority's function on behalf of the Contracting Authority for a specified period; (2) the private partner receives a benefit for performing the function through (i) compensation from a revenue fund, (ii) charges or fees collected by the private partner from users or customers of a service provided by it, or (iii) a combination of compensation and charges from fees; (3) the private partner is liable for the risks arising from the performance of the function; and (4) state facilities, equipment, or other state resources may be transferred or made available to the private party (The World Bank/PPP Mauritius country profile; Mauritius PPA, Section 2, 2018).

#### 3.1.2.2 Scope of the Mauritius Build-operate-transfer Act

Under a BOT PPP in Mauritius, a private contractor is given the right to build a capital infrastructure and to operate the infrastructure for a specified time, subject to a "transfer back" to a government entity at the end of the PPP contract period. The BOT Act's scope also covers other project delivery methods, such as (1) where the private sector project company assumes ownership of the project (build, own, operate, and transfer) and is also responsible for designing the project (design, build, finance, operate, and transfer) and (2) where the project involves the modernization of existing capital infrastructure (modernize, own/operate, and transfer).

The BOT Act provides for the greater integration of the design, construction, and operational skills of the private contractor more efficiently than what existed under the PPP Act and the Public Procurement Act. The BOT Act also allows the relevant government entity to have the capital infrastructure operational for a far lesser initial investment than conventional procurement methods; the cost of the project could be amortized over the lifetime of the concession. This allowance was one of the main points of the BOT Act when the National Assembly passed it.

The BOT Act does not affect any partnership between Mauritius and a foreign state under a bilateral agreement. Government to Government, arrangements are not affected by the BOT Act and are governed by the PPP Act and Public Procurement Act. The BOT Act supersedes the provisions of the Public Procurement Act and the PPP Act, although the rules of the Central Procurement Board on the assessment of bids would still apply. Under the BOT Act, it is also now mandatory for BOT agreements to be submitted before the National Assembly, which was not previously the case.

The procurement process begins when the government initiates a BOT PPP bid. The relevant governmental authority appraises the potential PPP bids and authorizes feasibility studies, in line with the requirements of the BOT Act on potential BOT PPPs. The procedure from authorizing feasibility report up to Concession award and the entry into the BOT capital infrastructure transaction is fixed under the BOT Act. The BOT Act creates more certainty by prescribing the minimum standard set of terms to be covered in the transaction documents which include, among others, (1) the rights and obligations of the Contracting Authority and private party; (2) the period of execution of the project; and (3) the financial terms and the management of the private party's performance.

The BOT Act is a change in procedural rules for PPP capital assessment and approval. It provides for more efficient, competitive, and transparent procurement and to fill in any gaps which the PPP Act had not addressed. Under the former PPP procurement rules, public procurement was a long process, often prolonged by challenges and lengthy appeals, resulting in several viable PPPs being prematurely terminated. The change to the new law accelerated the process and reduced the level of uncertainty and political risk associated with public sector PPPs.

The Public Procurement Act (2006) amended in 2014, and its PPP Regulations (2008) (PP{A and PPPR), lays out the terms and conditions for public procurement more broadly.

#### 3.1.2.3 Procurement and Contracting Procedures/Choice of the Private Partnership in PPP

The Mauritius procurement process involves:

*3.1.2.3.1 Preselection of Bidders.* Invitation to Bid (PPPA, Articles 8 and 9).

A Request for Proposal (RFP) covers the procedure for the submission of bids, the criteria for the evaluation of bids, and includes a model agreement (PPPA, Article 2).

*3.1.2.3.2 Award of a Public–Private Partnership Project.* According to the provisions of this Act, the Board approves all documents relating to the bid; authorizes, approves, and carries out preselection exercises; authorizes the advertisement, issues the invitation locally or internationally, and the call for bids; examines and evaluates bids; and approves the award of a PPP project in the manner provided for under the PPPA, 2004 (Public Procurement Act, 2006).

#### 3.1.2.4 Mauritius PPP Policy Guidance

The PPP Policy Statement, 2003: The PPP Policy Statement articulates the strategic rationale for the Mauritius government's use of PPPs, that is, to foster economic growth by developing new economic opportunities, increasing competition, and encouraging the private sector and foreign investment. The Policy Statement emphasizes the need for the government to increase opportunities for efficiency through better quality and more cost-effective service delivery, better capital infrastructure utilization, and clearer customer focus. Payments are linked to outputs, rather than service inputs, and accelerated delivery of projects (Mauritius PPP Policy Statement, 2003).

The *Mauritius Public–Private Partnerships Guidance Manual* sets the framework for implementing PPPs in Mauritius. It provides the overarching PPP policy goals of affordability, value for the money, and appropriate risk transfer. The PPP Unit advises the government on PPP policy formulation and development of guidelines and best practices. The Procurement Contracting Unit is responsible for maintaining the project from the beginning through the close of the project. They are also responsible for Feasibility Studies to demonstrate the benefit of a PPP option. The role of the Mauritius Ministry of Finance is regulatory, while the Central Tender Board ensures the legitimacy and transparency of the capital project procurement.

The government units responsible for carrying out Mauritius PPP law are the PPP Unit within the Mauritius Ministry of Economic Development, Financial Services, and Corporate Affairs, in collaboration with the Central Tender Board.

The Mauritius PPP Act does not apply to capital projects which include a construction phase. The BOT Act, discussed below, applies in those cases.

#### 3.1.2.5 Guiding Principle for Mauritius PPPs

Mauritius has embarked on an *Economic Agenda for the New Millennium*, which spells out the government's strategic policy emphases. The guiding principle for the Mauritius government is to invest massively in education, training, and information technology, as well as in capital infrastructure and the environment, to transform the county into full integration in the new global economic environment. In order to ensure that investment is sustainable, the government will restore soundness in public finances and bring down the budget deficit to a sustainable level. A major program to improve the quality and effectiveness of public expenditures has been implemented through the application of appropriate policy, as well as enhancement of the institutional and legal framework for encouraging the private sector to play a more significant role in procuring and financing capital infrastructure projects in the public sector through well-designed PPP (Mauritius PPP Policy Statement, 2003; The World Bank, 2018b).

#### 3.1.2.6 PPP Institutional Framework

The Procurement Policy Office in the Mauritius Ministry of Finance and Economic Development oversees managing PPPs in the country. Mauritius first developed a PPP Program in 2002 which defined a PPP as a financing option for financing infrastructure and other capital infrastructures. It provided the basis for subsequent PPP legislation and a joint task force to develop the legal and organizational framework.

### *3.1.3 United States Laws Governing PPPs*

A national legal/regulatory PPP framework does not exist in the United States (Abdel Aziz, 2007). The use of PPPs is mainly in the area of federally funded projects (Abdel Aziz, 2007), although that is beginning to change. While several federal laws and regulations are governing the use of PPPs on federal capital infrastructure projects, those laws and regulations are limited in scope. The US Constitution precludes the creation of a federalized system of PPPs, and the use of PPPs in the individual states is governed by state law and state policy.

The subnational governments of Indiana and New York are used as examples and are described in the next section.

#### 3.1.3.1 New York State Laws Governing PPP

*3.1.3.1.1 Infrastructure Investment Act.* The Infrastructure Investment Act, Chapter 56 of 2011, Part F, is the law governing the use of PPPs. The Act allows only the Design-Build PPP project method and designates authorized state entities: (1) the New York State Thruway Authority, (2) the Department of Transportation, (3) the Office of Parks, Recreation and Historic Preservation, (4) the Department of Environmental Conservation (DEC), and (5) the New York State Bridge Authority to enter into the Design-Build form of PPP (Mujica, 2019).

*3.1.3.1.2 New York State Procurement Act, PPP Act of State of New York, Chapter 56 of 2011.* According to this Act, expediting the delivery of capital projects would lead directly to job creation and increase the state's competitiveness. Businesses in New York State have extensive and diverse experience in alternative project delivery methods for the study, planning, design, development, financing, acquisition, installation, construction, reconstruction, improvement, maintenance, and management of capital infrastructure facilities. These alternative project delivery methods produce significant benefits to the public by reducing the public cost of delivering and obtaining services for capital infrastructure; expediting project delivery; encouraging life cycle efficiencies; providing better use and leverage of public human and capital resources, and enhancing capital formation for large projects; creating jobs; promoting performance efficiencies; and bringing additional benefits.

For specific projects, the Design-Build project delivery method has the potential to achieve projects delivered on guaranteed or accelerated schedules, lower costs, and risk shifting to the private sector generally retained in conventional design-bid-build as well as to accelerate capital projects throughout the state.

The Legislature seeks to accelerate capital investment in New York State's capital infrastructure; coordinate capital investment among New York State's agencies and authorities; encourage private sector capital investment; ensure job creation benefits New York workers; and assist in the use of the most efficient and effective procurement and project management for capital infrastructure projects in the transportation, energy, environment, public facilities, and economic development sectors (https:/www.nysenate.gov/legislation/bills/2015, p. 23) The act allows the Design-Build PPP contracts by authorized state agencies, but the total cost of each such project shall not be less than one million two hundred thousand ($1,200,000) (New York State Assembly, 2015).

#### 3.1.3.2 Definition of PPP

New York State PPP laws, Chapter 56 of 2011, Part F defines PPP as Design-Build PPP contracts issued by the state agencies authorized to use the Design-Build PPP contracts for capital infrastructure. These include, but are not limited to, highways, bridges, dams, flood control projects, canals, and parks. It covers (1) repair damage caused by natural disaster, (2) to correct health and safety defects, (3) to comply with federal and state laws, standards, or regulations, (4) to extend the useful life of or replace the state's highways, bridges, dams, flood control projects, canals, and parks (New York State Senate, 2011).

#### 3.1.3.3 Guiding Principle for New York State PPP

New York State continues to experience limited debt capacity. The use of PPPs could provide new infrastructure finance policy options for planning, financing, and building capital infrastructure. This flexibility should not come at the expense of cost-effectiveness, transparency, and accountability. Tax dollars, fees, tolls, and other public resources must be used in the most economical, efficient, and accountable way possible (DiNapoli, 2014).

An *Infrastructure Report, Planning and Financing New York State's Capital Investments* is prepared by the Comptroller's Office. This report serves as the State's Infrastructure Finance Policy. The report points out that from

FY2009–2014, the state has relied more on debt (pay as you use) to finance capital projects and less on currently available funds (pay as you go) compared to FY2004–FY2009. The report notes that the state continues to increase debt capacity as measured by the statutory cap on debt outstanding established in the Debt Reform Act of 2000. The report further notes that 60% of the $47.6 billion projected to be spent on capital purposes over the next 5 years is expected to be funded through the issuance of bonds (DiNapoli, 2014). The increasing use of debt has created a substantial debt burden for the state. The report states that PPPs could provide new options for planning, financing, and building capital infrastructure, but this flexibility should not come at the expense of cost-effectiveness, transparency, and accountability. The report recommends that any PPP legislation guard against financial risk and reflects the proper valuation of infrastructure, reasonable pricing, realistic expectations, and reasonable budgeting (DiNapoli, 2014).

#### 3.1.3.4 PPP Procurement and Contracting Procedures

There is a two-step tendering and contracting process, which begins with (1) generation of a list of entities that have demonstrated the capability to execute a Design-Build contract. The list must have a specified number of vendors determined by the state government agency and produced based on the responses to a publicly advertised Request for Qualifications (RFQs). The authorized RFQs includes a general project description, the maximum number of entities included on the list, and the selection criteria. The selection criteria include the qualifications and experience of the design and construction team, organization, demonstrated responsibility, ability of the team or a member or members of the team to comply with applicable requirements, including relevant provisions of the State Education Law, record of compliance with labor law, and other qualifications including project understanding, financial capability, and record of past performance.

The authorized state agency evaluates and rates all private organizations that respond to the RFQs. Following the generation of the list of rated private entities, the state agency sends a RFPs. The state agency must consider minority and/or women-owned firms. The second step in the process is (2) the selection of the proposal, which is the best value (New York State Assembly, 2015). The RFPs specifies the project's scope of work and other requirements as well as the criteria used to evaluate the responses and the relative weight of the criteria. The criteria includes the cost and quality of the proposal, the qualifications and experience of the Design-Build entity, and other criteria considered appropriate by the authorized state agency (New York State Assembly, 2015). Examples of other criteria include the quality of the proposals project implementation, ability to complete the work on time and on budget and in satisfactory manner, maintenance costs of the completed project, maintenance of traffic approach, and community impact (New York State Senate, 2019).

The authorized state agency may award a construction contract to the private contractor offering the best value or the private contractor using cost plus not to exceed guaranteed maximum price type of contract in which the state agency is allowed to monitor and audit all project costs, and the process is used in determining a guaranteed maximum price.

The contract between the state agency and the private contractor must (1) describe the scope of the work and the cost of performing the work; (2) include a detailed line item cost breakdown; (3) include a list of all drawings, specifications, and other information on which the guaranteed maximum price is based; (4) include dates for substantial and final completion on which the guaranteed maximum price is based; (5) include a schedule of unit prices; or (6) use a lump sum payment. Such a contract requires the contractor to accept a set dollar amount in a contract which comprises a single bid, without providing a cost breakdown for all costs such as for equipment, labor, materials, and the contractor's profit for completing all items of work for the project.

#### 3.1.3.5 New York State Finance Law 137

State Finance Law 137 requires general contractors on most public works projects to purchase payment bonds to protect against claims made by subcontractors and suppliers and others who provide work to a construction project. This requirement provides another way for subcontractors and suppliers to protect against claims for nonpayment by a general contractor or developer. A payment bond is required for any public construction project that, in the aggregate, exceeds $100,000, but only if those projects are not subject to New York State Wicks Law (New York State Finance Law, 2012).

#### 3.1.3.6 PPP Institutional Framework

New York State first developed a PPP capital infrastructure financing option in 2011, which defined a Design-Build PPP financing option for the delivery of capital infrastructure and other capital infrastructure. Certain designated state agencies are authorized under the State of New York, Infrastructure Investment Act, Chapter 56 of 2011 to enter into the Design-Build PPP project contract. The agencies are listed in the Infrastructure Investment Act section below.

New York State Works Task Force is responsible for advising on New York State Capital Planning for State Agencies. The Task Force leverages financing of capital infrastructure and develops the state's capital plan, in coordination with regional economic development plans. The New York State Works Task Force recommends prioritization of capital infrastructure projects and allocation of capital resources. The New York State Works Task Force also recommends financing options for capital infrastructure, including state-supported debt, federal funding, and other financing options, and advises state agencies and authorities on the use of methods of procurement and contract.

### *3.1.4 Indiana Laws Governing PPPs*

Indiana's PPP Program is under the general legal framework in the Indiana Code. The statutes authorizing PPP projects are IC8-15.5 for the Indiana Finance

Authority (IFA) and IC8-15.7 for INDOT. The statutes allow both tolled and nontolled transportation projects and for the development, financing, and operation of PPP projects.

#### 3.1.4.1 Indiana PPP Law

Indiana law permits the Indiana Department of Transportation and/or the IFA to contract with a private contractor to manage all or part of a transportation project (Indiana Code, 2016). Any PPP that involves tolls, long-term contracts in excess of 2 years, financing, or projects on Interstate 69 must be procured under the IFA statute. The contract is between the IFA and the private contractor. INDOT provides technical expertise and oversees the execution of/compliance with the contract. The contract is funded through INDOT appropriations, INDOT transfers funds to IFA, and IFA pays the expenses under the contract using those funds (INDOT, 2016).

The statute allows governmental bodies to enter into PPP agreements with private entities for the acquisition, planning, design, development, reconstruction, repair, maintenance, or financing of public facilities. The PPP may require a performance bond and provide for the payment of contractors and subcontractors under Indiana Code 4-13.6-7, 5-16-5, or 35-1-12, whichever is applicable.

#### 3.1.4.2 The Scope of the Indiana BOT Law

(1) The design, construction, operation, management, maintenance, or financing of the cost of a public facility is partially or entirely the responsibility of the operator.
(2) The governmental body leases the public facility and real property owned by the governmental body upon which the public facility is to be located to the private contractor for a predetermined period. The BOT agreement provides for ownership of all improvements by the government unless the government elects to provide for ownership of the public facility by the private contractor during the term of the BOT agreement. In that case, ownership reverts to the government body when the BOT contract is terminated (https://codes.findlaw.com/in/title-5-state-and-local).
(3) The BOT contract must identify which costs are the responsibility of the private partner and which costs are the responsibility of the public partner.
(4) The private contractor may be authorized to retain a mutually agreed-upon percentage of the revenues received in the operation and management of the public facility, or the private contractor may be paid an amount established by the governmental body, which shall be applied as follows: (1) capital outlay costs for the public facility and public service plus interest and principal repayment for any debt incurred; (2) costs associated with the operation, management, and maintenance of the public facility; (3) payment to the governmental body for reimbursement of the costs of maintenance, law enforcement, and other services if the governmental body performs the

services under the BOT agreement; and (3) an agreed-upon return on investment to the operator.

(5) The operator may pay the governmental body either a lease payment or a percentage of gross revenue per month for the operator's operation and use of the public facility.

(6) The BOT contract may require a private contractor to provide performance bond and to provide for the payment of all contractors and subcontractors under IC 4-13.6-7, IC 5-16-5, or IC 36-1-12, as applicable (Indiana Code 5-23-3-2, 2016).

Indiana Law allows PPPs for the development of transportation facilities for toll road capital projects. The private contractor or subcontractor engaged in the construction of a toll road capital project unless covered by federal law or this section is not required to comply with IC-4-13.6 or IC 5-16 regarding state public works; IC 5-17 concerning purchases of materials, suppliers; or other statutes concerning procedures for procurement of public works or personal property as a condition of being awarded and performing work on the project (Indiana Code 8-15, 5-6-2, 2016).

Indiana has entered into partnerships such as (1) Lease Agreements, (2) Design-Build-Finance-Operate-Maintain Agreements, (3) Provide-Operate-Manage-Maintain Agreements, and (4) Design-Build-Best Value Agreements.

#### 3.1.4.3 Indiana Definition of PPP

Indiana PPP is defined as a BOT agreement or an operating agreement (Indiana Code 5-23-2-15). A governmental organization may enter into a BOT agreement with a private contractor for the acquisition, planning, design, development, reconstruction, repair, maintenance, or financing of any public facility on behalf of the government (statecodesfiles.justia.com/Indiana/2016, Title 5-23-3-1).

#### 3.1.4.4 Guiding Principles for Indiana PPPs

*Performance*: Any capital project delivered through PPP should meet or exceed a traditional capital delivery method and provide innovations and efficiencies through private sector participation. Such participation should increase the delivery of public capital projects and enhance the State's overall capital program. The majority of INDOT capital projects use established methods of delivery.

*Strategic*: PPPs are unique, and the PPP process may be modified to adjust to specific projects. IFA/INDOT will endeavor to be consistent to ensure that potential PPP projects benefit from considering the costs over the entire life cycle of the project consistent with INDOT's overall infrastructure management strategy for the state highway system.

*Financial*: PPPs must be financially sound and compatible with IFA/INDOT's financial capacity to pursue a PPP delivery method. Projects leverage INDOT's existing capital budget by providing an alternative financing mechanism (Indiana PPP Guidelines, 2016; Indiana Code 5-23-1-1 to 5-23-7-2).

#### 3.1.4.5 Indiana PPP Procurement and Contracting Procedures

Traditional Indiana procurement is through Design-Low Bid-Build. The PPP projects usually require a two-stage procurement process RFQs and RFPs, depending on the characteristics and objectives of the capital project. The first stage is a RFQs. The IFA/INDOT develops the procurement documents. The RFQ contains a description and status of the project and requests that potential proposers submit certain information used to assess the qualifications of each bidder. Once IFA issues an RFQ, it provides public notice of the RFQ. The RFQ information includes:

Team experience
Technical competence
Past performance
Utilization of local and disadvantaged businesses
Workforce capacity to perform
Resume of key personnel
Financial capability, capacity, and approach to development

## 3.2 Strengths and Limitations of PPP Laws

This section will use specific country examples, cases, and laws to evaluate whether these legal systems strengthen the chances of PPPs to succeed or whether specific laws limit success and create more possibilities for PPP failure. It describes the importance of understanding the role of Common Law and Civil Law in evaluating whether PPP laws strengthen or weaken the use of PPPs.

### *3.2.1 Legal Systems to Support PPP Laws*

Before evaluating the strengths and limitations of PPP laws, understanding the role of Common Law and Civil Law is essential as a basis for understanding the use of PPPs in each country. Countries primarily follow either a Common Law or a Civil Law system, which are the two main types of legal systems in the world (The World Bank, 2018). Common law system features include (1) constitution or codified laws not always written; (2) judicial decisions are binding, but decisions of highest court can generally only be overturned by that same court or through legislation; (3) extensive freedom of contract with few provisions implied into the contract by law (though provisions seeking to protect private consumers may be implied); and (4) everything that is not expressly prohibited by law is allowed (The World Bank, 2018). There are limited conditions implied in a contract under common law, and as a result, contracts are often longer than in a country with a Civil Law system (The World Bank, 2018). Countries with a Common Law system include former British colonies, as well as the United States.

Countries with a Civil Law system follow a codified system of law that has its origins in Roman Law. Civil Law system features include (1) a written constitution based on specific codes (i.e., civil code, codes covering corporate law, administrative law, tax law, and constitutional law), enshrining fundamental rights and duties; administrative law is usually less codified, and administrative court judges tend to act more like common law judges; (2) only legislative enactments are considered binding, and there is little scope for judge-made law in civil, criminal, and commercial courts, but in practice, judges tend to follow previous judicial decisions; constitutional and administrative courts can nullify laws and regulations and decisions in those cases are binding for all; (3) writings of legal scholars can have significant influence on the courses; (4) courts specific to the particular code and usually separate constitutional court, administrative court, and civil court systems that speak on consistency of legislation and administrative acts and interpret the specific code (The World Bank, 2018). There are several provisions implied in a contract under civil law, and less importance is generally placed on setting out all terms governing the relationship between the parties to a contract within the contract document. The application of the law can resolve ambiguities. Contracts are often shorter than in a Common Law country. Countries with a Civil Law system include Central and South America, Central and Eastern Europe, and East Asia.

### 3.2.2 Albanian Legal System

The Albanian national legal system is based on Civil Law. The development of the judicial system in Albania follows other former socialist countries. Following the creation of the People's Republic of Albania in 1946, the model for the judicial system was based on the Russian legal system. The 1929 Penal Code of the Kingdom of Albania was in place at the time of the establishment of the Republic of Albania. Separate enactments on penal law and criminal procedures were adopted between 1945 and 1952 to remedy the immediate need for reform of the 1929 Code. A new penal code was adopted in 1952. During the constitutional reform of 1977, the penal code was also reformed. The 1977 Penal Code has been amended again, reflecting extensive changes in the constitution that were adopted between the end of 1990 and the beginning of 1991 (Albanian Civil Law, 2012; OECD, 2017).

Albania has three levels of courts: district courts, appeals courts (zonal courts), and Supreme Court or Court of Cessation (Albanian Law, 2012). The 26 district courts are the first place for most criminal and civil cases (Albanian Law, 2012). The courts are presided over by a legally trained judge, who usually is assisted by two lay assessors. In certain more critical cases, the judge will be assisted by four lay assessors. A majority vote makes decisions. The lay assessors do not receive any specialized training for their duties. The district courts are trial level. An appeal man is made to the Albanian Appeals Court and then to the Albanian Court of Cessation. At each of the judicial levels, the courts are divided into civil, criminal, and military chambers. Justices of the Supreme Court serve for 7 years (Albanian Law, 2012; OECD, 2017).

The district court judges are elected by district citizen vote and are subject to removal by the voters or the local council. Each case (including the preliminary inquiry used in the more difficult cases) is always dealt with by the full complement of judges and assessors. This situation has led to a heavy caseload in some courts. The average length of the case, from the commission of the offense to the court sentence, is estimated to be two months (Albanian Law, 2012; OECD, 2017).

The six zonal courts are courts of appeal. The courts are the first instance for certain urgent cases, as decided by the President of the Supreme Court, which is an exception to the rule. Zonal court judges are elected for a 3-year term by the district councils in the zone. Local councils may also decide on the removal of a judge (Albanian Law, 2012; OECD, 2017)

The Supreme Court is the highest judicial body in Albania. In addition to its appellate responsibilities, it is the first instance for the more severe offenses indicated by the President of the Supreme Court. It has three divisions: penal, civil, and military. The procedure before the Supreme Court in appellate proceedings is formalized. The Court Case (including the preliminary inquiry used in the more difficult cases) is always dealt with by the full complement of judges and assessors. This procedure has led to a heavy caseload in some courts. However, the average length of the procedure, from the commission of the offense to the court sentence, is estimated to be 2 months (Albanian Law, 2012; OECD, 2017).

Parliament appoints the seven members of the Supreme Court or Court of Cessation and five of the nine judges on the Constitutional Court, with the rest appointed by the president. A Supreme Judicial Council appoints all other judges. In 1992, the Supreme Judicial Council began to remove judges who had served under the former Communist regime.

There is also a Constitutional Court (also known as the High Court) with jurisdiction to resolve questions of constitutional interpretation that arise during any case on appeal. In a 1993 decision, for example, the Albanian Constitutional Court invalidated a law that would have disbarred lawyers active during the communist era. The Court ordered those lawyers reinstated. Constitutional Court justice serves a maximum of 9 years (Albanian Law, 2012). While the Albanian Constitution provides for an independent judiciary, the system is plagued by a lack of resources and trained staff and is subject to political pressure, intimidation, and corruption.

### *3.2.3 New York State Legal System*

New York State law is based on Common Law. The New York State judicial system is one of three coequal branches of state government. The New York judicial system, based on Common Law, has three levels:

***Court of Appeals***: This court is New York's court of last resort (the equivalent of the Supreme Court in most states).

***Appellate Divisions of the Supreme Court***: This division is made up of principal intermediate appellate courts.

***Trial Courts***: These courts include Supreme Courts, the state trial courts of general jurisdiction (New York in-depth, 2019).

The courts and appeal procedures have been in effect since the last judiciary amendment of 1962. A court reorganization of 2002 was extensive and required an amendment of the New York Constitution.

#### 3.2.3.1 Court of Appeals

New York State's highest court is the Court of Appeals. The Court is made up of a Chief Judge and six Associate Judges. Each judge is appointed for a 14-year term. New York's highest appellate court was established to set forth statewide principles of law in the context of deciding lawsuits. The Court thus generally focuses on broad issues of law as distinguished from individual factual disputes. There is no jurisdictional limitation based upon the amount of money at stake in a case or the status or rank of the parties (New York in-depth, 2019). The Court of Appeals also establishes the rules of the court.

#### 3.2.3.2 Appellate Divisions of the Supreme Court

There are four Supreme Court Appellate Divisions. There is one division in each of the State's four Judicial Departments (geographical divisions). These Courts resolve appeals from judgments or orders of the superior courts of original jurisdiction in civil and criminal cases and review civil appeals taken from the Appellate Terms and the County Courts acting as appellate courts (New York in-depth, 2019; New York State Unified Court System, 2019). New York County and the Bronx belong to the First Judicial Department. Kings, Queens, and Richmond Counties are part of the Second Judicial Department (New York in-depth, 2019; New York State Unified Court System, 2019).

#### 3.2.3.3 Trial Courts

The Supreme Court is the trial court of unlimited original jurisdiction but commonly hears cases that are outside the jurisdiction of other trial courts which have more limited jurisdiction (NY Courts, 2019).

The County Court is established in each county outside New York City. It is authorized to handle the prosecution of all crimes committed within the County. The County Court also has limited jurisdiction in civil cases involving amounts up to $25,000 (NY Courts, 2019).

City Courts outside New York City exist in 61 cities and have criminal jurisdiction over misdemeanors and lesser offenses and civil jurisdiction over claims of up to $15,000. Some City Courts have separate parts to handle small claims (up to $5,000) or housing matters. City Court judges act as arraigning magistrates and conduct preliminary hearings in felony cases (NY Courts, 2019).

District courts are in Nassau County and the five western towns of Suffolk County. District courts have criminal jurisdiction over misdemeanors and lesser offenses and conduct arraignments in felony cases. They have civil jurisdiction over claims of up to $15,000 and small claims matters not over $5,000 (NY Courts, 2019).

Town and Village Courts in New York State have criminal jurisdiction over violations and misdemeanors and civil jurisdiction over claims of up to $3,000. Town and village court justices hold arraignments and preliminary hearings for those charged with more serious crimes. Traffic infractions also are heard in these courts (NY Courts, 2019).

### *3.2.4 State of Indiana Legal System*

Indiana law operates within a Common Law system. The Indiana Court system is one of three branches of state government. The court system, based on Common Law, has four levels:

The Indiana Supreme Court is the highest court of last resort for the State. It has original jurisdiction in the following areas: (1) appeal by right, (2) felony-civil-other, (3) administrative agency-other; (4) appeal by permission criminal, civil, limited administrative agency, writ exclusive death penalty; and (5) exclusive original proceeding with the application, bar/judiciary, certified question, advisory opinion.

#### 3.2.4.1 Court of Appeals

The Indiana Court of Appeals consists of 25 judges, serving in five, three-judge districts. This Court is the second highest Indiana Court and hears appeals from the State's trial courts. The Court does not preside over trials and must accept all appeals sent to it, except for (1) cases in which the death penalty or life without parole is rendered (appealed directly to the Indiana Supreme Court); (2) cases in which statutes are declared unconstitutional by a trial court (automatically appealed to the Supreme Court); attorney disciplinary cases (which also go to the Supreme Court); and (3) cases involving taxation (which go to the Indiana Tax Court) (Indiana Court of Appeals, 2019).

#### 3.2.4.2 Trial Courts

There are 315 judges in the Circuit and Superior Courts. These courts are courts in general jurisdiction (Indiana Judiciary, 2019).

### *3.2.5 Mauritius Legal System*

Mauritius has a hybrid legal system, with aspects of both civil law and common law. The Judiciary of Mauritius is one of three branches of government. It is an independent judicial system, which upholds the rule of law, safeguards the rights and freedom of the individual, and has national and international confidence. The Mauritius Constitution provides for an independent judiciary based on the concept of separation of powers. Mauritius has a single-structured judicial system consisting of two parts, the Supreme Court and the Subordinate Courts. The Constitution of Mauritius is the supreme legal document of the country. The final appeal from decisions of the Court of Appeal of Mauritius is to the Judicial

Committee of the Privy Council in London as provided for under the Constitution of Mauritius (International Budget Partnership, 2015)

The basis of Mauritian law is derived from French codes: Civil Code as amended to adapt to Mauritian context, Penal Code, which has been revised as the Criminal Code, and the Code of Commerce to a lesser extent. The law of procedure and evidence are derived from English Law, but provisions of the French Civil Code are also still in force. The Mauritian court structure and the remedies they provide are based on Common Law. The Mauritian Constitution follows the Westminster Model, and Mauritian legislation has borrowed English Law regarding trade and commerce law for shipping, finance, banking, company law, and negotiable and bankruptcy instruments. Mauritian law is a hybrid of both English and French Law and has its own unique identity.

The next section assesses the strengths and limitations of each country's PPP legislation and legal framework using the European Bank for Reconstruction and Development (EBRD) Best Practices as applied to selected criteria.

## 3.3 Strengths and Limitations of the Legal System and Laws of Each National and Subnational Government

### *3.3.1 Albania Strengths and Limitations of Legal System and Laws*

#### 3.3.1.1 Albania Legal System and Laws

Albania's legal system is based on Civil Law. The first Albanian Law on Concessions was adopted in 1995 and repealed with the adoption of the Concession Law of 2013. The strength of the Albanian PPP legislation and legal framework is that the law spells out the specific PPP law. There is a clear definition of the boundaries and scope of application of the concession legal framework. Under civil law, only legislative enactments are binding, and there is little opportunity for judge-made law in civil, criminal, and commercial courts. The legislation defines PPPs, the sectors covered, responsible authorities, and private sector eligibility. The legislation limits the risk of a challenge to the validity of PPP contracts.

*3.3.1.1.1 Selection of Private Party.* The Albanian PPP Law on Concessions articulates a fair and transparent tender selection process. It provides for limited exceptions allowing direct negotiations, competitive rules for unsolicited proposals, and the possibility to challenge illegal awards.

*3.3.1.1.2 Project Agreement.* There is flexibility concerning the content of the provisions of the project agreements, which allow for the identifiable allocation of risks without unnecessary requirements from the Contracting Authority (obligations, tariff, termination, compensation).

*3.3.1.1.3 Settlement of Disputes and Applicable Laws*

There is a possibility to obtain proper remedy for breach of contract under the applicable law through international arbitration and enforcement of arbitral awards.

Existence and role of PPP Central Unit/Agency.

There is a specialized department, the Concession Treatment Unit.

Division of power between different public authorities involved in PPP is clear and coordinated.

Each bidder is entitled to request an Administrative Review of the selection process by the Concession Unit. Such a review provides for transparency in the bidding process

*3.3.1.1.4 PPP Limitations.* The division of power is spelled out in the Law. However, it is not clear in the regulations, which implement the law, and implementation can be problematic (EBRD, 2011)

*3.3.1.1.5 PPP Legal Challenges.* There are no court decisions concerning the performance of PPP contracts. There are court decisions concerning the selection process of bidders, when one of the bidder's appeals against the decision of the Concession Treatment Unit (EBRD, 2011).

#### 3.3.1.2 Limitations of the Albanian Law

*3.3.1.2.1 PPP Policy Framework.* In practice, a PPP policy framework consisting of an infrastructure finance policy for implementing PPPs is not present.

*3.3.1.2.2 PPP Institutional Framework.* The implementation of PPP law through regulation via line ministers is fragmented.

#### 3.3.1.3 Obstacles to PPP Contract Implementation

There are social obstacles between the Concessionaire and the private owners of the land where the concession project is to be established. In some instances, private landowners can pose obstacles to successful PPP projects. Local tariffs and local taxes constitute other obstacles to PPP implementation because they vary between local governments. This inconsistency can present problems for the Concessionaire. Some PPPs, such as hydroelectric power plants, can become an obstacle, such as reducing the number of water obstacles that can take a long time to work out (EBRD, 2011).

### *3.3.2 Mauritius Strengths and Limitations of Legal System and Laws*

#### 3.3.2.1 Mauritius Legal System and Laws

The PPP Policy Statement was written in 2003, and the PPPA was implemented in 2004. The strength of the Mauritius PPP legislation and legal framework is that in addition to the PPP Act, 2004, the Policy Statement and the Guidance Manual clearly explain specific PPP law. The legal framework consists of the PPP Policy Statement, 2003; the PPPA, 2004; the BOTPB, 2016; the Public Procurement Act, 2006, and PPP regulations, 2008, and the PPPs Guidance Manual.

*3.3.2.1.1 Selection of Private Party.* The Mauritius Public Procurement Act, 2006, and PPP Regulations, 2008, spell out a fair and transparent tender selection process. Both the act and the PPP regulations provide limited exceptions. Such exceptions allow direct negotiations in special circumstances where (1) the lowest evaluated responsive bid is substantially above the updated estimated costs and a rebid exercise is considered not practical; (2) direct procurement from a single source is resorted to, or (3) emergency procurement under Section 21 of PPP is resorted to (The World Bank/PPP; Act. 11, PPPA).

*3.3.2.1.2 Project Agreement.* There is flexibility in the content of the provisions of the PPP project agreements, which allow for the identifiable allocation of risks without unnecessary requirements from the Contracting Authority (obligations, tariff, termination, compensation).

*3.3.2.1.3 Settlement of Disputes and Applicable Laws.* There is a possibility to obtain a proper remedy for breach of contract under the applicable law through international arbitration and enforcement of arbitral awards.

*3.3.2.1.4 Existence and Role of PPP Central Unit/Agency.* There is a specialized department, the Concession Treatment Unit. The PPP Unit is established in the Ministry of Economic Development, Financial Services, and Corporate Affairs, in collaboration with the Central Tender Board. Division of Power between Different Public Authorities involved in PPP is clear and coordinated. The Central Tender Board has procurement responsibility, and the PPP agreement must be formally approved by the Cabinet (Article 11, PPPA).

Division of Power between Different Public Authorities involved in PPP is clear and coordinated and spelled out in the Law.

*3.3.2.1.5 PPP Legal Challenges.* Each bidder is entitled to request an Administrative Review of the selection process by the Concession Unit. Such a review provides for transparency in the bidding process.

There are no court decisions concerning the performance of PPP contracts. There are court decisions concerning the selection process of bidders, when one of the bidders' appeals against the decision of the Concession Treatment Unit (EBRD, 2011).

#### 3.3.2.2 Limitations of the Mauritius Law

### *3.3.3 PPP Policy Framework*

No limitations. A PPP policy framework consisting of an infrastructure finance policy and laws for implementing PPPs are present.

*3.3.3.0.1 PPP Institutional Framework.* The implementation of PPP Policy and Law through via line ministers is cohesive (EBRD, 2011).

#### 3.3.3.1 Obstacles to PPP Contract Implementation

There are some obstacles between the Concessionaire and the private owners of the land where the concession PPP project is to be established. In some instances, private landowners can pose obstacles to successful PPP projects. Local tariffs and local taxes constitute other obstacles to PPP implementation because they vary between local governments. This inconsistency can present challenges for some Concessionaires. Some PPPs, such as hydroelectric power plants, can become an environmental obstacle, such as by reducing the number of water systems.

There are occasional intergovernmental obstacles such as the Central Government who owns specific resources and the local government who give permits for the PPP. These obstacles may in some cases take a long time to work out (EBRD, 2011).

#### 3.3.3.2 Settlement of Disputes and Applicable Laws

The parties to a procurement contract may agree in the procurement contract, or by a separate agreement, to submit any dispute arising out under the procurement contract for settlement by arbitration. The PPP Guidance Manual provides that dispute resolution shall be specified in the PPP agreement (Mauritius PPP Manual, Section 67, and Mauritius PPP Act, Article 8.5.30).

#### 3.3.3.3 PPP Legal Challenges

There have been no court cases involving Mauritius PPP.

### *3.3.4 New York State Strengths and Limitations of Legal System and Laws*

#### 3.3.4.1 Legal Framework and Definition and Scope of Law

The primary PPP law is the Infrastructure Investment Act, Chapter 56 of 2011, Part F of the Budget Bill, New York State Procurement Act, the New York State Finance Law 137 (Guidelines for Posting a Payment Bond, New York State Finance Law 163, State Agencies). There is a clear definition of the boundaries and scope of application of the Design-Build PPP legislative framework. Under common law, there is extensive freedom of contract, with few provisions implied in the contract, and everything is allowed that is not expressly prohibited by law. The legislation defines PPP (Design-Build), the sectors covered, responsible authorities, and private sector eligibility.

*3.3.4.1.1 Selection of Private Party.* The New York State Infrastructure Investment Act on Design-Build PPPs articulates a fair and transparent tender selection process. It provides for limited exceptions allowing direct negotiations and competitive rules for unsolicited proposals.

*3.3.4.1.2 Project Agreement.* There is flexibility in the content of the provisions of the project agreements, which allow for the identifiable allocation of risks without unnecessary requirements from the Contracting Authority (obligations, termination, compensation).

*3.3.4.1.3 Settlement of Disputes and Applicable Laws.* There is a possibility to obtain an appropriate solution for breach under the applicable law.

*3.3.4.1.4 Existence and Role of PPP Central Unit/Agency.* There is not a specialized agency responsible for Design-Build PPP. Each of the five agencies listed in the legislation is responsible for their Design-Build PPP contracts.

*3.3.4.1.5 Division of Power between Different Public Authorities Involved in PPP is Clear and Coordinated.* The division of power is not spelled out in the Law. Each of the state agencies designated in the legislation is to enter into Design-Build PPP.

#### 3.3.4.2 PPP Legal Challenges

Each bidder is entitled to request an administrative review. There are no court decisions about the performance of PPP contracts under New York State Law.

#### 3.3.4.3 Limitations of the Law

*3.3.4.3.1 PPP Policy Framework.* The Design-Build legislative framework was enacted in 2011 through the Executive Budget Bill, which authorized the Infrastructure Investment Act. The act allows the private sector to design and build in one bid for new facilities and private sector bids for Operation and Maintenance (DiNapoli, 2014).

*3.3.4.3.2 PPP Institutional Framework.* The act authorized the Thruway Authority, the Department of Transportation, the Office of Parks, Recreation and Historic Preservation (Parks), the DEC, and the New York State Bridge Authority to use Design-Build procurement for the construction, replacement, or repair of highways, bridges, dams, flood control projects, canals, and parks or to correct health and safety defects or comply with federal and state laws (DiNapoli, 2014, p. 5). The above agencies are the only entities allowed to enter into a Design-Build PPP under the Infrastructure Investment Act.

#### 3.3.4.4 Obstacles to PPP Contract Implementation

None identified.

### *3.3.5 State of Indiana Strengths and Limitations of Laws*

The Indiana PPP legal framework is set forth under the Indiana Code. INDOT and IFA have the legislative authority to procure PPP projects. The statutes that provide authorization to procure PPP projects are IC8-15-5 for IFA and IC8-15-7 for INDOT. IFA has the lead in the procurement of most projects. INDOT is responsible for the technical aspects of the PPP projects and is authorized to commit appropriations for a project. IFA is responsible for the financial terms of PPP procurement.

#### 3.3.5.1 Selection of Private Party

Indiana articulates a fair and transparent tender selection process. It provides for limited exceptions allowing direct negotiations and competitive rules for unsolicited proposals.

*3.3.5.1.1 Project Agreement.* There is flexibility with respect to the content of the provisions of the Project agreements, which allow for the identifiable allocation of risks without unnecessary requirements from the Contracting Authority (obligations, termination, compensation).

*3.3.5.1.2 Settlement of Disputes and Applicable Laws.* There is a possibility to obtain proper remedy for breach under the applicable law.

*3.3.5.1.3 Existence and Role of PPP Central Unit/Agency.* IFA oversees State-related debt issuances and provides financing solutions to assist in the state, local government, and business financing arrangements in the State. INDOT is responsible for the planning and development of the state's transportation system. INDOT works with IFA to assist with the procurement of projects and with oversight of the work of developers involved in all technical aspects of projects.

*3.3.5.1.4 Division of Power between Different Public Authorities Involved in PPP is Clear and Coordinated.* There is a clear division of power between IFA and INDOT, and PPP projects are coordinated.

#### 3.3.5.2 Challenges to Indiana PPP Statutes

*3.3.5.2.1 Indiana Toll Road.* A joint venture made up of private partners submitted the winning bid of $3.8 billion for the Indiana Toll Road Concession PPP. The PPP partners had previously worked on the Chicago Skyway. The PPP Indiana Toll Road contract was completed in 2006, and two companies formed the private Indiana Toll Road Concession Company to operate the Indiana Toll Road (Puentes, 2014).

A lawsuit by opponents of the financing and delivery arrangement in 2006 was filed. The judge ruled in favor of the State of Indiana. The judge declared the lawsuit brought by opponents a public lawsuit and required plaintiffs to post a bond of $1.9 billion in order for the case to proceed. The plaintiffs appealed the judge's ruling to the Indiana Supreme Court (Puentes, 2014). In 2006, in a 4–0 decision, the Indiana Supreme Court upheld the lower court decision. That decision allowed the lease of the Indiana Toll Road to proceed as scheduled. Some state legislators had concerns that too much financing was going to the Indianapolis area and too little to the areas in the northern part of the state. The joint venture experienced financial problems, and a new consortium was awarded the Indiana Toll Road Concession. The problem for the ITR investors was the imprecise nature of traffic projections, coupled with the 2008 financial crisis. Traffic projects are historically unreliable. If investors guess too high, they could lose significant sums (Trenkner, 2011).

The Indiana Toll Road Concession Company (private partner) increased its fees by 35% for heavy vehicles such as trucks. A lawsuit was filed that alleged that the increase in tolls is discriminatory and excessive and violated the Commerce Clause and Privileges and Immunities Clauses of the United States Constitution (Clark & Hakim, 2019). According to the Governor, the new rates put the Indiana Toll rates in line with heavy vehicle toll charges in other states. The suit states that the tolls should be paid for by taxpayers and not by increases in toll charges (Clark & Hakim, 2019).

### *3.3.6 Whether Specific Laws and Legal System Limit Success or Create More Possibilities for PPP Failure*

Common law and civil law jurisdictions have different approaches to PPP-related issues. In many civil law countries, a separate administrative law governs PPP arrangements because the service in question is deemed to be a public service (The

World Bank Legal Resource Center, 2018; Son, 2012). The law stipulates government and contractor rights regarding PPPs, including the right of a Contracting Authority to unilaterally cancel a contract, the right of an operator to compensation following an unexpected increase in the cost of operations, or the right of an authority to make unilateral changes to the contract due to public interest. Also, in a civil law country, unless the contract specifies that the parties have agreed to arbitration, the contract will be enforced by the administrative courts (EPEC, 2011). Relying on laws alone in civil law countries can be difficult because rules are often ambiguous, and it is not clear what specific terms mean (The World Bank, 2014). A contract that uses administrative law principle and spells out exactly how it is to be applied will generally be effective. However, changing or overriding an administrative law principle may or may not be legally possible. It may not be possible to remove altogether the ability of a Contracting Authority to change service standards (The World Bank, 2014) unilaterally.

The United States and other common law counties such as the United Kingdom have greater flexibility in granting different types of security over capital infrastructure, which is an essential feature of PPP arrangements involving commercial funding such as BOTs. Common law forms the fundamental basis of all commercial transactions which support the allocation of risk. Common law forms also have the concept of trusts, which allow security interests to be held by a trustee for lenders in a syndicated loan situation without the need for formal transfer or reregistering of security interests in names of new lenders (The World Bank, 2014). Civil law does not have that concept, and so security interests generally have to be reregistered in the name of the new lender (involving additional registration costs and other related fees) (The World Bank, 2014).

## 3.4 Summary of PPPs Laws

This section summarizes PPP laws so that policymakers can be aware and informed of what laws or specific legislation to write to best ensure PPP effectiveness and efficiency. Such laws further amplify the PPP success rate and potential for positive impact. Further, the laws and legal systems demonstrate institutional processes which facilitate implementation. Chapter 8 recommends PPP laws and policies so that policymakers can see what are most effective in different legal contexts.

In addition to the Common Law or Civil Law context of PPP laws and institutional arrangements, an essential consideration in designing laws that support the use of PPP as an Infrastructure Finance Policy option is to ensure that the relevant laws support the Infrastructure Finance Policy goals of the national or subnational government. Those goals should include (1) a more efficient and effective overall capital management and budgeting system, (2) capital infrastructure projects delivered on time and within capital budget appropriation, (3) more effective management of the use of long-term debt, and (4) more enhanced public value and provide a better balance between traditional means of government capital improvements financing (long-term debt, equity financing, and capital reserves and alternative financing options).

### *3.4.1 Albania PPP Laws*

#### 3.4.1.1 Albanian Definition of PPP

A concession is defined as a PPP agreement between the government and the private contractor. Three types of Concession are defined in the PPP Law of 2013: (1) Public Works Concession, (2) Public Service Concession, and (3) Mixed Concession.

#### 3.4.1.2 Specific Albanian PPP Laws

Specific Albanian PPP Laws No., 125/2013 Albanian PPP Law No. 125/2013 on Concession.

PPP (PPP Law, 2013).

### *3.4.2 Mauritius PPP Laws*

#### 3.4.2.1 Mauritius Definition of PPP

Mauritius defines PPP as an agreement between a Contracting Authority and a private party, approved in terms of the act in which the private party performs a contracting function on behalf of the Contracting Authority and receives a benefit for performing the function in the form of revenue or fees or some combination. The Act does not apply to PPPs that include a construction phase. The BOT Act applies in that case.

#### 3.4.2.2 Specific PPP Law

The Mauritius PPP Act of 2004, the BOTPB of 2016, the Public Procurement Act of 2006, and PPP regulations of 2008.

### *3.4.3 New York State PPP Laws*

#### 3.4.3.1 New York State Definition of PPP

It allows authorized state agencies to use the Design-Build PPP contracts for capital infrastructure including, but not limited to, the state's highways, bridges, dams, flood control projects, canals, and parks, and also, including, but not limited to, to repair damage caused by natural disaster, to correct health and safety defects, to comply with federal and state laws, standards, and regulations, and to extend the useful life of or replace the state's highways, bridges, dams, flood control projects, canals, and parks (New York Senate, 2015).

#### 3.4.3.2 Specific New York State PPP Law

Infrastructure Investment Act, Chapter 56 of 2011, Part F is the law governing the use of PPPs. The law allows only the Design-Build PPP project method. It designates authorized state entities: (1) the New York State Thruway Authority, the Department of Transportation, (2) the Office of Parks, Recreation and Historic Preservation, (3) the DEC, and (4) the New York State Budget Authority to enter into the Design-Build form of PPP (Mujica, 2019).

### *3.4.4 State of Indiana PPP Laws*

#### 3.4.4.1 Indiana Definition of PPP

Indiana defines PPP as a BOT agreement or an operating agreement between a governmental body and an operator for the acquisition, planning, design, development, reconstruction, repair, maintenance, or financing of any public facility on behalf of the governing body.

#### 3.4.4.2 Specific Indiana PPP Law

The Indiana PPP statutes are set forth under the Indiana Code. The statutes that provide authorization to procure PPP projects are IC8-15-5 for IFA and IC8-15-7 for INDOT. The statutes provide authorization to procure PPP projects, and IFA has the lead in the procurement of most capital projects. INDOT is responsible for the technical aspects of the PPP projects and is authorized to commit appropriations for a capital project. IFA is responsible for the financial terms of PPP procurement.

## 3.5 Summary

Laws have been enacted in these countries to provide specific legislation enacted, which stipulates the legal basis for PPP contracts. The law is further expanded on in Part 6, Chapter 8.

New York State PPP law allows authorized state agencies to use the Design-Build PPP contracts for capital infrastructure. The Infrastructure Investment Act, Chapter 56 of 2011, Part F, is the law governing the use of PPPs. The law clearly defines PPP (Design-Build), the sectors covered, responsible authorities, and private sector eligibility. New York State Law provides a clear definition of the boundaries and scope of application of the Design-Build PPP legislative framework. Under common law, there is extensive freedom of contract, such as PPP contracts, with few provisions implied in the contract, and everything allowed that is not expressly prohibited by law.

Mauritius uses the legal term Concessions and, in the legal sense, has a standalone PPP law. Mauritius also has two sets of systems for PPP laws and Concessions independent of whether they regulate PPPs as a stand-alone system or whether it is in the broader context of their procurement law. Mauritius PPP legislative and legal framework consists of the PPP Policy Statement, 2003, and the Guidance Manual, which clearly explain specific PPP law. The legal framework consists of the PPPA, 2004; the BOTPB , 2016; the Public Procurement Act, 2006, and PPP regulations, 2008.

Albania PPP law covers Concessions and is defined as a PPP agreement between the Contracting Authority and the economic operator. Albania's legal system is based on Civil Law. Albanian PPP law clearly defines the boundaries and scope of application of the concession legal framework. Under civil law, only legislative enactments are binding, and there is little opportunity for judge-made law in civil, criminal, and commercial courts. The legislation defines PPPs, the sectors covered, responsible authorities, and private sector eligibility. The legislation limits the risk of a challenge to the validity of PPP contracts.

Indiana law defines PPP as a BOT agreement or an operating agreement Indiana PPP law. INDOT and IFA have the legislative authority to procure PPP projects. The statutes that provide authorization to procure PPP projects are IC8-15-5 for IFA and IC8-15-7 for INDOT. IFA has the lead in the procurement of most projects. INDOT is responsible for the technical aspects of the PPP projects and is authorized to commit appropriations for a project. IFA is responsible for the financial terms of PPP procurement.

# Part 2
# Public Sector and Private Sector Value Differences

Chapter 4

# The Role of in Infrastructure Finance Policy Shaping Public Value

This chapter begins with a discussion of the value differences espoused by the public sector and the private sector. Understanding the role of value in the public sector and especially which values form the guiding foundation in public sector decision-making is critical to understand how the use of PPPs fits in an overall Infrastructure Finance Policy design. The private sector's primary value clearly and unambiguously is profit maximization, while the public sector's primary value is social welfare maximization (Crocker & Reynolds, 1993; Koppenjan & Enserink, 2009). This distinction between the private sector's profit maximization value and the public sector's social welfare value forms a basis for serious consideration of how the public value of social welfare maximization can be articulated. The discussion begins by identifying and articulating the use of the private sector as a partner in infrastructure financing and construction as an option in a government's Infrastructure Finance Policy design, as implemented through the capital management and budget system. The market in which infrastructure financing and delivery takes place has the power to define value. However, it can only define value through individual transactions, not taking into consideration the way these transactions accumulate and without comprehensive design into broader macro patterns (Kettl, 2015). The government's role is critical in creating and defining public value (Kettl, 2015), which it can articulate through comprehensive policy design such as Infrastructure Finance Policy. The focus of this book is on the role of Infrastructure Finance Policy in articulating the rationale for a PPP policy option. The ultimate role of the public policy decisions in terms of creating public value needs to be defined in terms of policies that govern responsibility for and accountability to its citizens for social welfare maximization. One of the policies that can define public sector value and maximize social welfare is through Infrastructure Finance Policy that provides direction for resource allocation in shaping public value.

The role of public value in the context of Infrastructure Finance Policy is to serve as a consideration of what is created and sustained by the government on behalf of the public (Nabatchi, 2018) A government's public values are

**Public-Private Partnerships, Capital Infrastructure Project Investments and Infrastructure Finance, 103–132**

**doi:10.1108/978-1-83909-654-920201004**

communicated and implemented through its Infrastructure Finance Policy and form the basis for creating its multiyear capital investment plans. Managerial work in the public sector aims to create public value just as managerial work in the private sector aims to create private value (Moore, 1995). Public value is shaped and actualized when government policies receive political legitimacy, meet the needs of citizens, and are managerially feasible and sustainable (Nabatchi, 2018).

## 4.1 Public Value and Private Value

A private contractor that enters into partnership with a government through a PPP contract to finance and deliver a capital infrastructure does such dissimilar values than those of the public sector because of the different values and purposes as described above. A government's social welfare goal is maximized if goods and services are produced at minimum cost, in a competitive environment, and it does not create negative social externalities. The profit of a private contractor is maximized when goods or services are produced at a minimum cost and provided to a government for a price that exceeds the cost (Bajari, Houghton, & Tadelis, 2014). An Infrastructure Finance Policy that includes the option of capital infrastructure financing and construction through the use of PPP is an example of a public value that is articulated through public policy.

The critical issue is understanding the importance of public policies. In particular, such policies as Infrastructure Finance Policy are essential in that the design of such policies influences resource allocation (Rosen & Gayer, 2014). A government's Infrastructure Finance Policy that articulates the role of the private sector as a significant partner in delivering public goods and services, such as capital infrastructure, is an example of the expression of a public value through resource allocation. Public value can be best understood through several dimensions: (1) political, (2) legal, (3) organizational, and (4) the market. Taken together and as a whole, they provide meaning to public policies (Nabatchi, 2018), such as Infrastructure Finance Policy. Each of these dimensions is shaped by core content value, and additionally, they are guided by prevailing modes of rationality and a particular set of dominant methods (Nabatchi, 2018). The legal dimension, described in Chapter 3, establishes the rules of the game and creates the legal zone of discretion within which public administrators carry out their work (Moynihan, 2009). The market dimension is made up of market-oriented reforms (Nabatchi, 2018), such as the inclusion of the private sector in infrastructure capital infrastructure financing and delivery. The articulation of private infrastructure financing and delivery methods, such as the inclusion of PPPs in an Infrastructure Finance Policy and the use of PPPs, is an example of identifying the market dimension (including the private sector) as a public value. The economic (market) dimension, in particular, provides the predominant strategic Infrastructure Finance Policy dimension and value standards that, in turn, guide the systematic capital infrastructure management planning and implementation through the multiyear capital improvements plan.

## 4.2 Value Dimensions

The (1) political, (2) legal, (3) organizational, and (4) economic (market) value dimensions are used to create a policy framework to better understand the role of public value such as private participation in financing and delivering capital infrastructure through PPPs. These dimensions provide a basis for illustrating and understanding how value dimensions translate policy, such as Infrastructure Finance Policy, into public value.

### *4.2.1 Political Value Dimension*

The political values dimension shapes a government's macro level policies (and its decisions) and is carried out through voting, representation, and political responsiveness. The political values dimension uses substantive rationality to determine what a group's goals, values, and ideals should be (Nabatchi, 2018).

### *4.2.2 Legal Value Dimension*

The legal values dimension comprises individual substantive rights, procedural due process, and fairness (Nabatchi, 2018; Rosenbloom, 1983). Legal rationality is used to uphold these values. Statutes (laws passed by legislatures to address values problems) and common law (case law or precedent developed over time) are used as a basis to make legal determinations. As a values dimension, the law establishes the rules of the game and legal zone of discretion within which government administrators operate (Nabatchi, 2018). A comprehensive legal values dimension results in more explicitly articulated and regulated administrative behavior, and administrative discretion is narrowed (Nabatchi, 2018), as we see in the case of Mauritius described in Chapter 3. Problems emerge when a country's (or state's) legal values dimension is ambiguous, and the letter of the law is substituted for the legal values dimension that best explicates welfare maximization as a dominant value dimension, influencing administrative behaviors (Lynn, 2009; Moynihan, 2009; Nabatchi, 2018). From a welfare maximization reference perspective, a country's (or state's) legal values dimension is implemented in administrative decision-making through impartial administrative laws judges, hearing examiners, and regulatory commissions (Nabatchi, 2018; Rosenbloom, 1983). There are also various alternative dispute resolutions, such as negotiating and settling (Nabatchi, 2018; Rosenbloom, 1983).

### *4.2.3 Organizational Value Dimension*

The organizational value dimension core value is based on administrative efficiency. The other values on which the organizational value dimension is based are specialization and expertise, and merit, formalization, organizational loyalty, and political neutrality reinforce administrative efficiency (Nabatchi, 2018). The organizational values dimension uses technical rationality, which raises the scientific analytical mindset and the belief in technological progress (Nabatchi, 2018). The focus in this value dimension is finding the most efficient means to an end (Nabatchi, 2018).

### *4.2.4 Economic (Market) Value Dimension*

The primary values in this dimension are (1) cost savings and (2) efficiency, supplemented by other values such as productivity, flexibility, innovation, and customer service (Nabatchi, 2018). The market values dimension is guided by a focus on the most efficient or cost-effective means of achieving a specific end without refection on the value of that end. The emphasis is on cost-cutting and allowing public managers to manage according to private sector corporate practice (Nabatchi, 2018). The emphasis on cost savings and efficiency is seen in such methods as competition, contracting out, franchises, vouchers, and commercialization (Nabatchi, 2018).

The private sector, in general, may be better positioned in some cases to deliver large-scale capital infrastructure projects more efficiently because of greater skills, technology, and state of the art knowledge (Ghobadian, O'Regan, Gallear, & Viney, 2004). The reason for the private sector to enter into a PPP contract is the expectation of increased profit potential and business expansion (Jamali, 2004; Scharle, 2002) as we see in the case of Mauritius' use of PPP.

Aspects of the four values dimensions will be integrated into the four case examples to better bring into focus the role of the dimensions and will be used to illustrate their impact on Infrastructure Finance Policy.

## 4.3 Value Dimension Case Examples

### *4.3.1 Case Example 1: Mauritius*

In Mauritius, the government's Infrastructure Finance Policy is communicated as a public value primarily through both the economic (market) value dimension and the legal value dimensions. Because of governmental budgetary constraints, the need for the private sector to be substantially involved in the implementation of public services (e.g., roads, public transport, hospitals, schools) is being increasingly recognized as crucial to ensure the delivery of better facilities faster and generally cheaper over the long term through risk-adjusted and whole-life costs of a particular service (Mauritius NDP, 2004). In identifying the need for the private sector to be substantially involved in the implementation of public services, Mauritius is articulating a public value. A government policy objective in implementing its Infrastructure Finance Policy is that a portion of its infrastructure financing should come from the use of Public–Private Partnerships as we see to varying degrees in Albania, the United States (in New York State and Indiana), and Mauritius.

### *4.3.2 Case Example 2: Albania*

In Albania, the government's Infrastructure Finance Policy is communicated as a public value primarily through the political values dimension. There is still limited government legal and organizational capacity and capability and, as a result of the imbalance, undue political influence (UN, 3/17). One example of the over-emphasis on the political values dimension in articulating public values is that the government has produced overly optimistic revenue forecasts to support spending increases that have, in turn, negatively impacted capital financing (MoF, 2014; as cited in Beckett-Camarata, 2019). Political pressure to justify and maintain growth in spending in the operating budget has negatively impacted financing capital infrastructure. The guiding principles in Albania for implementing PPPs (especially service concession contracts), (1) transparency, (2) nondiscrimination, (3) proportionality, (4) efficiency, (5) equal treatment, (6) mutual recognition, (7) nondiscrimination, (8) mutual recognition, and (9) legal certainty, are clearly articulated. The evolving political values dimension and its undue influence in administrative decisions have hampered the ability of Infrastructure Finance Policy to guide capital management and budgeting and Albania's appropriate use of PPP for financing and constructing capital projects.

### *4.3.3 Case Example 3: New York State*

New York State's Infrastructure Finance Policy is communicated as a public value primarily through both the political and legal organizational values dimensions. The state's Infrastructure Finance Policy is evident in communicating its public values both in its laws and in the state's executive budget. In approving the use of design-build PPP contracts by authorized state agencies, the state is articulating a public value. A New York State government objective in implementing its Infrastructure Finance Policy is for certain projects the design-build delivery method has the potential to achieve projects delivered on guaranteed or accelerated schedules, lowers costs, and risk shifting to the private sector to accelerate capital investments in New York State's capital infrastructure (NYS PPP Act, p. 23 [see Chapter 3]; schoolconstructionnews.com, 2007). As noted in Chapter 3, New York State has limited debt capacity. The state has used long-term debt extensively in financing capital infrastructure, and the increasing use of debt has created a substantial debt burden (60% of the $47.6 billion projected to be spent is expected to be funded through the issuance of bonds [see Chapter 3]). Because of the state's limited debt capacity (due to extremely heavy reliance on long-term debt to fund capital projects), expanding its policy on the use of PPPs could provide the state with new options for planning, financing, and constructing capital infrastructure.

### *4.3.4 Case Example 4: Indiana*

Indiana's Infrastructure Finance Policy is articulated as a public value primarily through the legal and organizational values dimensions. The state's

Infrastructure Finance Policy, as spelled out in the Indiana Code, allows both toll and nontoll transportation projects and for the development, financing, and operation of PPP projects. PPPs are carried out through two agencies: (1) the Indiana Financing Authority and (2) the Indiana Department of Transportation. The state's public values, legal values dimension, are further articulated through the Indiana Code. The Code provides the guiding principles in Indiana, as described in Chapter 3.

## 4.4 The Role of Capital Improvements Planning within Capital Management and Budgeting Processes in Identifying Infrastructure Financing

This section covers the role of capital improvements planning, within capital management and budgeting process, in identifying specific capital projects financing. It discusses the process that the capital improvement plan provides in setting capital infrastructure financing priorities and their identified financing sources. Given the long-term nature of capital projects, most projects in the capital budget for a given year will be financed with some combination of public and/or private financing sources.

Public managers are responsible for setting budget policy and driving the capital management and budget process. Different agencies within a government are explicitly charged with responsibility for various aspects of the budget process, such as legislative or executive budget offices or ministries. In contrast, other agencies with a government that may contribute to the capital management and budget process are implicitly charged with contributing to the budget process, such as program staff. Collectively, these public managers translate the often-abstract public values of citizens and those of politicians. In effect, they are cocreators of public value, and as applied to budgets, particularly capital improvements plans, they are also the translators of public value into concrete budget priorities (Chohan, 2019). Individual citizens are recipients of resource allocation through the budget process. Citizens, collectively, through civil society, are also recipients of resource allocation through the budget process. Public values, as they apply collectively to citizens through the allocation of resources through the budget process, may have different effects on different citizens (Chohan & Jacobs, 2017), both individually and collectively. The capital improvement plan is one way that public values, expressed through citizens, politicians, and translated by public managers, are articulated.

A greater understanding of capital management and budget processes in different national and subnational governments, and in particular, the role of the capital improvements plan, is important in understanding Infrastructure Finance Policy implementation. Most of the attention is paid to the Governmental Funds within the Operating Budget, especially the General Fund, and financing policies pertaining to those funds. Less focus has been on capital management and budget system. The particular capital improvements plan will vary based on the size of the government and its staffing capacity and capability, as we see in the case examples. However, a purpose of capital infrastructure planning within the capital management and budget system is to provide continuity between the annual or biennial budget process and strategic Infrastructure Finance Policy and provide for an integrated and coordinated decision support process for capital improvements financing and delivery. The following four case examples illustrate the capital management and budgeting process.

### *4.4.1 Case 1: Mauritius Capital Management and Budgeting Process*

#### 4.4.1.1 Capital Improvements Planning

Capital improvements planning, capital budgeting, and financial management in Mauritius are based on the Mauritius National Development Program. For example, the plan provides the basis for multiyear capital investment plans. In Section 14.4 of the Program, one of the critical planning objectives is to provide strategic guidance and context in the improvement and provision of new capital infrastructure to enable the planned capital infrastructure to be achieved and provide guidance for strengthening the institutional and legal framework (Mauritius NDP, 2004, p. 4).

#### 4.4.1.2 Capital Management and Budgeting

A significant component of the Mauritius Program strategy is the use of Public–Private Partnerships at the planning stage to bring forward projects for early implementation (Mauritius NDP, 2004, p. 29). To that end, legislation was passed to support the strategy. In the National Development Program, Section 19.3.5 on Public–Private Partnerships further articulates the Infrastructure Finance Policy. That noted that because of governmental budgetary constraints, the need for the private sector to be substantially involved in public services (e.g., roads, public hospitals, schools) is being increasingly recognized as critical to ensure delivery of better facilities faster and generally cheaper over the long-term through risk-adjusted and whole-life costs of a particular service.

A PPP Secretariat Unit was been set up in the Mauritius Ministry of Finance (MoF) and Economic Development, and the unit reviews projects for potential PPP financing. PPP can be a useful mechanism for implementing land-use planning projects contained in local plans or Action Area Plans and through MTEP, other ministries, and agencies scheme (Mauritius NDP, 2004).

The Capital Improvements Project Plan Committee under the Finance and Audit Act was initiated to ensure that capital projects are prepared, designed, and implemented, and risks are adequately assessed so that projects are implemented on time and within budget. The project implementation unit is in five ministries and departments. There is a multidisciplinary project unit made up of technical officers and consultants in engineering, economics/finance, and project management. An Asset Register has been developed in the Accountant General Department to improve the recording of capital infrastructure to help in the determination of capital infrastructure value and budgeting for capital infrastructure, including acquisition, upgrading maintenance, and disposal. An asset replacement program (buildings, vehicles, equipment) has been developed with line ministries.

Mauritius has identified Government borrowing on the domestic market as its primary source for financing capital infrastructure. As part of the Investment Implementation Plan, the government overhauled its Public Investment Management Framework to speed implementation, transparency in procurement, and obtain value for the money. It also set up an alternative method for procurement through Build Operate and Transfer (BOT) for line Ministries for implementation of capital projects. The BOT Act (see Chapter 3) provides for private sector participation in capital infrastructure financing and delivery. The Act provides a legal framework for a simple and effective process for facilitating the expeditious implementation of BOT projects and ensures value for money, transparency, and accountability (Mauritius Investment Guide, 2015).

Mauritius has a *Public Sector Investment Program* document that lays out the Infrastructure Finance Plans for 5 years based on its Strategic Plan. The plan is updated when the budget is presented. The capital projects in the document reflect the priorities and values articulated in the needs, objectives, and priorities and laid out in the Medium-term Expenditure Plan. The capital projects list in the document the objectives, project benefits, and community priorities and are prioritized in the budget document. The Mauritius Budget describes how capital projects are prioritized in the budget and the method used for systematic project selection. The 2019 capital budget of Rs 9.5 million is financed through loans and equity, bringing the total capital outlay in the budget to Rs 27.4 billion (Mauritius 2019/20 Budget speech, p. 67). The government is borrowing Rs 2.6 billion from foreign sources and repaying Rs 2.6 billion from foreign sources and repaying Rs 4.4 billion of foreign loans (Mauritius 2019/20 Budget Speech, p. 67). The government is also raising Rs 27.4 billion from domestic sources (Mauritius 2019/20 Budget Speech, p. 67).

Based on revenue and expenditures contained in the budget document, public sector debt is forecast to decline to 63.1% of GDP by June 2019, and the share of foreign debt is forecast to be reduced from 19.5% to 18% (Mauritius 2019/20 Budget Speech, p. 67). The government forecasts revenue to be MUR121.7 billion for FY 2019/20, increasing by 10% from MUR120.7 billion collected in 2018/19 (KPMG-mu, 2019). The collections are mainly from tax revenue and grants receivable. Tax receipts represent 78% of revenue, of which 69% of tax receipts will be from taxes on goods and services, and 31% will be from income and profits (KPMG-mu, 2019). Revenue from grants represents 5% of total revenue (KPMG-mu, 2019).

Budgeted government expenditures are forecast to increase to MUR138.6 billion for the fiscal year 2019/20, increasing by 9.5% from MUR 126.5 billion expensed in 2018/19. Spending on social protection and general public services, ~MUR74 billion, is the largest category of expenditures. The category represents 53% of total forecasted expenditures (KPMG-mu, 2019).

### *4.4.2 Case 2: Albanian Capital Management and Budgeting Process*

#### 4.4.2.1 Capital Improvements Planning

The Albanian Prime Minister's Office is responsible for long-term fiscal projections. Long-term capital improvements planning and capital budgeting and financial management in Albania are based on its Medium-term Budget and Forecasts prepared by the Department of Planning and Budget within the Albanian MoF (Beckett-Camarata, 2019). The projections provide the basis for planning multiyear capital financing. The Albanian process for initiating, appraising, prioritizing, approving, and contracting for capital improvements planning does not consistently follow the steps in an organized manner (Beckett-Camarata, 2019) because the process is politicized, fragmented, and lacks adequate staffing (see Chapter 5).

In Article 8(5) of Law No 125/2013, one of the key planning objectives is the approval of a strategic policy document for defining the primary sectors for capital financing based on Public–Private Partnerships, preferred forms of Public–Private Partnerships and other issues related to the overall policy framework for Service Concession Agreements and other forms of Public–Private Partnerships.

#### 4.4.2.2 Capital Management and Budgeting

Capital projects in Albania are identified in the capital budget proposal, but only capital projects listed in year one of the capital improvement plan (capital budget proposal) are budgeted. The Albanian MoF is responsible for compiling the government-funded capital budget. The Albanian Budget includes both government-funded projects and foreign-funded projects. Albania includes a list of multiyear capital projects in rank order. The projects are ranked based on political priorities (the primary factor), funding availability, and national sector strategies. Albania's capital budget process has been much less orderly than would be intended and desirable (Albania MoF, 2014) because of political involvement. Albania has no budget balance rules (Beckett-Camarata, 2019). In the past, revenue from privatization has been used to finance the Albanian Operating Budget, and no distinction was made between revenue from privatization in the operating and capital budgets (Beckett-Camarata, 2019). This approach resulted in the undermining of the capital budget and increased pressure on the capital budget.

In the Albanian case, the starting point for identifying a possible PPP project in Albania is considered within (1) the national, regional/local, or sectoral planning process, (2) the analysis of the capital infrastructure status, (3) identification of service shortages and financing needs, and (4) projects-based policy priorities.

The Albanian Budget, as described below, reveals high debt levels, which in turn impact its ability to fund capital projects.

#### 4.4.2.3 Albania Revenue and Expenditure Analysis

Based on revenue and expenditures contained in the budget document, public sector debt is forecast to be 69.8% of GDP as of July 2019, and the share of foreign debt is forecast to be in 9.6% in March 2019 (Salim, Shijaku, Guxho,

2019). The budget forecasts government revenue to be 467.6 billion leks for FY 2019, increasing by 4.05 % from 449.4 billion leks collected in 2018 (IMF Country Report, 2019). The collections are mainly from tax revenue and grants receivable. Tax receipts represent the largest percent of revenue, of which 91.98 % of tax receipts are from taxes on goods and services (IMF Country Report, 2019). Revenue from grants represents 14.6% of total revenue (IMF Country Report, 2019). Budgeted government expenditures are forecast to be 510.1 billion leks, of which 82.9 billion leks is budgeted for capital expenditures for the fiscal year 2019.

### *4.4.3 Case 3: New York State Capital Budgeting and Management Process*

#### 4.4.3.1 Capital Improvements Planning

Annually, each New York State agency is required to prepare a 5-year assessment of its capital infrastructure and maintenance needs, which is then incorporated into the State Capital Plan. This Plan provides a broad overview of (1) capital spending enacted in the state budget, (2) financing sources, and (3) spending by public authorities from state-supported bond proceeds (off-budget capital spending) (DiNapoli, 2014). The State Capital Plan also includes projected spending by appropriation over the life of the Plan (www2.osc.state.ny.us/reports/capital_report 20).

The FY 2012–13 Enacted Budget contained a section establishing a New York Works Task Force. The Task Force s appointed by the Executive and Legislative Branches, to advise on coordinating the capital plans of New York State agencies and authorities, including leveraging and accelerating funding streams and financing mechanisms to enhance capital infrastructure investment throughout New York State (DiNapoli, 2014; Article 5-E, NY State Finance Law as amended by Part HH of Chapter 58, 2012). The capital infrastructure provision requires the Task Force to (1) develop a coordinated capital infrastructure plan among state agencies and authorities, focusing on the efficient and accelerated deployment of resources to meet regional and statewide capital infrastructure needs; (2) recommend prioritization of and financing options for capital infrastructure projects and the allocation of capital resources; (3) make recommendations regarding state actions necessary to advance priority capital infrastructure projects; and (4) advise state agencies and authorities.

In 2013, the Task Force published the *New York Works* Plan covering FYs 2013–14 through FYs 2022–23 as its long-term Capital Plan. The purpose of the *New York Works* Plan is to provide a strategic plan designed to break down the silo-based approach to capital investment (New York State Finance Law, Article 5-E, as amended by Part HH of Chapter 58, 2012). The *New York Works* Plan lengthened the state's capital planning timeframe from 5 to 10 years and expanded the scope of comprehensive capital planning by providing a broader picture of planned capital spending. The Plan does not include detail on existing capital infrastructure and financing arrangements, including the use of PPPs, but provides a summary of forecasted investment commitments by sector and by capital category. The funding source, such as bond financing, state pay as you go, is also provided for each agency within each sector.

#### 4.4.3.2 Capital Management and Budgeting

New York State uses an Executive Budget Process. Formal budget requests are submitted annually by agencies several months before the introduction of the Executive Budget by the governor. The requests are initiated through a formal process that requires agencies to submit spending requirements and goals for the upcoming fiscal year. Agency proposals are reviewed by the Budget Director, with recommendations to the Governor for inclusion in the Capital Projects Budget Bill as part of the Executive Budget submission to the Legislature. The Division of the Budget is responsible for publishing the Capital Program and Financing Plan twice a year, with the Executive Budget and the Enacted Budget. The enacted budget contains the final budget provisions. The Enacted Capital Program and Financing Plan (the Capital Plan) provides capital spending and debt issuance. It describes the state's multiyear capital program, the way it will be financed, and the impact of debt on the state's financial plan (NYSFY2020 Enacted Capital Program, 1999).

Based on revenue and expenditures identified in the budget document, debt is $53,528,000, and debt service is $6,753,000 as of July 2019 (NYSFY2020 Enacted Capital Program, 2019, p. 8). The Legislature, through the Conference Committee, made up of the Assembly and the Senate, has about 2  months to officially review, deliberate, revise, and reach an agreement on the budget. The legislature may not change an appropriation bill submitted by the Governor, but it may add items to the appropriation bill. Those appropriations must be passed by both houses to be a law immediately without further action by the governor (Article VII, 4, NYS Constitution).

Budgeted government capital expenditures are forecast to be 15,165 for the fiscal year 2020, increasing by 13.50% from expensed in 2018/19. This represents 53% of total forecasted expenditures (NYSFY2020 Enacted Capital Program, 2019). The New York State Budget reveals high debt levels and high levels of spending.

### *4.4.4 Case 4: Indiana Capital Management and Budgeting Process*

#### 4.4.4.1 Capital Improvements Planning

Analysis of agency spending requests is conducted by involving Government Efficiency and Financial Planning in the early stages. The Indiana Department of Administration has the responsibility for managing capital projects but does not manage the capital improvement plans of individual agencies. The Budget Agency reviews the submitted budget requests and formulates recommendations. The Budget Director reviews budget requests and formulates recommendations and discusses the analysis and recommendations with the governor. The requests are adjusted as approved by the Governor and then presented to the Budget Committee. The Budget Committee holds public hearings with state agencies, and the committee then makes a comprehensive recommendation to the Governor. Revenue forecasts are made annually in December and in April before the final enactment of the appropriation.

#### 4.4.4.2 Capital Management and Budgeting

Funding requests are also tied to program metrics. The State of Indiana uses an Executive Budget Process. Formal budget requests are submitted annually by agencies several months before the introduction of the Executive Budget by the Governor. The requests are initiated through a formal process that requires agencies to submit spending requirements and goals for the upcoming fiscal year. The Budget Director reviews agency proposals.

Based on revenue and expenditures contained in the budget document, debt is $15,095.6 million, and debt service is $45.5 million in July 2019 (Mujica, 2019). The budget forecasts government revenue to be $37.99 billion for FY2020, increasing by 8.8% from $34.99 billion collected in 2019 (Mujica, 2019). The collections are mainly from tax revenue and federal funds. Tax receipts represent the percent of revenue, of which % of tax receipts will be from taxes on goods and services, and percent will be from income and profits (2019). Revenue from grants represents 40.8% of total revenue (Mujica, 2019).

Budgeted government expenditures are forecast to increase to $39,178.3 million for the fiscal year 2020, increasing by 13.6% from $34.4487.7 expensed in 2019. Spending $37566.1 million social protection and general public services is the largest category of expenditures. This represents 95.88% of total forecasted expenditures (Mujica, 2019).

## 4.5 Role of Infrastructure Finance Practices in Achieving Infrastructure Finance Policy Objectives

This section discusses the role of infrastructure finance practices in achieving Infrastructure Finance Policy objectives and discusses determining how much debt a government can afford as critical to capital projects investment planning and in managing debt.

A government's outstanding long-term debt, its authorized, but unissued long-term debt capacity, and long-term debt of other local governments that tax the same citizens or property (overlapping debt) can impact a government's ability to finance future capital projects (Marlowe, Rivenbark, & Vogt, 2009). If a government has substantial long-term debt, requiring it to make large debt service and lease payments from general revenue, it faces a scenario that will continue for many years. If balancing future operating budgets will require significant tax increases or spending cuts, its ability to take on new long-term debt may be difficult. If the government has modest debt, annual debt service payments that will decline in future years, revenue growth that meets or exceeds expected spending growth in future years, then taking on planned new long-term debt to meet policy objectives will be manageable (Marlowe et al., 2009).

### *4.5.1 Managing Use of Long-Term Debt in Infrastructure Finance Planning*

If appropriately managed, long-term debt financing can be an effective tool for paying for infrastructure capital infrastructure. Sources of long-term debt financing are discussed in Chapter 1. Because of the large amount of capital infrastructure financing that is needed in all countries, only a fraction of the financing needed to fund capital infrastructure projects can come from pay-as-you-go (cash) revenue sources. In some countries, such as the United States, the use of long-term debt has been the predominant method of financing government capital infrastructure (Hou, Xu, & Wang, 2009). While using cash to finance a share of capital infrastructure presents some limitations, the use of pay as you go (cash) does afford the benefit of reducing the amount of debt service and the accompanying interest payments (Hou et al., 2009). Pay as you go, however, is rarely a viable option for major capital projects and acquisitions (Marlowe et al., 2009), especially large and complex capital infrastructure projects. As a result, the use of debt to finance capital infrastructure projects is a policy option.

#### 4.5.1.1 Government Debt Affordability

The use of debt to finance a capital project can be a policy option in a successful capital project financing strategy. The first step is to determine a government's debt affordability. Governments have many different financing options that can be used in different combinations to finance capital infrastructure projects, as discussed and described in Chapter 2, that will allow them to manage the amount of debt within their debt limits. The capital infrastructure financing process typically starts with the identification and analysis of available financing sources. A combination of financing sources may be used by a government to pay for the capital infrastructure, depending on the type of capital infrastructure project. A selection of infrastructure financing sources may include (1) general tax revenue, (2) revenue from other specific tax revenue sources, (3) user fees such as toll roads, (4) proceeds from bond sales, (5) designated capital improvement fund, (6) Public–Private Partnership financing (NASBO, 2014), or (7) reserves. Some capital infrastructure project financing is carried out entirely or primarily through long-term debt (pay as you use) and/or through the use of reserves. In most instances, there are constitutional or legal limits on a government's use of long-term general obligation debt because it is backed by the full faith and credit of the government. Factors such as the useful life of the project, timing of cash receipts, availability of general revenue, intergovernmental transfers, and the bond market also impact the use of long-term debt (NASBO, 2014). Finally, intergenerational equity, political acceptability, and the project's potential impact on economic growth also affect long-term debt as a way to finance capital projects.

Considering all these factors and changing political climate, governments face a delicate balance between long-term borrowing to build and maintain needed capital infrastructure and affording the additional debt repayment and debt service payments involved. The process for evaluating government current and future debt affordability, and by what amount, can be challenging for many governments because of a lack of useful data to assess future debt affordability. The goal of assessing long-term debt affordability is to use evidence-based analysis to assist in determining the type and level of debt the government can manage. In some instances, policymakers do not know the full amount of long-term debt that is owed because of what is known as overlapping debt. Overlapping debt is the proportionate share of the debts of local governments located wholly or in part within the limits of another government reporting entity that must be borne by property owners within each government. Confounding the issue is that different overlapping government entities issue long-term debt, and the data on that debt are not centralized in some cases (Murphy, 2017), which can result in a lack of complete data to determine the total long-term debt burden.

The long-term debt burden is basically a tax incidence problem in an intergenerational setting and the burden of debt is hard to pinpoint (Rosen & Gayer, 2014, p. 471). The existence of a debt burden, which is present when a government incurs a long-term debt, depends on, among other things, whether the debt is internal or external and what kinds of projects are financed by the long-term debt (Rosen & Gayer, 2014). From an efficiency standpoint, the question is whether debt or tax finance generates a higher excess debt burden. The key in is answering the question of whether the use of debt or tax finance generates a higher excess debt burden is to understand. Every increase in government spending must ultimately be financed by an increase in taxes. The choice between tax and debt financing is just a choice between the timing of the taxes. With tax finance pay as you go, one large payment is made at the time the expenditure is undertaken. With debt finance pay as you use, many small payments are made over time to finance the [principal and] interest due on the debt. The net present values of the tax collections must be the same in both cases (Rosen & Gayer, 2014).

Government long-term capital borrowing provides financing to commit resources for current public use (Mikesell, 2014). The long-term debt that results from borrowing, along with interest on the long-term debt, must be repaid and, as a result, commits future budgets to the debt repayment. Debt service costs, if not managed well, can grow so large that they can result in the inability of a government entity to provide needed services, as occurred in the case of Detroit, Michigan. The rule of thumb in debt financing is not to issue debt for a maturity longer than the financed project's useful life (Mikesell, 2014).

If the long-term debt is higher than the useful life of the capital infrastructure, the capital infrastructure's actual annual cost is understated, and citizens will continue to pay for the capital infrastructure long after the project is completed. If the useful life of the capital infrastructure exceeds the debt period, the capital infrastructure's cost has been overstated, and citizens will receive benefits without payment (Mikesell, 2014). However, this could mislead decision-makers to understate future replacement costs.

As indicated in Chapter 1, there are many different types of options that can be considered to finance and deliver capital infrastructure projects. Following the analysis of financing sources available to pay for individual capital projects, a combination of financing sources may be used, as identified in Chapter 1. Some capital projects may be financed solely through the use of debt financing, while other capital projects may be financed through a combination of debt, general fund revenue, and reserves. Most governments have some limits on the use of long-term debt to fund capital improvements. Governments issue different types of bonds to finance capital projects. The bonds are issued based on security pledged for debt. The security pledged for debt is the guarantee that the issuer will repay the debt with interest. The investors require the issuer to pledge some collateral as a guarantee of repayment. Examples of collateral pledged are (1) property taxes, (2) specific revenue, or (3) property being financed with debt (Marlowe et al., 2009). If the government defaults on its contractual obligation to make debt service payments, the investors may enforce the terms of the contract to satisfy the terms of the debt repayment. If specific revenue is used to secure debt, it may be used to fund debt service payments.

The security pledged to guarantee the government debt classifies the types of government debt to fund capital infrastructure improvements. Constitutional conditions and laws may limit the security that the government can pledge for debt. Interpretations by courts on such legal limits are essential in shaping a government's debt practices (Hildreth, 2009). Types of government debt authorized in one country and the subnational government may not be authorized in a different country and subnational government (Krane, Rigos, & Hill, 2001).

There are four different kinds of government long-term debt classifications:

(1) *General obligation bonds* backed by the full faith and credit of the issuing government.
(2) *Revenue bonds* backed by specific revenue associated with a self-supporting (enterprise) government activity.
(3) *Lease or lease-purchase debt* security backed by property financed with the debt. Security for some lease debt involves both property and lease revenues.
(4) *Special obligation debt*, backed by limited tax debt, special assessment debt, nonproperty tax debt, and moral obligation debt (Marlowe et al., 2009).

In the United States, government entities responsible for issuing debt, such as a Treasurer or independent financing authority work with bond attorneys, financial underwriters, bond insurers, and other institutional players involved in raising funds and taking a bond offering to market to sell to investors or underwriters (NASBO, 2014). Following the sale of the bonds, the debt becomes outstanding and needs to be repaid. The government must monitor the status of its outstanding debt through the use of a repayment schedule, amounts still owed, and terms of a bond agreement to ensure that funds are available for payment without disrupting current operations (NASBO, 2014).

Debt repayment pledges from subnational governments in the United States, for example, come in various forms and are secured by one of the different pledged securities described above. The government issuer of general obligation bonds is obligated to repay the debt because the issuer's taxing power guarantees it. Revenue bonds, however, are obligated only to pay principal and interest on the bonds from the specifically pledged source according to the bond agreement.

Limits on revenue bonds are less restricting and may change depending on the purpose of the debt and/or issuing authority guidelines (NASBO, 2014). Many subnational governments in the United States, especially state governments, use revenue bonds to finance capital projects (Guzman & Moldogaziev, 2012). Borrowing costs of general obligation bonds tend to be lower than revenue bonds (Guzman & Moldogaziev, 2012). Many subnational governments also limit the amount that can be spent on debt service. Limits on debt service do not diminish the risks from issuing new debt, though it is prudent to assess debt affordability before issuing new debt. Debt affordability assessment is especially important for governments to understand when viewed in the context of changes in the government's tax base (NASBO, 2014). It is important to recognize that investors can either be creditors or equity holders, and some investments, such as PPP contracts and Service Concession Agreements, may have debt-like characteristics due to contracted cash flows (OCED, 2015).

Financial policies, especially infrastructure finance policies, are a critical aspect of capital infrastructure financing decisions, as implemented through the unified capital management and budgeting process, primarily through the capital infrastructure planning and financing decision phase. Capital expenditures typically increase and decrease according to economic conditions (Srithongrung, 2017), so it is crucial to understand how the long-term decision on capital infrastructure financing and construction will impact the operating and capital budgets. These economic conditions impact (1) total revenue receipts (Pagano, 2002), (2) business cycles (Marlowe, 2012), (3) recessions, and (4) annual cycle trends (Srithongrung, 2017).

## 4.6 Infrastructure Finance Policy Design, Implementation, and Evaluation

As introduced in Chapter 1, an articulated Infrastructure Finance Policy should be the basis for capital infrastructure financing and delivery decisions, capital improvements planning and project financing, and acquisition (Beckett-Camarata, 2019) and to achieve public Infrastructure Finance Policy goals. To date, there has been insufficient recognition of the importance of the Infrastructure Finance Policy implementation phase of capital infrastructure planning and financing in identifying potential uses of PPPs (Beckett-Camarata, 2019). The importance of Infrastructure Finance Policy is critical to guiding the activities that support Infrastructure Finance Policy implementation. The activities include comprehensive and strategic physical planning, capital needs analysis, project cost estimation, project priority ranking, and capital project programming based on the sequential order of projects (Bunch, 2013; Marlowe et al., 2009; Millar, 1988; Srithongrung, 2018; Steiss, 2005; Vogt, 2004).

### *4.6.1 Infrastructure Finance Policy Design*

Since a PPP is only one financing and capital project delivery option among many infrastructure financing and delivery policy options, it is crucial to consider the other activities that are needed to support and underpin the Infrastructure Finance Policy. It is critical to consider the context in which the policy will be designed and implemented; thus, the policy should be specific to the individual country and/or subnational government. Specifically, the political, legal, regulatory, and organizational dimensions discussed previously, as well as the business environment, must also be well thought out. Infrastructure financing policy should consider the nature of the infrastructure in setting policy preferences. The policy should be designed so that it provides the foundation for practical infrastructure financing approaches that will broaden the options available for financing capital infrastructure delivery and diversify the investor base. As a result, the cost of financing can potentially be lowered and may increase the pool of potential investors where investment gaps may exist (OCED, 2015).

In designing an Infrastructure Finance Policy, it is important to consider the context, that is, the government's need to achieve and/or maintain economic stability and its need to balance the budget (considering the impact of the capital budget on the operating budget) and to achieve and to maintain long-term fiscal sustainability. Multilateral lending organizations use cash balance to measure fiscal sustainability (Mintz & Smart, 2006). A primary role of any balanced budget measure is judging the sustainability of a fiscal measure. Government solvency ultimately depends on the taxing capacity of the government economy (Musgrave, 1959). The argument for a government incurring long-term debt is not based on capital infrastructure held on the balance sheet, but that the public investment will directly or indirectly lead to increases in government revenue (Mintz & Smart, 2006). When a government's capital infrastructure are like private sector infrastructure, such as communications and transport, they could be sold to pay a debt (other than GO debt in the United States) if needed (Mintz & Smart, 2006). Long-term debt, in that case, is sustainable to the extent that the government can assure lenders that their investment is secured. Since the marginal cost of public finance is an increasing function of government tax revenue, the case for borrowing is strong for using debt to finance capital infrastructure (Mintz & Smart, 2006).

The argument for public capital infrastructure is based on the idea that resources allocated to such investment translate into an equivalent value of public capital stock. By lowering the cost of production or distribution, public investment benefits the private sector and affects the overall growth process. This effect is typically measured by the rate of economic or social return from public investment (Rajaram, Kaiser, Le, Kim, & Frank, 2014). Conducting a cost–benefit analysis is essential for determining the expected rate of return; however, the rate of return will depend on the effectiveness of public investment management. This analysis applies in the budgeting and the execution of the capital project (Rajaram et al., 2014).

The policy choice to use PPPs as an Infrastructure Finance Policy option (depending on the form and contract) provides the opportunity for a government to pass operational roles in capital improvements to the private sector while keeping the government's focus on retaining and improving core government services. Properly implemented, this approach can result in a lower cash outlay for the government and more efficient and effective service to the citizen (Asian Development Bank, 2012). A government's track record of finance policies (including infrastructure finance policies) is a standard for attracting private investment (Hammami, Ruhashyankko, & Yehoue, 2006). The sustainability of PPP contractual relationships depends on the quality of the legal dimension (see Chapter 3), which is formed by the organizational dimension.

### *4.6.2 Infrastructure Finance Policy Implementation*

A government's organizational dimension quality matters for potential investors through its direct influence on country risk (Hammami et al., 2006). A PPP is based on a legal contract, as discussed in Chapter 3. Capital infrastructure financing is complex and requires substantial knowledge and comprehension of legal contracts, infrastructure finance, budgeting, accounting, and reporting. Thus, it is critical to have organizational and legal expertise to implement an Infrastructure Finance Policy.

Infrastructure Finance Policy provides the basis for strategic identification of country-specific effective capital infrastructure financing and delivery approaches, instruments, and vehicles that broaden the financing objectives available for capital infrastructure projects and increases and diversifies the investor base, which lowers the cost of capital infrastructure financing (OCED, 2015). The Infrastructure Finance Policy presents available financing options to promote a common understanding of infrastructure financing priorities. Implementation of the Infrastructure Finance Policy will also provide a basis for a risk-based regulatory framework to support financing mechanisms such as PPPs (OCED, 2015, discussed in more detail in Chapter 2).

### *4.6.3 Infrastructure Finance Policy Implementation Assessment*

As noted previously, there are many different competencies needed to assess the risk and return of capital infrastructure investments (OCED, 2015). A clearly articulated Infrastructure Finance Policy will provide a foundation for evaluating the most efficient and effective financing and delivery method. Some PPP financing and delivery approaches, particularly PPP Service Concession Agreements, may have debt-like characteristics due to contracted cash flows. Financing categories are defined by their nature (creditors, equity holders, or creditors with equity options and participation rights), with the debt-like characteristic derived based on whether an investor receives priority claims in corporate or project cash flows (creditors) or residual claims to cash flows (equity) (OCED, 2015).

At the capital infrastructure project level, the PPP contract implementation assessment should be based on the likelihood of a given capital infrastructure project to attain financial and delivery closure and to yield a positive result during project implementation (The World Bank, 2018). Reviewing prior assessments will assist not only in understanding financing issues that may have developed in similar contracts and in structuring future PPP projects but also in designing PPP contracts (The World Bank, 2018). The use of (1) an economic analysis, (2) a fiscal affordability assessment, (3) an identification and allocation of potential risks, (4) a comparative assessment with traditional procurements (or value-for-the-money assessment), (5) an assessment of the market for potential investors, and (6) an environmental impact assessment will aid in assessing the likelihood of a successful decisions based on Infrastructure Finance Policy (The World Bank, 2018). The use of assessment tools to assess PPP contract implementation can help to assure that the use of PPPs contributes to the quality of public infrastructure financing and delivery and other policy objectives.

## 4.7 Benefits and Contributions of PPPs to Improved Access to and Quality of Infrastructure Financing and Delivery

As described in Chapter 1, capital infrastructure has typically been delivered by the government soliciting private contractor involvement through a traditional procurement process. In that case, the government issues a bid for solicitation of proposals; a private contractor responds with a bid, and the private contractor selected fulfills the terms of the contract. Once completed, the private partner turns over the completed service and/or capital infrastructure to the government. The salient feature of traditional procurement is that the government separately and externally procures each phase of the capital project and takes responsibility for potential project risks. As a result of the procurement of different contracts for each phase of the capital project, in some instances, capital projects have experienced inappropriate project designs, used outdated or inadequate technology, had substantial cost overruns, and/or ineffective capital project management and budgeting.

Having a PPP as a policy option with which to structure the financing and delivery of capital infrastructure, the government increases financing policy options to deliver a capital infrastructure project in addition to the use of traditional financing and delivery. If the PPP is structured correctly, the PPP financing alternative can help overcome the complex challenges with conventional government financing and construction of capital infrastructure.

Benefits from the use of PPPs as an infrastructure financing and delivery policy option are the improvement in overall quality of infrastructure capital improvements financing and delivery. While governments are the principal source for setting and implementing financing policies regarding the use of infrastructure financing instruments, PPP financing overall is still a small, but growing, share of infrastructure financing at about 5%–10% (AfDB, 2018) in most countries that use PPPs as a capital infrastructure financing and delivery policy option. The scope of the public agency's liability in PPP financing is generally different, however, than in non-PPP financing (Thomson Reuters, 2019). In traditional capital infrastructure financing, the government is generally responsible for all construction costs, including any cost overruns. Also, the government may have to pay to correct any design or construction defects (as described in Chapter 1). As a result, the government cannot completely know the full extent of its financial liability at the outset because traditional capital contracts are bid in phases. This lack of complete information is especially an issue if the government is relying on limited tax revenues or grants to pay these capital project costs. The government can have a more definite sense of its financial exposure in a PPP financing project because the private contractor's cost to construct the project is typically determined in advance by contract because the phases are bundled, and the costs are generally fixed. In a PPP, if additional financing is required to complete construction, the private partner is typically required to make up the shortfall, depending on the contract and the use of government guarantees.

## 4.8 Macro and Micro Level Risks

### *4.8.1 Macro Level Political, Economic, Stakeholder, and Force Majeure Risks of PPPs*

The macro level political, economic, stakeholder, and force majeure risks of PPP. This section introduces the macro level political, economic, and force majeure (unforeseen circumstances that prevent contract fulfillment) risks and describes how PPPs at the micro, project level can allow for risks to be transferred from a government to the private partner. Governments typically identify, manage, allocate, and assess risk transfer. The section discusses the optimum balance of risk between a government and a private partner in PPP.

The Infrastructure Finance Policy, the capital management, and budget processes and institutional capabilities such as PPP legal and organizational framework form the support system for managing PPP risk. The absence of a sufficient legal and organizational framework can cause the required PPP project procurement process to be canceled or postponed. Thus, the existence of the legal framework (described in Chapter 3) and administrative expertise presence are essential as a basis for the government's PPP procurement and contracting process. Having adequate laws and administrative rules and regulations in place is necessary, but not sufficient, to support a PPP project (Caribbean PPP Toolkit, 2017). Political, economic, and stakeholder risk mitigation are also critical to the success of a PPP project. As described in Chapters 1 and 2, the organizational/institutional capacity is also critical to the success of PPPs. Measures to reduce the organizational/institutional risk include capacity building, recruitment, and involvement of experienced staff, and timing external expert consultants in support of PPP projects.

Albania, as described above, is an example of a country that has experienced the need to build institutional PPP capacity and has done so by the use of external consultants such as the International Monetary Fund to build capacity. Part of capacity building is the need to have a coherent organizational framework and process. Insufficient funding and access to long-term financing are risks inherent in moving forward with a capital project and point to the need to have an Infrastructure Finance Policy in place. Addressing and overcoming bureaucratic inertia necessitates internal collaborative efforts consisting of the agencies or unit(s) within the government that have responsibility for developing and implementing PPPs. Stakeholder support is critical to the success of a PPP project.

Stakeholders include the general public and key political actors who support the PPP projects.

A qualitative micro level risk assessment assists in prioritizing risks and in distinguishing between significant and insignificant risks. The micro level qualitative risk assessment identifies the likelihood of a risk occurring and the consequences of a risk occurring.

### *4.8.2 Micro Level Risk Assessment and Management*

On the micro level, project risk management is a dynamic process that should be used throughout all phases of the capital project. A reliable risk assessment is critical for providing detailed ongoing guidance on identifying, mitigating, and allocating potential capital infrastructure project risks (Caribbean PPP Toolkit, 2017). The four main steps in risk management are

Step 1: Risk identification:

What are the project risks?
What are the sources of the risks?
What is the impact of the risk?
What is the probability of occurrence?

Step 2: Risk mitigation:

How can we reduce the probability of occurrence?
How can we lessen the impact of the risks?
Can we simply avoid a particular risk?

Step 3: Risk allocation:

Who can better manage the risks?
Can a partner credibly commit to managing risks?
Can it devolve risks to the government?
Can it cope with these risks?

Step 4: Risk monitoring:

Which risks shall government monitor?
How will the government monitor the risks?
What are the contingency plans?
How shall government report on the risks?
*Source:* Caribbean PPP Toolkit (2017).

Table 4.1 provides an example of a Risk Assessment Analysis for Albania.

## 4.9 Balancing Multiple Macro and Micro Level Potential Risks

This section will focus on the balance between political, economic, and social macro level risks. A PPP contract provides for the allocation of potential risks to

Table 4.1. Risk Assessment Analysis for Albania.

| **Source of Risk** | **Relative Likelihood** | **Impact if Realized** | **Policy Advice** |
|---|---|---|---|
| Poorly designed PPPs and increased contingent liabilities | High | Medium<br>Engaging in poorly designed PPP contracts for infrastructure Investment and create large contingent liabilities, which, if realized, could under mine fiscal and debt sustainability | Strengthen government and transparency in PPP implementation<br>Upgrade the capacity of the Ministry of Finance to undertake financial analysis of new PPP contracts |
| Rollover of public debt | Low | Medium<br>Concerns about debt sustainability may make banks reluctant to roll over government debt, a significant part of which is short term | Diversity the debt holder's base.<br>Improve market communication and coordination with the Central Bank<br>Continue fiscal adjustment and debt reduction |
| Domestic political instability | Low | High<br>Volatile domestic politics and social tensions could hinder the implementation of the structural reforms and fiscal consolidation agenda. Reforms, including those to strengthen the rule of law, are key for medium-term growth and Prospects for EU accession talks | Ensure that reforms are grounded in careful policy analysis and a consultative preparation process |

*Source:* Adapted from IMF Albania Staff Report 19/207 (2019) and Annexure l: Risk Assessment Matrix.

the partner that is best suited to manage and mitigate the risk over a long time. The period may include postconstruction operation and maintenance in some contracts (Smith et al., 2019). Risk management and mitigation for PPPs is different from other capital project financing types' risk management and mitigation because of increased complexity due to the PPP private partner's broader scope and involvement in all phases of the capital project as compared to traditional government financing which arises from bundling the phases (see Chapter 1). Because PPP risk assessment at the capital project level is unique to each potential capital project and requires an individual analysis for each capital project, assessing risk is complex and requires a detailed and specialized analysis of the potential risks before allocating the risk (Smith et al., 2019). Risk allocation decisions typically involve the use of performance incentives to manage risk (Smith et al., 2019). A government should identify potential risks during the preaward phase of the PPP contract to consider the most cost-effective measures in the contract negotiations before the contract award. For example, in the preaward stage, the incidence of government changes and/or violence and social unrest may influence investors' choices of the project's location, size, type, and length (Baker, Khater, & Haddad, 2019) and must be considered in identifying and managing risk.

### *4.9.1 Potential Political Risks of PPPs*

While traditional government financing remains the primary source of funding capital projects, the private sector is recognized as a source of financing capital infrastructure projects. However, in many countries and states, private sector financing, such as through PPPs, is still not utilized to its full potential, as noted previously. The success of a PPP depends in part on a government's openness to market-oriented types of capital infrastructure financing, which may vary depending on the political party in office. A change in government leadership, which results in a lack of support for market-oriented types of capital infrastructure financing arrangements, or particular political groups in power, which do not support such financing arrangements, can result in political risk for the use of PPP financing. Political risks are arbitrary or inequitable actions taken by governments, political groups, or individuals that have an adverse impact on international trade or investment transactions (irmi.com/articles/expert-commentary; Sachs, Tiong, & Wang, 2007). Some political risk can be ascribed to government actions, such as restrictions on converting or transferring currencies, political violence, expropriation, or breach of contract, and are insurable through public and private sector political risk insurance providers. Other political risks such as sudden changes or laws or governments are borne by the private sector (Sachs et al., 2007). Political risks also arise from the perception of an unstable political environment often found in many emerging economies such as Albania.

Political risks:

Lack of technical capacity
Failure to achieve closure

Political interference
Corruption
Civil disorder
Political upheaval
*Source:* Caribbean PPP Toolkit (2017).

Economic risks:

Economic volatility
Budgetary constraints
The creditworthiness of the private partner
The creditworthiness of the government
Exchange rate volatility
Foreign exchange availability
External economic shocks
*Source:* Caribbean PPP Toolkit (2017).

Force majeure risks:

Hurricanes
Torrential rains
Earthquakes
Tsunamis
Storm surges
*Source:* Adapted from Caribbean PPP Toolkit (2017)

The presence of potential risk involved in PPP contracts must also take into consideration transaction cost.

### *4.9.2 PPP Contract Cost Risk*

As discussed in Chapter 2, the decision to use a PPP as an option in the Infrastructure Finance Policy implementation stage involves time and expense, as well as the costs of negotiating and drafting the PPP contract documents (Thomson Reuters, 2019). The costs can be managed in some cases by standardizing PPP procedures and agreements (Thomson Reuters, 2019). Both the public and the private partner can take actions to mitigate contract risk (Petersen, 2019). Identifying transaction cost expenditures can help manage contract risk (Mooi, 2015; Petersen, 2019). The contract can be precisely written, detailing the terms across a range of contingencies (Petersen, 2019). Public and private partners can coordinate financing and allocate costs, such as mutual performance monitoring systems, to ensure that the contract delivers the greatest gain for both partners (Petersen, 2019). When transaction cost in connection with risk is translated into spending, it is recorded in the government's accounts when the government expends funds to mitigate the risk (Petersen, 2019).

Governments' contract management capability and fiscal capacity are critical aspects of a procurement contract transaction, especially PPP contract procurement, that can impact transaction costs and the resulting expenditures. Effective management of contract activities can help mitigate contract risks (Petersen, 2019). Effective management includes hiring and training administrative, legal, and contract management employees, but such hiring is costly and impacted by the government's fiscal capacity. Those government employees who have contract management expertise, especially about complex contract management such as PPPs, can lower transaction cost expenditures because of their prior knowledge of contract management, which they can draw on for similar contracts. Tacit knowledge and standard operating procedures are more likely to transfer over time for similar types of PPP contracts.

Governments typically incur basic transaction cost expenditures such as writing requests for proposals, soliciting and reviewing bids and reviewing proposals, before negotiating contract terms. By bundling capital project contracts, such as occurs in using PPPs, governments may be able to influence transaction costs over the life of the bundled PPP contract and, in some cases, reduce the transaction cost. Transaction costs can increase with contract complexity, and fiscal capacity can decrease without requisite government expertise in negotiating complex contracts such as PPP contracts. The ratio of transaction cost expenditures to total cost is lower for a higher value than for lower value contracts, which suggests that economies of scale impact contract spending (Petersen, 2019) such as occurs in bundling.

## 4.10 Balance of Potential Risk between Public and Private Partners

Appropriate allocation of potential risk between the public and the private partners is crucial to successful PPP project outcomes (Caribbean PPP Toolkit, 2017). Project risk allocation is based on the concept that each partner to the contract bears the risk they are best equipped to manage (Caribbean PPP Toolkit, 2017). The potential risks are allocated based on the ability of the partner to (1) control the risk; (2) anticipate and/or respond to the risk factor, or (3) absorb the risk (Caribbean PPP Toolkit, 2017).

The choice of Public–Private Partnership type will dictate the use of specific provisions not commonly included in the government's other traditional contracts. For example, for PPP projects involving the transfer of revenue risk, the government should consider limitations, including setting toll rates or other user fees, and include appropriate provisions in the contract to ensure the requirements are evident over the long term. The contract should include performance requirements to ensure the project will achieve operational and policy objectives, specify processes to resolve performance failures, and provide sufficient incentives to assure compliance and performance throughout the term of the contract for PPP projects involving concessionaire payments. Legal advice should be consulted regarding the availability payment system, if used, to ensure that provisions for deductions from payments are legally enforceable. Risk allocation methods may include performance-based payment and penalty and provision of government guarantees or indemnities as a way for accepting or sharing on those risks it believes it is best positioned to manage and will not offer general guarantees on overall project returns (Caribbean PPP Toolkit, 2017). In some cases, to provide incentives for risk transfer, a minimum level of equity finance may be necessary (Caribbean PPP Toolkit, 2017). Also, performance bonds may be required in cases or project stages where the equity exposure of the private party is inadequate (Caribbean PPP Toolkit, 2017).

## 4.11 The Use of PPPs to Leverage Infrastructure Financing

PPP as an Infrastructure Finance Policy option to leverage capital project financing. This section covers the government's use of PPPs to leverage infrastructure financing. An effective Infrastructure Finance Policy includes an analysis of available options financing infrastructure.

The specific capital financing options are generally prescribed by law, as described in Chapter 3. The private partner is typically responsible for raising financing, depending on the PPP type. As discussed throughout the book, PPPs do create fiscal obligations for the government. Depending on the PPP type, the obligations may be similar to traditionally procured capital infrastructure projects financed with government debt. It is crucial for a government that intends to use PPPs to have an Infrastructure Finance Policy in place which articulates its PPP strategy.

PPP as an Infrastructure Finance Policy option at the strategic level should be the government's statement of intent and contain the principles in financing and delivering capital infrastructure, such as the statement of intent to use the private sector (World Bank Institute, Reference Guide, 2012) (see Mauritius as an example). Based on the strategic PPP policy perspective, PPP policy goals, PPP program goals, PPP program scope, and implementation principles and procedures follow, including Infrastructure Finance Policy options. Establishing the strategic PPP policy and the Infrastructure Finance Policy, in particular, depends on the legal values dimension of the country and the political values dimension for establishing government policies, procedures, institutions, and rules, as well as the dimensions, described previously. The essential underlying philosophy on whether to use a PPP to finance and deliver a capital infrastructure project is that the combination of both public and private sector strengths to achieve their respective goals working together as a partnership. Conditioned by the prior successful experience with private partner involvement in capital infrastructure financing and delivery, the PPP strategic policy becomes the basis for creating and ensuring support from potential capital investors concerning the priority placed on private sector involvement. For example, PPP policy allows the government to determine how it wishes to introduce PPPs; sets the scope and framework for implementing PPP projects; sends a clear signal to the public and private sectors as well as civil society about the government's commitment to implementing PPPs in an open, transparent manner; sets out the action plan or priorities for implementing PPPs; defines institutional responsibilities and key approvals; and defines any support measures required to facilitate PPPs (Caribbean PPP Toolkit, 2017).

Once the Infrastructure Finance Policy is in place, and the capital projects have been selected in the capital improvements plan, analysis of capital infrastructure financing options is critical to the success of the capital project. Different competencies are needed to assess the potential risk and return of infrastructure financing options. Direct investment involves significant expertise and resources from the private investor. Potential investors in certain types of capital infrastructure projects must also assess the risk/return profile of the investment throughout its economic life. This assessment includes the construction phase and the operational phase (OCED, 2015).

### *4.11.1 Analysis of Infrastructure Finance Policy Options*

Identifying and planning for potential risks and steps the public sector can use to mitigate the risk can encourage the use of private sector financing options, especially the use of institutional investors (for example, guarantees, grants, fiscal incentives) (OCED, 2015). Policy actions to identify potential risks and actions to mitigate the possible risk can also foster trust building and create a more accommodating infrastructure finance environment and mitigate project-specific risks, which further increases acceptability to a bank (OCED, 2015). An advanced level understanding of market instruments can align the risk of financing and delivery of capital infrastructure with the risk tolerance of those involved in financing infrastructure. This understanding is essential to choosing the appropriate infrastructure financing policy option. Such expertise creates the range of different competencies required to assess the risk and return of infrastructure capital project financing. Direct investment requires a high level of expertise generally provided by the infrastructure management company/general partner who has the expertise and acts on behalf of investors (C40 Cities, 2017; OCED, 2015), as discussed below.

In some national and subnational governments, PPP financing is managed separately from traditionally financed capital infrastructure funding. Thus, in some governments, PPPs may not be regulated in the same way as traditional capital infrastructure expenditures (The World Bank, 2014). In these countries, the infrastructure financing mechanisms, direct or market-based, each have their unique set of characteristics with implications for lending or investment portfolios. Market-based financing can be an efficient method to allocate potential risks to those private partners willing to bear the risk at a reasonable rate of compensation.

The World Bank has identified four reasons for inefficient management of infrastructure finance, as follows:

First, the project may be proposed by one agency or line ministry and subject to review by the Albanian MoF or budget agency. Weak organizational coordination may cause delays in infrastructure financing.

Second, political priorities for infrastructure financing may differ from established timelines and interfere with the capital financing process.

Third, the allocation of resources to a project is a multiyear commitment and can present problems to a weak budget process and result in negatively impacting the operating budget.

Fourth, large capital infrastructure projects can involve issues with site acquisition and environmental challenges that can cause significant delays and cost escalation. Fourth, weak government management and accountability systems can create the conditions for corruption and negatively impact capital investment management. In countries where public resource accountability systems are weak, the likelihood of resource mismanagement is high and will require a systematic, transparent approach to capital financing (The World Bank, 2014).

The private sector can provide state-of-the-art expertise and skills to finance, deliver, and operate capital infrastructure projects more effectively and efficiently (Ramlugan, 2014). The public and private sectors have different values, goals, and unique characteristics (Ramlugan, 2014) as discussed in Chapter 2.

Capital projects financing management and budgeting for PPPs at the national and global levels involves screening of all project investment proposals or compatibility and consistency with national and local priorities (The World Bank, 2014). All project financing must have an economic assessment and be legally feasible, socially sustainable, and economically viable (The World Bank, 2014). Before capital projects are approved for funding, the proposed project should undergo an assessment to determine whether the project is feasible (The World Bank, 2014).

When PPP financing and delivery is used, large amounts of future government revenue are committed (such as guarantee payments), and it is critical to analyze from a fiscal perspective whether a government can maintain fiscal soundness and sustainability while promoting PPP (The World Bank, 2014), as an Infrastructure Finance Policy option. Project investment commitments from PPPs and a hard budget constraint is a significant challenge for managing PPP fiscal risks. The capital budget connects capital investment decisions with procurement and financing. The capital budget communicates the government strategy for carrying out the Infrastructure Finance Policy. In some countries, such as Albania, PPPs commitments have been off budget without a systematic and consistently followed Infrastructure Finance Policy and capital review process. As a result, some public financing has been exposed to high-risk commitments and potentially high amounts of contingent liabilities, such as the case example of Albania.

Thus, a decision whether to use a PPP for financing and delivering a capital project should involve a choice about whether the project should be (1) solely a government responsibility and thus be undertaken as a traditional capital project or (2) undertaken in partnership with the private sector (The World Bank, 2014). An ideal decision process would involve the preparation of two capital project proposals – one as a PPP and the other as a public sector comparator (traditional financing) with the decision determined by an [expert] independent review of the best value-for-the-money and risk-sharing arrangement (The World Bank, 2014).

Once the choice between the two capital infrastructure financing and delivery alternatives (traditional or PPP) is made, based on the Infrastructure Finance

Policy, a unified, comprehensive, and effective capital budgeting and management system needs to be in place to effectively carry out the financing decision. In many countries, there is neither a unified and systematic capital budgeting nor a management framework in place to support either a traditional infrastructure financing system or a PPP financing framework. One of the distinctive features of a unified, comprehensive, efficient, and effective capital management and budgeting system is that the operating and capital budgets are separate but interconnected, with adequate funding for operations and maintenance of completed capital infrastructure. In some national governments, and subnational governments, medium-term fiscal budgets are in place, but the selection of capital investment options are still made on an annual basis. While this is typically the case when the capital budget (the first year of the capital improvement plan) is in place, the updated financing and delivery decision should be based primarily on the preliminary financing and delivery option previously identified in the capital improvement plan. Although volatile revenues can negatively impact spending for capital infrastructure, a systematic Long-term Revenue Trend Analysis, which is consistently monitored and updated, can provide a basis for future decisions on capital infrastructure financing options. Articulation of an Infrastructure Finance Policy and alignment of the policy with a unified and comprehensive capital budgeting and management system can provide a solid foundation for efficient and effective financing options. Also, a robust system of checks and balances can strengthen the systematic approach to capital budgeting and finance and reduce the politicization of public investment decision-making (The World Bank, 2014).

## 4.12 Summary

This section summarizes the different public versus private sector goals in the context of capital projects investment and Infrastructure Finance Policy and introduces capital projects investment management and budgeting processes and PPPs at the national and global levels.

This chapter describes the value differences between the public sector and the private sector. The role of values in the public sector and especially which values form the guiding foundation in public sector decision-making is critical to understanding how the use of PPPs fit in an overall Infrastructure Finance Policy framework. The private sector's primary value clearly and unambiguously is profit maximization, while the public sector's primary value is social welfare maximization (Crocker & Reynolds, 1993). This distinction between the private sector's profit maximization value and the public sector's social welfare value forms a basis for serious consideration of how the public value of social welfare maximization can be articulated. The discussion begins by identifying and articulating the use of the private sector as a partner in infrastructure financing and construction as an option in a government's Infrastructure Finance Policy as implemented through the capital budget and management process. The market in which infrastructure financing and delivery takes place has the power to define value. However, it can only define value through individual transactions and the way these transactions accumulate, without comprehensive design into broader patterns (Kettl, 2015) such as the use of Infrastructure Finance Policy.

The public partner has a critical role in creating and defining public value, which is articulated through comprehensive Infrastructure Finance Policy design, as in the case of Mauritius. The role of Infrastructure Finance Policy in articulating the option of selecting PPPs as an infrastructure financing and construction option in capital improvements planning and budgeting, the ultimate role of the public sector in terms of public value, is defined as policies governing responsibility and accountability to its citizens for social welfare maximization. One of the policies that can define public sector value is through Infrastructure Finance Policy because it provides direction for resource allocation.

# Part 3
# Infrastructure Finance Policy and PPPs at the National, Subnational, and International Levels

Chapter 5

# Infrastructure Finance Policy, Capital Management and Budgeting Processes, and PPPs as an Infrastructure Financing Option

## 5.1 Infrastructure Financing

This Chapter describes infrastructure financing as well as the capital management and budget processes as an output of its Infrastructure Finance Policy and Public–Private Partnerships (PPPs) as a policy option. This section introduces the connection between capital management and budgeting processes, precisely the capital improvements plan (CIP), infrastructure financing, and PPPs as a financing option within its Infrastructure Finance Policy. Capital infrastructure projects connect economic growth, job creation, and poverty reduction (The World Bank, 2018). Appropriate financing of large capital projects, especially in Emerging Market Economies (EMEs) (estimated USD 1.3 trillion per year), is critical to attaining a country's long-term sustainable development goals (The World Bank, 2018). These financing policy goals are stressed as a priority by the G20, along with an explicit mandate for Multilateral Development Banks (MDBs) (G-20 Infrastructure Action Plan, 2019). In the past, government revenue, banks, and international donors were the traditional funding sources in most EMEs (although not always banks in some Low Income Countries). The section discusses issues and constraints facing many capital infrastructure projects when making Infrastructure Finance Policy decisions.

The connection between a national or subnational government's capital management and budgeting processes, Infrastructure Finance Policy, and PPPs is through the capital improvement plan (CIP). Government capital financing (including capital infrastructure) is an investment in the acquisition or building of new capital infrastructure; or major repair and replacement of existing infrastructure that have an economic life longer than 1 year and a value above a specified threshold (The World Bank, 2011). Capital financing sources are identified for specific capital projects in the CIP, based on the Infrastructure Finance Policy. The Infrastructure Finance Policy is implemented through the policy-based, capital infrastructure financial strategy.

**Public-Private Partnerships, Capital Infrastructure Project Investments and Infrastructure Finance, 135–176**

**doi:10.1108/978-1-83909-654-920201005**

A policy-based capital infrastructure financial strategy at the capital project Pre-Commitment Stage (see pp. 139 and 141) consists of a forecast of capital improvements financing capacity. At the Post-Commitment Stage, it involves (1) ongoing monitoring of capital projects financing sources versus outstanding long-term debt, (2) accounting for appropriated capital project expenditures, and (3) annual financial report. At the Post-Completion Stage, an audit report forms the basis for fiscal strategy within the capital management and budget system. A government's written policies, implemented through the practices it follows and approved by the governing board, provides the most reliable and most consistent basis for selecting, financing, and delivering capital projects (Marlowe, Rivenbark, & Vogt, 2009).

At the national and subnational levels, in some cases, there is a fragmented system of capital infrastructure financing strategies or plans which are rarely accompanied by a formal systematic public sector financing program or by a strategic approach to attract private investment to key sectors (OCED, 2015). In the case of Albania, for example, although the capital budget cycle begins with the National Development Plan (which is the basis for multiyear investment plans), there are significant deficiencies. These deficiencies are: (1) the absence of clear policy priorities for PPP financing within the national development plan and, in some cases, (2) unreconciled differences between the government's proposed capital projects and legislature-approved capital projects. The disconnect can result in the deletion of some capital infrastructure projects, and others included without adequate capital project analysis and evaluation. The situation is the result of the lack of coherence between ministry capital project micro policies and national planning macro policies. The lack of coherence between ministry policies and national planning policies, in turn, impacts the execution of budget and procurement policies and may be part of the reason for the high levels of contract renegotiation in Albania. A coordinated and integrated strategic national or subnational Infrastructure Finance Policy can provide the direction for providing financing sources such as PPPs as a viable alternative policy option to traditional capital infrastructure financing. This direction is especially critical for large-scale capital infrastructure projects that must be financed within the overall context of capital infrastructure financing and debt management.

### *5.1.1 Infrastructure Financing at the National and Subnational Levels*

One of the main determinants of capital infrastructure capacity to fund a capital project is a forecast and analysis of the size of the government's revenue and expenditure base. The basis for a government to collect and expend revenue is in the law. There are two primary revenue sources: (1) operating budget revenue sources and (2) capital budget revenue sources. Operating budget revenue sources such as property taxes, sales taxes, and fees fund the annual operating budget. Capital budget revenue sources include long-term debt, equity financing, and capital reserves, as described in Chapter 2.

In Albania, for example, government revenue forecasting, which forms the basis for identifying government capital project financing, is fragmented. The Prime Minister's Office prepares the long-term (6–7 years) fiscal projections and revises these projections every 7 years. The Albanian Ministry of Finance (MoF) prepares medium-term revenue forecasts, which are the basis for the CIP. The MoF creates 3-year forecasts and publishes summary tables in the Macroeconomic and Fiscal Framework at the beginning of the medium-term budget process. The MoF forecasts (with input from the Budget Analysis, Policy and Programming Directorate, and Budget Management and Monitoring Directorate) are set out in the medium-term budget and are updated and published after the final budget is approved (IMF, 2015). While the Albanian long-term fiscal forecasts are updated regularly, the new/updated forecasts do not explain how or why the new/updated reports differ from the previous forecast, nor do they compare how the forecasts differ from the actual revenue (Beckett-Camarata, 2019).

The long-term capital improvements planning process should be the place for deciding future capital project financing and acquisition (Beckett-Camarata, 2019). This part of capital improvements planning is critical, as noted in Chapter 4, since it connects Infrastructure Finance Policy, with revenue and expenditure forecasting and capital infrastructure finance planning. The capital planning process should include formal coordination across departments, including estimated benefits of the project and projected life-cycle costs (Beckett-Camarata, 2019).

Capital planning, including capital infrastructure finance planning, begins with detailed knowledge of the government's Infrastructure Finance Policy and the capital investment sources that are legally allowed. In deciding whether a government has the fiscal capacity to incur additional debt for capital infrastructure, the government must perform a debt capacity analysis as well as identify the potential revenue source(s) for financing the capital improvement project. The government also needs to assess their capacity and capability to monitor and control capital project costs. In some countries, a government receives grants for capital improvements financing from a higher-level government as the primary financing source (Kaganova, 2011), but regardless of funding source, capital project cost overruns can be a potential problem in managing debt.

In this context, the capital infrastructure planning process should include analysis of capital infrastructure projects and financing alternatives for inclusion in the CIP. This evaluation process should be done in a separate phase of the capital improvement planning process, in which every capital request is subjected to economic analysis (Marlowe et al., 2009) such as Value for Money (VFM), as described below. Also, it is essential to consider input from stakeholders, such as citizens, into the capital planning process. From a public policy analysis viewpoint, cost–benefit analysis (CBA) is another policy tool for evaluating individual public capital expenditure decisions (Marlowe et al., 2009).

The CIP identifies potential capital infrastructure financing sources, including both public and private. The government must evaluate and prioritize the projects included in the CIP. Governments, however, encounter challenges in prioritizing and planning for financing and delivering capital infrastructure projects:

Demands and needs for capital financing are always higher than available funding. There is an intrinsic timing challenge. On the one hand, allocating funding for capital projects should be done annually. On the other hand, before external financing can be arranged, complex capital infrastructure projects may require several years' preparation and packaging before external financing (grants or debt). Contemporary approaches to evaluate financial options for complex capital infrastructure projects usually exceed technical capacity. Capital infrastructure financial planning is a growing area of public financial management (The World Bank, 2011).

One of the analytical tools for analyzing capital infrastructure financing options is VFM analysis, discussed below.

### *5.1.2 Analytical Tool for Evaluating Infrastructure Finance Options*

#### 5.1.2.1 Value For Money Analysis

VFM is an analytical tool defined as the identification and analysis of capital infrastructure life-cycle costs. VFM analysis involves the use of cost analysis as a factor in the decision process, selection of the best possible financing option, one which results in the most efficient delivery of the best quality capital infrastructure to meet the long-term needs of the user. Some governments use VFM analysis as part of an overall PPP project versus traditional financing decision process. The selection of a PPP as an infrastructure financing option, compared to traditional procurement, can provide superior VFM over traditional procurement if the advantages of risk transfer and private partner performance and innovation incentives result in value-added efficiencies over the life of the capital project.

In some countries such as South Korea, VFM analysis involves the whole PPP financing decision-support process, as opposed to only one factor in the PPP financing decision-support process (The World Bank, 2013). The use of VFM, regardless of whether it is the only factor or just one factor in the whole PPP financing decision process, analysis in PPP financing decision support can provide challenges to some governments. Not all capital financing options are equally available or feasible from the standpoint of a government's assessment of its organizational dimension, that is, its capacity and capability to finance capital infrastructure projects. Some capital infrastructure projects may be characteristically unattractive for potential private partners and require public partner's higher assumption of risk and/or enhanced provision. During the capital improvements planning process, especially as it pertains to infrastructure capital financing, it is crucial to understand the government's financial capacity to generate enough additional future revenue, and the timing of that revenue, to fund the capital infrastructure project and to evaluate capital infrastructure financing options based on objective analysis.

The reason for applying VFM analysis to a capital project is to provide a method of decision support that will aid in the decision as to whether to finance proposed capital infrastructure projects using PPPs or through traditional capital project financing. VFM analysis usually includes both quantitative and qualitative analytical techniques (The World Bank, 2013). Many governments choose a threshold for the use of VFM analysis, such as the dollar size of a capital infrastructure project. In cases of similar types of capital projects, VFM does not necessarily need to be used for each project. VFM analysis uses both quantitative and qualitative methods of analysis. VFM quantitative analysis involves a comparison of VFM for a proposed PPP project through a Public Sector Comparator (PSC) model. The PSC model is used to analyze capital project financing, if implemented, using traditional public procurement. Most governments who use the PSC model adjust the cost comparison for government risk. The model builds the cost of bearing the risks to be transferred to the private partner under a PPP financing option for comparison into the model. In the United States, for example, the Commonwealth of Virginia assesses a range of possible contractual arrangements other than traditional financing, such as (1) PPP pure toll Concessions, (2) PPP different levels of availability payments or (3) PPP Design-Build-Finance approach using the PSC model. A VFM qualitative analysis provides an assessment of whether the project is suitable for private financing based on the country's or subnational government's PPP law and its Infrastructure Finance Policy. The Commonwealth of Virginia screens potential PPP capital infrastructure road projects against specific criteria in the Public–Private Transportation Act to determine whether a project will: (1) benefit from private sector innovation, (2) achieve the appropriate level of risk transfer, (3) determine if it has stakeholder support, as well as the fit within the Infrastructure Finance Policy (The World Bank, 2013).

Timing of VFM analysis in capital improvements planning capital project selection and financing, as well as the capital budget process, is critical because of its use as a factor in the infrastructure financing decision-making process. In some countries, VFM analysis is applied only to capital projects screened for possible PPP financing. If, based on VFM analysis, a capital project is determined not to provide VFM but has a positive Cost–Benefit ratio, some countries earmark the project for possible traditional infrastructure financing. If the VFM analysis is conducted late in the Capital Management and Budgeting process, then the VFM analysis can be used (if appropriate) to aid in decision support to finance the capital project using a PPP. Timing in the use of VFM analysis, in any event, produces trade-offs at the initial stages of the capital improvements planning process between availability and accuracy of preliminary information used in the VFM analysis, and its level of influence on the PPP financing decision. If the quantitative analysis is conducted later in the capital budget process, it has the potential to create pressure to rationalize the VFM analysis in order to justify the earlier financing decision, rather than an objective analysis. If the VFM analysis is conducted later in the process, it may not receive as much scrutiny. The usefulness of quantitative VFM analysis in the capital budget process is that it can be helpful with the political and public perception of a proposed capital project using PPP financing and capital infrastructure project delivery; however, it can result in an oversimplification of the decision (The World Bank, 2013). In conducting VFM quantitative analysis, one of the challenges is to accurately quantify the cost of significant risk to be transferred when using a PPP financing and capital infrastructure delivery option (The World

Bank, 2013). In quantifying risk, France, for example, uses the mean value for smaller projects (less than 50 Euros) calculated by estimating the probability and impact of significant risk. Large projects use Monte Carlo simulations. In that case, probability distributions are assumed for the likelihood and impact of each risk to calculate the distribution of possible costs (The World Bank, 2013). Analysis of this type requires specific expertise as well as data on previous similar projects to inform the assumptions on probability distributions. It is for those reasons that many countries are not able to adjust for risk either for traditional financing or for PPPs for large-scale capital infrastructure projects.

Another aspect of quantitative VFM analysis in calculating VFM of PPP capital infrastructure financing versus traditional government financing is the calculation of the Net Present Value (NPV) of government payments for each financing option. Government cash flow forecasts vary significantly depending on the discount rate used and thus can have a significant impact on the decision based on a comparison of PPP versus traditional financing. Many governments use the government borrowing rate to discount cash flows under both procurement options. The justification is the cost of bearing the risk built into the analyses explicitly through its impact on cash flow, and the cost of financing is built into the PPP analysis. Risk-reflective discount rates are typically used to capture the riskiness of capital infrastructure project income streams rather than payment streams (The World Bank, 2013). Some governments, such as British Columbia, use a risk-adjusted Internal Rate of Return (IRR) based on their previous experience to discount cash flows under both traditional and PPP models. Bidders then use the same discount rate to calculate the NPV, which allows direct comparison of bids with the traditional and PPP calculations (The World Bank, 2013).

VFM analysis can also be used during the capital infrastructure project procurement process in addition to the capital improvements planning process and updated in the capital budget process as verification in the final bid of the initial VFM analysis. In some cases, VFM analysis provides a hard limit on acceptable bids, while in others, it is a guide in the procurement decision. In Korea, VFM analysis is used in the bid process for unsolicited proposals as a basis for a bonus award to the contractor and as a bottom line for price bidding to achieve VFM. In France, VFM analysis can be communicated to bidders as part of the project documentation so that all bidders have the same information regarding cost assumptions. This approach helps to avoid bids that differ significantly from the government's project call for bids (The World Bank, 2013).

Other PPP analytical tools typically include feasibility studies and economic analysis. In considering a PPP financing and delivery option of a capital infrastructure project the critical issue is the likelihood that the PPP will be able to provide an adequate return on investment (ROI) to attract quality investors and is affordable for the private partner. The capital projects selected for financing are listed in the CIP once the analyses and studies are complete.

The CIP (6 years) is the list of capital projects identified for financing, prioritized by year, with estimated beginning and completion dates, annual estimated costs, and proposed financing methods. The legislative body then approves the CIP.

The information included in the CIP is:

Project Justification
Full Description of the Project
Alternative Approaches
Total Project Cost
Cost for the Budget Year
Cost for Two Out Years and Remaining Cost
Recurrent Cost Impact because of Project Financing
Forecasted Project Revenues, if any
Donor Funding, if any
Net Budget Cost.
*Source:* The World Bank (2013).

#### 5.1.2.2 Infrastructure Project Selection Process

The process for evaluating and selecting capital infrastructure projects to include in the CIP is critical because the type of financing used for the capital projects funded through the Capital Budget will have a long-term financial impact on the operating budget. The Operating Budget repays the long-term principal and interest on Infrastructure Financing. The monitoring and management of capital projects, which is part of the budget process, helps ensure adequate recurrent funding to maintain and operate existing capital infrastructure (The World Bank, 2014). How to fund recurrent capital project costs in the Operating Budget needs to be considered (The World Bank, 2014) in the financing decision process.

A macro-level Infrastructure Finance Policy framework consists of broad strategic policy guidance on capital infrastructure financing, anchors government capital project decisions, and guides micro-level decision-making toward national and subnational priorities. Capital project selection is one of the most challenging parts of the capital infrastructure financing process because it is often one of the most controversial (The World Bank, 2014) parts of the CIP process. The controversy stems from stakeholders (including ministries and departments that will gain from the capital infrastructure project, political patrons, legislative patrons, as well as contractors who want to secure contracts) who work to influence capital project selection (The World Bank, 2014). Emerging economies, such as Albania, tend to have uneven capital infrastructure system capability, with some areas of relative strength, but weakness in their overall system (The World Bank, 2014), which impact Infrastructure Finance Policy option choices. More advanced economies tend to have organizational capabilities, such as:

*National finance strategy*. The strategy documents guide capital infrastructure financing new projects. Capital projects are evaluated, costed, and integrated with the operating budget (if there is not a separate capital budget).

*Formal capital financing policy*. The policy includes PPPs as an option for financing a capital project.

*Public hearing*. In some countries, large capital infrastructure projects are subject to public hearing before the end of the appraisal stage.

*Independent evaluation.* Only projects that have been subject to a thorough and independent evaluation is included in the CIP.

*Managing and recording project costs.* There is a strong focus on managing project costs, and the accounting system records the annual project costs and the total project costs.

*Capital Project Status Reports.* There are regular capital project status reports.

*Ministry Authority.* There is one ministry designated as responsible for managing capital financing.

*Procurement.* Contracting is carried out by staff with expertise in contract procurement and management.

*Project Review.* Capital projects are subject to rereview if there are material changes to the project.

*Asset Register Maintenance.* Capital asset registers are maintained and subject to external audit. In some countries, such as the UK, full accrual Balance Sheets are in place across the central government. There is a significant effort in after-the-fact project reviews, that is, comparing completed projects to identify factors affecting project cost.

*Source:* The World Bank (2014).

The micro-level implementation of the Infrastructure Finance Policy establishes the specific types of capital infrastructure project financing that are eligible for consideration and inclusion in the CIP and identifies the types of analysis that should be included in the decision.

There are many issues facing capital infrastructure projects financed with high debt/equity ratios. A national or subnational government that takes on the excessive long-term debt will have its bond rating downgraded and will have to pay interest rates that increase as the debt increases. Beyond the marginal cost of new bond-financed capital projects begins to increase sharply (Bosworth & Miluseva, 2016). Therefore, financing a new capital project through increased debt is not only more expensive but more importantly, it raises the cost to service all existing debt as it is rolled over (Bosworth & Miluseva, 2016). Therefore, the ability to take on additional debt is controlled to a certain extent by the government's constraints on its ability to increase long-term debt to finance capital projects.

#### 5.1.2.3 Ongoing Monitoring of Capital Projects Financing

When a capital project is selected for financing, regular monitoring of the capital and operating budgets are critical to making sure that the capital projects are implemented, as appropriated, through the capital and operating budgets. Ongoing capital project monitoring is also critical to ensure that the capital projects are making progress and to be able to adjust, if needed, based on changes that have occurred after budget appropriations are made, and contracts are signed. A government should communicate how often it monitors capital projects and the capital budget and compares the budget-to-actuals as part of the monitoring process.

As part of the ongoing monitoring of the capital project, a government should ensure that:

(1) Each capital project is consistent with debt capacity laws, procurement procedures, and SEC regulations.
(2) Reporting requirements are met; relevant data are compiled, such as capital project milestones, performance measures, and stakeholder needs based on legal and fiduciary requirements.
(3) There is a review of project-related transactions to support budget review, auditing, and asset management.
(4) A review of expenditures compared to the current budget and the project phases.
(5) Validation of continued appropriation of revenue sources.
(6) Verification of cash flow adequacy relative to project obligations.
(7) Comparison of the timing of investment maturities to project status.
(8) Review of financing sources and uses.
(9) Comparison to established performance measures.

Reporting on Project Status, especially large-scale, high-profile projects
(10) Comparison of actual results to the project plan, including:

Percent of Project Completed
Percent of budget expended
Progress on key project milestones
Funding commitments
Remaining available appropriation
Project closeout
Confirm contract encumbrances closeout
Confirm that all closeout and reporting requirements, such as bond covenants, have been completed
Confirm project closeout. Data are recorded in the fixed-asset schedule
Confirm that procedures are in place to meet any continuing disclosure or reporting requirements.

*Source:* Government Finance Officers Association Executive Board (2007).

Capital project monitoring and evaluation should occur at different stages of the capital project cycle. For example, the contract management team should carry out a range of regular monitoring responsibilities during the construction phase, such as:

Monitoring actual work progress versus the schedule
Monitoring actual work accomplished against the total work to be completed
Monitoring work performance versus applicable laws and regulations
Quality control and materials monitoring
Partnership relationship management
Monitoring identified potential risk versus actual risks and risks not contractually allocated

Monitoring performance measures in the PPP contract, including the project output specifications, the private partner's performance management reporting requirements, and any penalties that apply as a result of noncompliance

### *5.1.3 Infrastructure Finance Policy Implementation Issues and Constraints*

In infrastructure finance policy implementation, there are several micro-level issues and constraints which must also be considered, such as (1) Hard Operating Budget Constraints, (2) External Balanced Budget Rules, and (3) Changes in International Accounting Standards impacting recording of contingent liabilities.

#### 5.1.3.1 Budget Constraints

*5.1.3.1.1 Hard Operating Budget Constraints.* In situations involving Hard Budget Constraints, the policy choice to finance a capital infrastructure project through the use of PPPs may be more costly than traditional financing. PPPs, however, may still be the best financing policy option given the capital infrastructure priority and the current critical need for financing the particular project. Public managers often face conflicting priorities in meeting their responsibilities to manage the organization (Buso, Marty, & Tra, 2014). As a result, public managers may consider the use of a PPP under a hard budget constraint to the organization's fiscal advantage (PwC, 2010). Some PPPs are classified as nongovernmental according to the 2004 Eurostat risks and rewards criterion (Buso et al., 2014). Under this criterion, a government can account for capital project work under specific PPP concession-type arrangements as off-balance sheet when the construction risk and at least one of either availability or demand risk are transferred to the private partner. The debt related to PPP financing, in that case, is recorded in the accounting system as an accrued liability.

Consequently, some governments may have an increased incentive in favor of the use of some types of PPP arrangements for reasons other than the PPP is the most efficient and effective financing arrangement compared to traditional financing methods. Those reasons include long-term debt levels. There is a strong correlation between the use of PPPs and debt levels at the subnational government level (Buso et al., 2014 citing Russo & Zampino, 2010).

Some governments that are operating under Hard Budget Constraints may be more likely, in some cases, to underreport long-term debt in their Annual Financial Reports (Buso et al., 2014). Some governments also may adjust their accounting and external reporting based on the introduction of external fiscal rules, such as International Accounting Standards and International Financial Reporting Standards (IFRS), which impacts what is included in reporting the long-term debt. For example, there is some evidence that some governments may have circumvented fiscal rules such as the 1997 Stability and Growth Pact in the European Union (EU) (Buso et al., 2014). In the one study reported by Buso et al., the reported long-term debt levels were lower than the actual long-term debt levels. Melesi-Ferretti and Moriyama (2006) also analyzed the reduction of long-term debt levels in the EU. The authors found a strong correlation between debt reduction and capital asset sales, in addition to reductions in public financing in the previous year. This difference in reported long-term debt levels suggests a misleading picture of the evolution of the fiscal condition (Buso et al., 2014) and to underreporting the actual long-term debt burden. IFRS introduced a change from a risks and rewards approach to a financial control criterion. Under the new IFRS standard, if the public authority controls one of the following five aspects of the capital project, the related debt should be recorded on the balance sheet as an Asset, while the paid investment and related debt should be recorded as Liabilities: (1) the private operator is not able to sell or take out a loan on the equipment; (2) the occupation of a public-owned domain; (3) the definition of the equipment's main features; (4) public services' management; (5) the revenue paid to the private partner for service (Buso, Marty, & Ra, 2014).

The use of PPPs in a Hard Budget Constraint environment (which is based on an Infrastructure Finance Policy options and unified and comprehensive capital management and budgeting process) can provide the basis for a government to achieve its strategic infrastructure financing goals by focusing the financing choice on the strategic capital financing direction. Some governments record PPPs off Balance Sheet when the construction risk and at least one of either availability or demand risk are transferred to the private partner (Melesi-Ferretti & Moriyama, 2006). In that way, the PPP is recorded using an accrual basis. Under the accrual basis of accounting, the annual payment related to investment, financial, and operating costs is reflected in the public account. The remaining principal and interest on the debt are recorded as a multiyear payment schedule. As a result, the debt related to a PPP did not appear on the balance sheet.

Large-scale use of PPPs by a country could result in reduced government borrowing in the short term (depending on PPP type), and a lower level of increases in Net Debt. Some European governments are obligated, as member states under the Maastricht Treaty or other similar European level requirements, to avoid excessive budgetary deficits (Buso et al., 2014). The Maastricht Treaty requires that member governments' annual deficit and debt should not exceed: (a) 3% for the ratio of deficit to GDP and (b) 60% ratio of government debt to GDP (Buso et al., 2014). Some evidence exists that French public managers do not use PPPs to hide long-term debt on their financial reports, but instead, they use PPPs when resources are scarce, and alternative long-term financing options are needed to continue economic growth (Buso et al., 2014).

When faced with Hard Budget Constraints, governments need to especially consider reviewing their current financial policies and adding Infrastructure Finance Policy to their overall financial policies if not already in place. Governments also need to enact legislation regarding the use of PPP to finance and deliver capital infrastructure projects through establishing policies that demonstrate the commitment to support the use of the private sector as a policy option in infrastructure capital project financing and delivery. The government policy is implemented through a comprehensive set of legislation and regulations and supported through independent PPP units with the expertise needed to attract private sector participation in financing and delivery of capital infrastructure and face the increasing demand for providing quality infrastructure.

*5.1.3.1.2 External Balanced Budget Rules.* EU and the European Monetary Union (EMU) rules on member state budget deficits and debt require balanced budgets, which may also impact a member state's long-term borrowing ability. For example, the Scottish Lothian Regional Council criteria for capital funding was first to determine if it was unable to procure the necessary funding via traditional procurement routes (McQuaid & Scherrer, 2010). The Council examined different PPP financing types that resulted in its capital expenditures off balance sheet after the financing determination was made (McQuaid & Scherrer, 2010).

*5.1.3.1.3 International Public Sector Accounting Standards.* The International Accounting Standards adopted by the EU limited the use of PPPs to avoid increases Operating Budgets by transferring capital financing to "off-balance sheet" (McQuaid & Scherrer, 2010). Depending on the exact interpretation of the International Accounting Standards by an individual government and the financial condition under which a government adopts the standards, there now may be a modest budgetary advantage in using PPPs as compared to traditional public sector funding or debt (McQuaid & Scherrer, 2010). This change in International Accounting Standards brought the use of a PPP financing option into a more level playing field with other financing sources for operating and capital budgeting, accounting, and reporting, and also give a more realistic assessment of future public long-term liability commitments and debt. In that case, PPP financing options, compared to traditional funding, is based more on their efficiency and effectiveness (VFM, for example) than on budgetary considerations (current general capital expenditures do not appear as increased borrowing or long-term liabilities) (McQuaid & Scherrer, 2010). In those governments where financial accounting and reporting impact the governmental fund balance (McQuaid & Scherrer, 2010).

The International Public Sector Accounting Standards Board (IPSASB) standards move governments away from the cash-based system of accounting to an accrual-based accounting system. The standards allow for disclosure of contingent liabilities on the government's balance sheet rather than off-balance sheet (which avoids investors' and analysts' scrutiny; Toudas, Poutos, & Balios, 2013). However, although a government may recognize the need for, and importance of adopting an accrual-based accounting system, their capability to adopt an accrual-based system may, in some cases, be inadequate (Bhatia, 2019). Europe has developed its budgetary standards, as well as adopted public sector accounting standards, the European Public Sector Accounting Standards (EPSAS) (Biondi & Sierra, 2016). As of 2017, for OCED countries, almost 75% of the member countries adopted accrual accounting for their year-end financial reports (Bhatia, 2019). Overall, however, outside of OCED countries, adoption by national of international accounting standards by governments is low (Bhatia, 2019).

Many national and subnational governments do not require full costs of PPPs to be budgeted for upfront at the time the PPP project commitment, and the contract is signed (ECA Special Report, 2018). In many such governments, annual capital project charges are recorded several years after contract approval and completion of capital construction. The reporting of PPP actual project cost occurs well after PPP project change-order decisions have been made. In some cases, PPPs are scrutinized less carefully than traditional capital procurement contracts because capital expenditures for traditional capital projects are budgeted for more closely in the capital budget and compete with other capital projects for funding (ECA Special Report, 2018).

In some cases, capital improvements procurement procedures do not require a recognized analytical tool to be used as a basis to demonstrate value-added, VFM when analyzing specific PPP project features and selecting the most suitable financing option and lack analytical documentation, such as VFM, regarding the procurement decision (ECA Special Report, 2018). Analytical tools such as VFM analysis are essential in capital project procurement decisions because private partners, depending on the PPP contract, usually bear higher financial costs and require higher compensation depending on their risk (ECA Special Report, 2018). Private partners tend to minimize long-term maintenance costs by improving construction quality, which implies also higher construction costs (ECA Special Report, 2018). Cost savings in operation and maintenance costs need to be forecasted and be sufficient to compensate for higher construction and related financial costs (ECA Special Report, 2018). The forecasting and maintenance cost forecasting is an essential step in determining whether a PPP is the best financing option for a capital infrastructure project. A government can manage its operation and maintenance costs by balancing their cost savings in maintenance with the higher construction costs. The more the capital infrastructure requires high maintenance costs, and the lower the difference in interest rates paid by the government and private partner, the more likely that PPPs can achieve sufficient long-term savings (ECA Special Report, 2018, p. 37). Capital infrastructure projects financed through traditional funding generally do not include funding for operating and maintaining the capital infrastructure project (Pagano, 2019). PPP contracts, depending on the type of contract, include private partner responsible for operation and maintenance (ECA Special Report, 2018).

Capital infrastructure projects delivered through traditional funding have separate phases for bidding and funding purposes. PPP projects, on the other hand, need a minimum size in order to justify the cost (due to complexity from bundling) of financing needed for enhanced efficiency in completing the capital project. The challenge is that the enormous scope of the capital project may, in some cases, reduce the number of contract bidders (ECA Special Report, 2018). Fewer private partner may have the capability to bid on and/or subcontract to complete the bundled contract. This situation may place the government in a position of being dependent on one contractor to complete the project (ECA Special Report, 2018). PPPs, on the other hand, may require the contractor (depending on the type of contract – usually Service Concession Agreements [SCAs]) to finance the project and be paid during the operational phase of the contract. Choosing a PPP policy option, the government has the advantage of immediate initiation of the capital infrastructure project and the potential to achieve the benefits from the use of a PPP to complete the project. However, to award a contract using PPP, all aspects of the capital infrastructure project, such as financing and project construction details, must be identified and negotiated upfront, and usually require more time than a traditional capital infrastructure procurement. In a few instances, however, the private partner may experience financial problems after the procurement contract is signed, and the PPP is underway, resulting in the need to renegotiate the contract and considerable delays in completing the project.

The risks identified and allocated between the public and the private partner and specified in the contract must align with the contract award criteria, and the private partner must be held accountable for the terms of the contract. Risk allocation between the public and private partners is a critical component of a PPP contract. Recording PPP capital infrastructure on the government's Balance Sheet helps ensure a more level playing field between the traditional and PPP procurement options and keeps the focus on VFM analysis (ECA Special Report, 2018).

*5.1.3.1.4 Contingent Liabilities.* PPP contracts obligate the government to pay future costs in connection with the timing of financing capital infrastructure projects. Government guarantees, which are typical in many PPP contracts, constitute explicit contingent liabilities (Sfakianakis & van de Laar, 2012). Assessment of potential financial risks that may arise from PPP government guarantees is critical to identify in the context of its financial condition. For the first years of a government's use of PPP, its impacts on the government's surplus or deficit are less than a traditional government-funded capital infrastructure project.

In Mauritius, for example, the legislative framework regarding capital infrastructure project construction, operation, and maintenance concerning the use of PPPs incorporate flexible contracting procedures, the establishment of mutual rights and obligations between the public and private partner, as well as the use of incentives for private participation (See Chapter 3). Some PPPs (depending on the type) consist of subsidies, such as government guarantees and revenue sharing arrangements, as described in Chapter 1. Government guarantees, for example, can be a minimum revenue level established in the contract for the private partner in order to minimize financial risk. Another example is one where the government shares a portion of project revenues when the revenue reaches a certain threshold established in the contract. These guarantees constitute a government's contingent liabilities.

Contingent liabilities in PPP financing is critical to assess in the process of infrastructure finance policy implementation and capital project decision-making. In soliciting bids, contract negotiation, and in managing long-term debt, the use of certain types of PPPs (depending on the contract) constitutes a government contingent revenue guarantee and resulting contingent liability (Sfakianakis & van de Laar, 2012). For example, if the expected revenue from the capital project is less than the guarantee that is forecast in the contract and any renegotiations, the remaining amount constitutes a government's contingent liability (Sfakianakis

& van de Laar, 2012). The effect of the PPP risk then is the contingent financial risk arising from the PPP contract. Sfakianakis and van de Laar (2012) provide a case study demonstrating the valuing of a country's net contingent flows for PPP projects and their impact on the deficit/surplus. The Sfakianakis and van de Laar (2012) study is useful in understanding how both valuing and comparing various Infrastructure Finance Policy options can be part of unified, systematic capital management and budgeting process under the infrastructure finance policy.

In the first option, a traditional infrastructure funding option, the government funds and constructs the project in phases and bids the construction and funding of the project in phases. The direct funding impact is recorded in the years that the funding for the phases of the contract are appropriated and the years that the contract expenditures are made, based on the project phases. The revenue source (whether long-term debt, current revenue, or some combination) is recorded at the time of appropriation and expenditure, and the effect on the budget is recognized. This scenario affects long-term liabilities, which, in turn, will impact the deficit/surplus for PPPs involving large-scale projects. The initial impact calculated by taking the deficit/surplus, minus investment costs, plus expected discounted revenue for each year (Sfakianakis & van de Laar, 2012). From a debt sustainability perspective, with traditional capital infrastructure financing, the traditional self-finance approach seems to be beneficial in an economy with good fiscal performance. A similar analysis for economies that face difficulties in maintaining a sustainable fiscal path would be a good counterfactual scenario and an issue for further research (Sfakianakis & van de Laar, 2012).

In the second financing option, a new participant is added but in a different way, i.e., with the private contractor as a partner, who bundles the investment and construction of the capital infrastructure investment. The private partner provides the financing, usually by borrowing from an external lender, to design and build the project. The private partner finances the capital project and is responsible for the repayment of principal and interest to the external lender. The private partner bears the construction and management costs as well as receives the projected revenue (tolls in the case of a SCA), depending on the terms of the contract. In this option, there are two new government contingent flows: (1) the government guarantees with a negative effect on the current future account and (2) the revenue sharing flows with a positive effect on the current future account (Sfakianakis & van de Laar, 2012).

In the third financing option, a PPP option with Credit Default Swaps (CDS), the valuation of the contingent liabilities uses derivatives valuation techniques, i.e., CDS valuation. Most of the cash flow is the same as the second financing option, and the participants are generally the same. In this financing policy option, contingency valuation using derivatives valuation techniques and CDS valuation. Th PPP financing option with CDS assesses the price of the guarantee without considering counterparty risk. The guarantee is directly connected to the credit risk of the project, and the CDS serves as a tool to reduce the credit risk exposure of the government. The credit risk result is the triggering of the minimum revenue guarantee. If the toll revenue falls behind a certain threshold articulated in the PPP contract, the government will have to activate the guarantee.

However, the government can buy protection against this possibility by ensuring the contingent amount through a CDS that will reimburse the private partner (Sfakianakis & van de Laar, 2012).

The flow of payments related to loans, construction and maintenance costs, revenue, and contingent flows (guarantees and revenue sharing) have the same direction. The additional participant in the PPP option with CDS is a Financial Intermediary, such as an insurance company. There are two flows between the intermediary and the government: (1) a cash outflow from the government as a purchaser of the CDS structured as periodic payments to the intermediary unless a private partner defaults (or the expiration of the CDS) and (2) a contingent cash inflow to the government. The contingent liability is the payoff in the case of private partner default.

The flow of actual and contingent amounts is also applicable in the fourth PPP option with CDS and counterparty default risk. The project's default probabilities are considered in order to value the PPP risk in CDS valuation.

The unconditional default probabilities calculation uses the average default rate from Standard and Poor's Ratings Definitions. The CDS is computed as the Present Value of the expected payoff of the PPP investment less than the Present Value of the CDS payment, plus any accrual payments (Sfakianakis & van de Laar, 2012).

The fourth option is PPP with CDS Counterparty Default Risk. This option follows the valuation method in option three to price PPP guarantees. The assumption is that the government ensures the PPP project using a CDS, but also considers the default risk of the government. The government, in that case, may not meet its contractual obligations in the form of payments, fees, or guarantees to the private partner. This issue must be considered in emerging economies such as Albania, which may have unstable economies. The valuation includes the credit ratings for both the reference unit and the counterparty. If the credit index for the reference party drops below its default limit before the credit index for the reference entity does, payments continue up to the time of the default, with a final accrual payment. In this case, there is a final payoff. If the counterparty defaults first and the credit index for the counterparty falls below its default barrier before the credit index for the reference entity does, payments continue to the time of the default, with no final accrual payment. In this case, there is no final payoff. If neither the counterparty nor the reference entity default, then payments continue for the lifetime of the CDS, and there is no payoff. The CDS expected payments are recalculated, including the default probability of the counterparty (which may be the government itself) to estimate the CDS spread. Since the accruals and payoffs do not apply in the case that the counterparty defaults first, the amounts are the same as Option 3. The expected CDS payments must be recalculated to consider the default probability of the government. This recalculation provides the NPV of the CDS payment, which includes the risk of default from the counterparty (Sfakianakis & van de Laar, 2012).

In this fourth PPP financing option, in absolute terms, considering that the notional principal is the total maximum amount of guarantees covered via the CDS, then the mid-market CDS spread is the total discounted values of the guarantees times the spread (Sfakianakis & van de Laar, 2012). The price of the government's risk exposure is the CDS spread as the measure for the guarantee valuation.

To summarize, the first option in the Sfakianakis and van de Laar (2012) study described above is the traditional infrastructure financing policy option funded by the government. In that option, there is a direct effect on the government budget when the funds are appropriated, based on the initial project cost. Positive flows from user fees gradually offset this effect once the project is complete, though in a later budget cycle. In the second scenario, the fiscal effect of the net contingent liability flow for the government is the difference between the forecasted revenues and any guarantees should the guarantees be triggered. In the third and fourth financing options, the assumption is that the government can reduce its exposure to financial risk from the guarantee by purchasing protection, through the use of CDS, against the likelihood of liability. In this study, the mid-market CDS spread within the fourth option, and CDS spread without in the third option considering the government's probability of default. For a complete analysis of the application of these options, please see the Sfakianakis and van de Laar (2012) study.

This section introduced the connection between the capital infrastructure projects financing and the capital improvements planning and described the financial analysis risk process as an output of its Infrastructure Finance Policy options. The next section describes capital infrastructure projects financing in the context of the comprehensive capital management and budgeting framework.

## 5.2 Infrastructure Finance Policy Implementation through the Capital Management and Budgeting Stages and Framework

This section describes the comprehensive capital management and budget framework. The framework includes (1) Capital Management and Budget Policy, (2) Capital Management and Budget Process, (3) Centralized Capital Management and Budget Execution and Capital Project Management, (4) Infrastructure Maintenance (Srithongrung, 2016, p. 3). The Infrastructure Finance Policy should guide the critical components of a Unified and Comprehensive Capital Management and Budgeting Framework.

### *5.2.1 Capital Management and Budget Stages*

#### 5.2.1.1 Precommitment Stage

Updated CIP based on: strategic and comprehensive plans, needs assessment, financing strategy based on Infrastructure Finance Policy, and prior CIP.

#### 5.2.1.2 Postcommitment Stage

Centralized capital budget execution, accounting, capital project management, and financial reporting for capital infrastructure (Beckett-Camarata, 2019).

#### 5.2.1.3 Postcompletion Stage

Capital maintenance (Ammar, Duncombe, & Wright, 2001), including maintenance planning and funding, capital asset management, and auditing of Capital Projects Expenditures.

*Source:* Adapted from Srithongrung, Yusuf and Kriz (2019).

Srithongrung et al. (2019) describe the first two components of the PreCommitment Stage: (1) long-term capital improvements planning and (2) capital budgeting and financial management. Srithongrung et al (2019) added, (3) centralized the execution and project management components which take place during the postcommitment stage and (4) capital infrastructure maintenance is the postcompletion stage (Srithongrung et al., 2019). Each element at each stage can be examined both separately and together because the strength of the government's overall capital management and budgeting system depends on the activities in each of the components (Srithongrung et al., 2019).

This book introduces three new components: (1) Infrastructure Finance Policy as an additional component to the Srithongrung et al. (2019) model at the policy adoption stage before the Precommitment Stage long-term capital planning and (2) Postcommitment Stage of Accounting and Reporting (Beckett-Camarata, 2019) and (3) Auditing in the Postcompletion Stage.

Srithongrung et al. (2019) have built on the Ammar et al. (2001), model by emphasizing the unifying nature of the component, centralized Execution, and Project Management. Srithongrung et al. (2019) point out that the first two components, (1) long-term capital planning and (2) capital management and budget, which are the subject of this section, make up the precommitment stages of public financing. However, (3) centralized execution and project management take place during the postcommitment stage. Component (4), auditing and capital infrastructure maintenance, is the postcompletion stage (Srithongrung et al., 2019). The following framework expands on these stages.

## 5.3 Capital Management and Budget Framework

The following Framework expands on the Srithongrung Model and describes the stages as follows:

### *5.3.1 Capital Management and Budget Policy*

#### 5.3.1.1 Precommitment Stage

*5.3.1.1.1 Infrastructure Finance Policy as a Guide to Infrastructure Financing Decision.* Infrastructure Finance Policy is the formal written strategic policy that guides the long-term policy planning and implementation phase of long-term capital planning in identifying potential financing sources such as PPPs (Beckett-Camarata, 2019), for example, the Mauritius Infrastructure Finance Policy. A government's Infrastructure Finance Policy is implemented at the Precommitment stage through a unified, systematic CIP. The CIP identifies the methods used to pay for the improvements and encourages private investment in PPPs by connecting the Policy to the Capital Budget implementation procedures.

The Infrastructure Finance Policy framework then becomes the basis for long-term, 6-year capital fiscal planning and the CIP. The critical components of Infrastructure Finance Policy planning and implementation framework are: (1) Strategic Plan, (2) Needs Assessment (as identified by public and private sector stakeholders) translated into a statement of strategic objective(s), (3) Priority Project Ranking based on objective criteria, and (4) Identification of Capital Project Financing. The first year of the 6-year CIP is the Capital Budget or is the basis for the Medium-Term Expenditure Budget, as in the case of Albania and Mauritius. The remaining 5 years continue as part of the CIP, and an additional year is added based on the yearly CIP process.

The Infrastructure Finance Policy should cover a period of at least 5–7 years and should list and describe the types of financing options eligible for inclusion in the CIP. The Policy should also include minimum criteria for a capital project to be included in the CIP.

The Policy should identify which types of capital projects are eligible to be included, for example, reconstruction of existing facilities, new facilities, and the acquisition of land. The policy also should state which budget the capital project expenses come from, i.e., operating or capital budget. The policy should state the available funding options that the government intends to use, including any operating surplus and fee revenue. The policy should also briefly spell out the debt limits and provide a reference to the broader government Debt Policy.

The Capital Improvements Planning Process should consist of (1) CIP, (2) Capital Budget, (3) Centralized Execution and Project Management, and (4) Capital Infrastructure Maintenance, Accounting, and Auditing (adapted from Srithongrung, 2006). The updated CIP based on Infrastructure Finance Policy, strategic and comprehensive plan, needs assessment, financial plan, and CIP.

*5.3.1.1.2 Strategic and Comprehensive Plan.* The comprehensive plan should be the basis for the strategic plan. The comprehensive plan describes objectives for a community's land use (Srithongrung, 2006). The strategic plan, based on the comprehensive plan, sets the specific organizational strategies for a government. The specific objectives of capital improvements, in the strategic plan, are driven from the organizational strategies. The goals, objectives, and strategies have implications for capital needs and provide the basis for identifying capital requirements (Beckett-Camarata, 2003; Robinson, 1993) (See also Mauritius Strategic Plan, 2019).

A consistent approach to the successful implementation of strategic plans is to tie strategic planning directly to the budget process (Beckett-Camarata, 1998). A strategic plan is a long-term guide for implementing policies, programs, actions, decisions, and/or resource allocations. The strategic plan defines what an organization is, what it does, and why it does what it does (Beckett-Camarata, 1998). Strategic financial performance measures evaluate the success of strategic objectives (Beckett-Camarata, 1998) Financial goals are critical for evaluating the results of the strategic plan by assisting in diagnosing and correcting problems, and in implementation of policy decisions (Beckett-Camarata, 1998).

Infrastructure Finance Policy, along with other policies such as Capital Asset Management Policy, Debt Management Policy, plays a vital role in providing a balanced and sustainable basis for financing option decision support. These policies provide standardization of capital infrastructure financing options, including the use of PPPs, and their selection as a policy option, and serve as a basis for efficient and effective financing decisions. The use of these micro-level financial policies is especially important in shaping the capital planning and budgeting process because of the complexity of the planning and decision-making process and the impact that long-term financing has on current and future resource allocation decisions. With such strategic infrastructure finance policies in place in Mauritius, for example, such policies help to provide the framework in which to shape unified, systematic capital management and budgeting decision-support process. This unified, systematic capital management and the budget decision support process will, in turn, have a long-term, positive impact on managing capital costs and the ways that capital costs impact the operating budget.

The micro-level implementation of the Infrastructure Finance Policy should include the period covered by the policy, such as 6–7 years, to align with the CIP timeframe. The strategy should also define the types of capital project costs funded through the capital budget and the types of capital project costs funded through the operating budget. The policy should define a capital asset, including capital infrastructure. For example, the policy could state that a capital infrastructure eligible for financing through the capital budget is 100,000 USD or higher with a construction period not less than 2 years. It should also identify and define the types of analysis used in the capital project decision-support process. It should identify the types of capital infrastructure construction that are eligible for traditional financing and PPP financing such as rehabilitation, replacement, reconstruction of existing capital infrastructure, and public-use facilities, as well as new construction of capital infrastructure, the criteria for project justification, and acquisition of land for such construction. The policy should also state the priority for financing new construction versus rehabilitation of existing capital infrastructure. The micro-level implementation of the Infrastructure Finance Policy should also articulate which specific revenues, such as the one-time sale of government-owned land and property, are earmarked only for spending on capital projects. Other revenue sources that are earmarked for spending only on capital projects are land development fees, revenues from selling development rights, and lease fees. It should also reference the debt policy and include a summary of debt limits, which may impact future borrowing capacity. The more detailed analysis of the role of debt limits in capital infrastructure project financing will be conducted during the CIP process and updated in the Capital Budget preparation process.

Capital expenditures tend to be uneven because of such an imbalance in the timing of expenditures of large-scale capital projects. Financing through the planned use of long-term debt has advantages in that it allows a government to acquire financing, and at the same time, to allocate relatively stable amounts of current revenue for debt service. The role of the CIP simplifies forecasting the need for the use of long-term debt to fund capital infrastructure because the approval and prioritization of infrastructure capital projects are separate from the actual budget deliberations and considered on their merits (Bland & Rubin, 1997). Funding for approved capital projects in the Capital Budget becomes available as appropriations become available. Revenue to fund debt service comes either through the retirement of old debt or by committing additional new amounts for debt service. Debt capacity is impacted by bond ratings (discussed in Chapter 1) and by the political process (Bland & Rubin, 1997). Bond ratings primarily impact the cost to service debt for capital projects. These ratings reflect the underlying economic condition of the government. If bond rating agencies downgrade the government's bond ratings, the cost of debt for the government will increase.

*5.3.1.1.3 Capital Improvements Plan.* The CIP should operate under the guidance of the Infrastructure Finance Policy. The Precommitment Stage CIP of the capital management and budget process is the most critical stage because it is through the CIP that potential financing sources are identified and ultimately linked to the capital budget (the first year of the CIP). That is the reason that the decisions on financing and delivery capital infrastructure should be grounded in the Infrastructure Finance Policy. The CIP should also be coordinated with the strategic and comprehensive plan (Beckett-Camarata, 1998, 2008; Srithongrung, 2018) and should be based on a range of factors such as citizen needs, demographics and changes in demographics, population changes, underlying economic base changes, and technology changes.

The use of a CIP helps a government to consolidate, prioritize, and organize large, uneven capital infrastructure requirements, which generally vary from year to year (Giannakis & McCue, 1999; Srithongrung, 2018). A CIP usually covers a 6-year budget period and identifies capital infrastructure needs; provides cost or expenditure estimates for those needs; identifies possible sources of financing; evaluates, priorities, schedules projects and acquisitions, and forecasts the likely impact of projects and acquisitions on the operating budget.

Once the strategic plan incorporated into capital improvements planning process, it should include the following steps:

*Step 1.* Identify Capital Needs. The first stage of capital improvements planning is identifying capital needs for a 6–10-year period. Identify capital needs based on current and projected data on capital inventories, demographics, and economic conditions independent of financing requirements. A capital asset life cycle is created for major capital infrastructure. The life cycle should include costs to operate, maintain, administer, and repair or replace the capital asset in order to identify capital asset needs and schedule capital asset replacement or significant renewal. Further, using information such as development projections and comprehensive plans, the government should identify present and future service needs that require capital infrastructure or equipment.

A needs analysis connects a strategic plan to capital infrastructure needs. Assessment of capital needs includes inventorying current capital infrastructure, assessing their current condition, and identifying factors that may affect the ability to maintain the capital infrastructure in the future (Srithongrung,

2019). The needs assessment should also include capital maintenance and replacement and deferred maintenance of existing capital infrastructure, operation, and maintenance of existing capital infrastructure and additional new capital infrastructure (Srithongrung, 2019). The next step is to evaluate and prioritize the identified capital infrastructure needs. Operation and maintenance of capital infrastructure are normally considered current capital outlays. As such, they are identified in the CIP but budgeted for in the operating budget rather than in the Capital Budget. Operation and maintenance needs identified for significant road reconstruction (as opposed to filling potholes) or major building renovation (as opposed to carpet replacement) are categorized as capital outlay and included in the CIP.

The capital asset condition management framework, consisting of a capital infrastructure management plan based on life-cycle cost analysis is the basis for the government's accountability for sustainable capital asset performance. Knowing the condition of the government's capital infrastructure is the basis for capital infrastructure management. The capital asset inventory condition assessment information should be grouped by asset classification [infrastructure and type], location, age, performance history, historical cost, and replacement value, estimated remaining service life, and any significant issues. It should also include asset condition assessments related to asset performance. The condition of each asset is the basis for maintenance requirements and determines the need for repair or replacement.

An asset condition assessment system that allows for easy tracking throughout the life cycle of each capital asset should form a base for the updating and driving decisions regarding the CIP. Local governments are better able to complete and accurately update CIP if they continually assess capital improvement needs that must be maintained at the present level or enhanced to meet increased demand or need for higher quality service level. An ongoing needs assessment can be used as a basis for prioritizing capital project requests and in coordinating identified capital needs with an Infrastructure Finance Policy–based financing options. A life-cycle cost analysis includes the entire life cycle of the capital asset. Preventive maintenance schedules asset in reducing repair costs and in extending the life of the capital asset. Such a system will help ensure that asset conditions drive the CIP, and the capital budget help determines decisions on financing rather than the capital budget driving capital improvements financing decisions. An asset condition financing strategy can help identify specific capital projects based on the asset condition/needs assessment and potential funding options.

An asset condition assessment includes capital maintenance and replacement. This assessment usually is included in the operating budget because expenditures for maintenance and replacement are considered current operating capital outlays (Marlowe et al., 2009). Capital infrastructure project expenditures to renew or rehabilitate (as opposed to maintenance and replacement) capital infrastructure that involve structural change and extend the useful life of capital infrastructure, such as road reconstruction, are typically classified as capital outlay and included in the CIP and capital budget.

A government's asset condition assessment usually has a significant impact on its financial resources. The government should have a long-term capital asset financing plan based on its asset condition life-cycle costing as well as long-term expenditure forecasts and sources of financing.

*Step 2*. Update annual capital inventories. The second stage involves an updated annual capital inventory. Many capital infrastructure projects may function indefinitely if adequately preserved and maintained. In effect, the expense of maintaining infrastructure becomes a surrogate for depreciation expense. GAAP does not allow reporting depreciation expenses in connection with networks or subsystems of capital infrastructure if the government has made a commitment to maintaining them at a predetermined condition level (of its choosing) and has established an asset management system that is adequate for that purpose. A small number of governments use this approach. The modified approach is available for all capital infrastructure networks and subsystems, including those of business-type activities (enterprise funds). If a government fails to preserve and maintain that network or subsystem at the predetermined condition level (as indicated by the periodic condition assessment), it must then begin to depreciate the affected network or subsystem on a prospective basis (DiNapoli, 2016).

Alternatively, the government could elect to lower the predetermined condition level. To qualify for the modified approach, a government must have an asset management system which ensures that:

An inventory of eligible capital assets, including capital infrastructure, is maintained up to date;

Condition assessments are performed at least every 3 years; and

Annual estimates of the amount needed to maintain and preserve the capital infrastructure at or above preestablished condition levels are met. A government that chooses to use the modified approach must disclose extensive details about its capital infrastructure in its financial statements. Supplementary information schedules must show the assessed physical condition of all eligible capital infrastructure based on at least the three most recent assessments. The condition assessments must be performed at least once every 3 years. The dates of the assessments must be disclosed. The schedules must also show, for each of the past five reporting periods, the estimated annual amounts deemed necessary to maintain and preserve the capital infrastructure at or above preestablished condition levels, compared with the amounts spent. Certain disclosures must accompany the schedules, such as:

The basis for the condition measurement (such as the distress found in pavement surfaces);

The measurement scale used to access and report the condition (from zero for a failed pavement to 100 for pavement in perfect condition); and

The condition level in which the government intends to preserve the capital asset including capital infrastructure (DiNapoli, 2016; Governmental Accountings Standards Board, 2019).

*Step 3*. Determine Financial Impact. The third stage is to estimate a capital project's cost, revenues, and/or life-cycle costs. For capital projects that are programmed beyond the first year of the capital plan, cost projections should be adjusted based on anticipated inflation. A precise estimate of all major components required to implement a project should be outlined, including land acquisition needs, design, construction, contingency, and postconstruction costs. The ongoing life-cycle costs associated with each capital project should be calculated, and the sources of funding for those costs should be identified (including PPPs). This step is vital since life-cycle costs will impact future annual operating budgets, which must be considered as project requests are prioritized.

*Step 4*. Forecast the complete individual project financial burden and identify all potential financing sources. Analyze and compare traditional financing and delivery methods to PPP financing and delivery methods (i.e., debt financing and current revenue) at the project level (Ammar et al., 2001; Ebdon, 2004; Government Performance Project, 2005; National Association of State Budget Officers, 1999, 2014; Srithongrung, 2006).

The financial planning phase (see Stage 6) of capital budgeting is based on forecasts of revenues, expenditures, and debt burden forecasts (Aronson & Schwartz, 2004). The government should forecast future revenues from different traditional tax and nontax sources, potential grants, long-term debt (Srithongrung et al., 2019; Steiss, 2005), and private financing such as PPPs. Long-term financial projections should classify the total resources available for capital projects based on the individual project sources of financing (Singhvi, 1996; Srithongrung et al., 2019).

Based on the Infrastructure Finance Policy, a government should identify capital infrastructure project financing from different sources such as tax and nontax revenues, potential grants, long-term debt, and alternative financing sources such as PPPs. This identification of financing at a strategic level is essential to be able to specify the aggregated level of potential capital project financing (Srithongrung, 2019; Steiss, 2005). The aggregated level of potential capital project financing is critical at this stage so that long-term capital investment is not competing with short-term resource allocation and decision making via the operating budget (Srithongrung, 2019). Capital project financing in the CIP at the micro-level should identify sources of financing and amounts by the capital project (Singhvi, 1996; Srithongrung, 2019), including financing sources such as PPPs. The costs and benefits of a capital project must be analyzed and should be matched with its proposed financing source(s) so that the public dollars match with the benefits received (Fisher, 2016) to ensure that social costs are distributed in an efficient manner (Srithongrung, 2019).

*Step 5*. Prioritize Capital Requests. Legal requirements and/or mandates may impact the initial prioritization process. Priorities, however, should still be based priorities. Such priorities include (1) Health and Safety such as high safety risk issues that require a capital infrastructure/project to correct, (2) Asset Preservation which involves capital infrastructure that require renewal or replacement based on capital asset life cycle, (3) Service/Infrastructure Expansion/Addition which involves capital infrastructure improvements needed to support government policies, plans, and studies. As part of the capital request prioritization, the government should: (a) incorporate feedback from major stakeholders and citizens, (b) the impact of planned capital projects on operating budgets, (c) evaluate projects based on such techniques as NPV, CBA, life-cycle costing.

An example of a capital project priority ranking system is the United States, the Commonwealth of Virginia's SMART SCALE (System for the Management and Allocation of Resources for Transportation) project prioritization process (Chicago Federal Reserve Board, 2019). The system, which was passed unanimously by the state legislature, requires the state Transportation Board to use quantifiable and objective measures for scoring capital infrastructure projects. The system receives political support because of the recognition by the Department of Transportation that different parts of the state have different capital infrastructure needs, and that one specific mode of transportation is not favored over another mode of transportation (Donohue, 2019). Also, there is a statewide citizen engagement process that includes individual meetings being held with planning organizations and stakeholders in every transportation district throughout the state.

The categories in the ranking system used to evaluate capital infrastructure projects are (1) Congestion Mitigation, (2) Economic Development, (3) Accessibility, (4) Safety, (5) Environmental quality, and (6) Land use (in areas with populations over 200,000) (Donohue, 2019). The score is submitted for every potential capital project for financing. One of the benefits of the priority prioritization process is that it creates an incentive for an agency to submit a capital project to consider creative ways to achieve its goals at a considerably lower cost. Further, by having the project scores available publicly, the reason behind why some projects are selected for funding and other projects rejected is transparent. The financing source is identified in the CIP when a project is selected. Additional priority ranking systems are discussed in Chapter 5.

*Step 6.* Develop a comprehensive financial plan. A viable overall multiyear financial plan should cover the multiyear period of the capital plan to ensure that the proposed capital plan is achievable within expected available resources. Financing strategies should align with expected project requirements while sustaining the financial health of the government. The Financial Plan should include revenue and expenditures forecasts and their relationship to multiyear financial plans and ongoing impacts on the operating budget.

The CIP provided the 6-year (year one is the Capital Budget) rolling schedule of proposed capital projects and proposed financing sources based on evaluation methods such as CBA, life-cycle costs, and VFM. At the time that capital infrastructure projects are initially proposed, it is not realistic or practical to conduct all project analyses and to make complete cost estimates before including a capital project in the CIP. Preliminary analyses and cost estimates are conducted for the first phase of capital improvements project selection. In a second phase, more detailed analyses are prepared for those projects that meet the criteria for inclusion in the CIP. For large capital infrastructure projects, the CIP should show the forecasted project expenditures. Usually, the initial capital project phase costs associated with initial studies are identified in the Capital Budget before the start of the construction phase. A process needs to be in place to record those capital projects that are not selected for inclusion in the current CIP.

Given the complexity and time commitment in preparing a CIP, the process involves coordination within the organization and preparation of proposed capital projects as well as a systematic and efficient method for ensuring that the proposed capital infrastructure projects meet Infrastructure Finance Policy, Debt Policy, and other relevant policies.

In many governments, regardless of size, given the large scope of the capital projects proposed and the high level of future commitment of funds for several years, a CIP Committee is formed and charged with responsibility to oversee the CIP process, review capital project proposals, organize public participation (especially at the subnational level), assign priorities according to the policies, criteria, and strategic priorities, and make recommendations on capital projects for selection in the CIP. Having knowledgeable and impartial representation on the Committee, including competent technical staff, is essential to being successful in balancing the capital needs with interest group agendas. For the CIP committee to be effective, a committee member (a committee member selected by committee consensus) should be designated as responsible for coordinating the CIP process.

Some capital projects considered for inclusion in the CIP, such as capital infrastructure projects, require a more detailed and accurate proposal analysis and preparation since they usually require external financing at some point in the process. If a decision to include a capital infrastructure project in the CIP is made, that project will go through a second, comprehensive analysis. This second, comprehensive analysis is critical in aiding the Committee to identify those capital infrastructure projects that meet the Infrastructure Finance Policy and apply relevant criteria in recommending PPP financing and project delivery. In some cases, a government will use governmental funds in the operating budget to fund an initial analysis of the feasibility of selecting a PPP for project financing and delivery. In the process of analyzing the feasibility of a PPP, as discussed on in Chapter 5, qualitative analyses, in addition to quantitative analyses, may also be utilized through input from procurement and finance department staff who may know about similar prior capital projects funded and delivered through the use of a PPP.

The result of the initial committee project selection process is a detailed list of proposed capital projects for inclusion in the CIP. The detailed list is developed based on preliminary capital project analyses. The capital project forecast of costs should also be included. If debt funding is anticipated and alternative financing such as the use of PPPs is identified as an option that should also be formally recognized. A CIP containing a capital project list in rank order is produced, based on more detailed project input using the financing policies and criteria for selecting a project for financing and delivery. The CIP should also include the identified financial sources for funding the capital projects for the first year of the CIP, with forecasts for the remaining years in the plan. Usually, continuing large-scale capital projects have priority for funding, and the other capital projects financing is matched with the available financing sources. Year One of the CIP becomes the capital budget after the CIP is approved, and the updated Year One capital budget is appropriated.

Once the capital projects have been identified for possible PPP financing and project delivery, they should be compared with other financing methods using tools of analysis such as CBA. The long-term financial effects of the use of PPPs should also be identified as well as their recording recorded in the budget, accounting, and financial reporting systems. Separate feasibility studies should be conducted on potential capital projects to be financed and delivered using a PPP to assess the project's likelihood to succeed. These studies should include both a preliminary assessment of risks and a market assessment. The preliminary assessments can be updated and included with the procurement documents if the projects are included in the CIP and updated in the capital budget.

Unified and comprehensive capital management and budgeting, including long-term capital improvements planning, is necessary in order for governments to respond to citizens' needs, while at the same time maintaining sustainable financial condition in an appropriate timeframe (Mikesell, 2014). Such systematic capital management and budgeting practices need an Infrastructure Finance Policy framework in order to:

(1) have a more efficient overall capital planning, management, and budget program,
(2) provide capital improvements on time and within capital budget,
(3) more effectively manage the use of long-term debt,
(4) provide for more enhanced social value, and
(5) provide a better balance between traditional means of government capital infrastructure financing (long-term debt, equity financing, and capital reserves) and PPP.

As noted previously, the long-term CIP is especially crucial in capital infrastructure project design and delivery.

#### 5.3.1.2 Postcommitment

*5.3.1.2.1 Capital Budget Implementation.* Systematic capital management and budgeting practices are supported by an (infrastructure) investment policy goal (King, 1995). An example is the Mauritius Infrastructure Finance Policy. As described in Chapter 1, Infrastructure Finance Policy expresses the basis for the strategic allocation of resources to capital infrastructure. An Infrastructure Finance Policy is also important because it will receive scrutiny from potential private investors. A sustainable long-term capital management and budgeting practices should be based on and support its Infrastructure Finance Policy. Systematic long-term capital planning and management practices (i.e., separate capital budget, impact analysis of capital spending, the proportion of capital outlay funded through a dedicated resource in capital project funds and bond ratings) (Srithongrung, 2018) and are developed based on the strategy as articulated in the Infrastructure Finance Policy.

The Capital Budget proposal (year one of the CIP) contains more up-to-date and detailed information on the design, cost, and updated recommendation on financing. The project costs listed in the CIP are estimated based on financial projections at the time that the CIP was updated. The projects in the Capital Budget become finalized based on the updated project cost estimates. Once the capital budget is appropriated, expenditures from the capital budget are authorized for capital projects. The government must also reassess the economic viability of each capital project based on any changes in the external or internal environment that will impact project financing and delivery. It is during the time that full financing options are reassessed and updated, and any changes to financing available from current revenue (taxes, special assessments) are made. Accurate and up-to-date capital infrastructure project cost estimates listed in the capital budget are critical at this stage because the capital budget, like the operating budget, is based on such factors as revenue projections and limitations on issuing new debt. Capital infrastructure financing also requires decisions in the context of debt affordability.

When the first year of the CIP becomes the Capital Budget, the timing of updating and preparing Year One (capital budget) is essential (Bland & Rubin, 1997) because preparing the operating budget and updating the capital budget simultaneously focuses legislative attention on operating and capital budget issues at the same time. However, preparing both at the same time also has the potential to overload agency and legislative staff with preparing and analyzing operating and capital budgets together. How a government approaches updating the first year of the CIP, and the appropriation as either as separate budget documents or as a unified operating and capital budget depends on past practices, management philosophy, the size of the budgets, and staffing. Some subnational governments use simple lists of approved CIP projects, and some have more detailed CIPs, depending on the size of the government (Bland & Rubin, 1997) and staffing.

Capital expenditures are not all reported in the Capital Budget. Instead, a government identifies a minimum dollar threshold for inclusion in its capital budget. Capital project acquisitions that fall below the threshold are included in the operating budget. The minimum value depends on the size of the capital budget and the government's policy preferences (Bland & Rubin, 1997).

The Operating and Capital Budgets have different focuses and timeframes. The operating budget is planned, prepared, and appropriated by line-item, based on operating spending categories, and is generally funded with tax revenue for 1–2 years. The operating budget appropriation ends at the end of the budget cycle (except for Federal funds). The capital budget, the first year of the CIP, is presented by project, source(s) of funding, and forecasted project expenditures. The appropriation remains for the life of the capital project, which can be several years. Capital budgets have different funding sources than operating budgets. Governments use long-term debt (as described in Chapter 1) in part to fund the cost of capital improvements. Capital infrastructure debt repayment is spread over the life of the infrastructure. If a government uses General Obligation Debt, they must obtain voter approval before a bond sale. A government can also establish a capital reserve fund to accumulate sufficient resources to construct or replace a capital infrastructure when needed. Governments typically use a mix of current revenue and debt to fund large capital infrastructure projects (Bland & Rubin, 1997; Marlowe et al., 2009).

When Operating Budget expenditures are authorized, they are charged to the General Fund. Capital project expenditures in the operating budget are reported in a Capital Projects Fund. Separate funds are set up for each major capital project, such as the construction of a new government building or road. Revenue that goes into the Capital Projects Fund can come from bond proceeds (debt), current revenues, or grant income if traditional financing is used. Expenditures from the Capital Projects Fund are recorded as the total of the expenses of all the individual capital projects such as construction materials and payments to contractors. When each general capital project is completed, the individual project financing within the Capital Projects Fund is closed. Any remaining individual general capital project balances are transferred to another general capital projects fund.

A government should have a Capital Reserve Fund earmarked for capital improvements to provide financial flexibility and help to manage unplanned debt. A Capital Reserve Fund should be established for each capital infrastructure class such as roads and buildings, as well as unplanned maintenance and repair, based on data in the asset management plan. The reserves can also help fund future capital infrastructure expenditures that fluctuate significantly from year to year and protect against unexpected expenditures or revenue reductions.

The Capital Budget provides information on the project design, cost, and financing option, based on the Infrastructure Finance policy that is recommended for the individual capital project. The capital budget appropriation provides the government with authorization to expend for capital improvements in the same way that the operating budget appropriation provides the government with authorization to expend for recurring expenditures.

*5.3.1.2.2 Accounting and Reporting Capital Projects.* The cost of acquiring, purchasing, adding to, leasing, planning, designing, construction, extending, and improving all or any part of a capital project and of paying principal, interest, or premiums on any indebtedness incurred for these purposes are accounted for as a capital expenditure. Using the Budgetary Basis of Accounting for an Enterprise Fund, for example, actual revenues and expenses are recorded on a full accrual basis following GAAP.

#### 5.3.1.3 Postcompletion

*5.3.1.3.1 Closeout PPP Accounting and Reporting.* There are different PPP accounting and reporting standards, depending on the country and the type of PPP. ESA 95 and GFSM 2001 cover some PPP type. PPPs are designed to share certain risks, but because each PPP contract is unique to the specific capital project, any identified potential risks and contingent liabilities must be identified, quantified, and disclosed.

Traditional public capital budget expenditures are based on cash flow and do not account for the future capital outlays that may result from contingent liabilities. As a result of possible contingent liabilities in capital infrastructure projects, the actual capital infrastructure project cost may not be fully known, and, therefore, the government may not have complete data on such liabilities that they may face. Additionally, the potential impact on the government's financial condition may also not be known. If such contingent liabilities are not recognized and an unforeseen event occurs, which results in an actual liability to the government, it may result in a severe negative impact on their financial condition. Some governments are assessing their future contingent liabilities in order to manage their exposure to such future contingent liabilities better. If those liabilities are not identified or recorded, they cannot be appropriately managed.

Some types of PPP arrangements, such as Concession, provide for a private partner to assume debt related to the capital project, and the public partner compensates the private partner either directly or indirectly through user fees over the life of the capital project. This arrangement allows the government to amortize any debt related to the capital project and may pay the debt to a project sponsor or concessionaire that has assumed the debt. Some governments do not recognize this type of debt.

The US Congressional Budget Office has identified six criteria for not recognizing PPP project expenditures as not part of government liabilities:

(1) The Capital Asset serves a general purpose
(2) The Capital Asset also has a market in the private sector
(3) The private partner has ownership title to the capital asset which is not transferred to the government during the life of the PPP contract
(4) The contract does not stipulate a bargain price purchase option
(5) The contract term does not exceed 75% of the estimated economic life of the capital asset
(6) The present value of the minimum rent payable during the contractual term may not exceed 90% of the fair market value at the beginning of the contract term.

*Source:* CBO (2012).

For a SCA, the government contracts with a private partner to operate or maintain (depending on the contract) the government's capital infrastructure. The asset's availability is either based on the physical condition of the asset or the achievement of specific performance measures.

For PPPs, receivables should be recorded for installment payments. Deferred Inflow of Resources for the capital infrastructure should also be recorded, including payments received from the private contractor at or before the initiation of the PPP contract. If the underlying asset is a new asset or an existing asset that has been improved, and the PPP is a SCA, also record the capital asset at acquisition value when placed in operation. Otherwise, recognize a receivable for the capital asset, measured at the operator's estimated carrying value at the future date of ownership transfer.

Long-term liabilities in connection with PPP financing obligations should be recorded and reported in the appropriate budgetary account. In many countries, control of long-term debt in connection with PPP financing is managed at the fund level. OECD countries that are members of the EU, as discussed in Section

5.3.1 Post Completion, are subject to the European System of Accounts, which provides for specific budgeting and accounting treatment of PPPs. As a result, they must adhere to the European System of Accounts for recording long-term liabilities in connection with PPPs.

One strategy to reduce the risk of political instability is to involve international organizations which can provide expertise to emerging countries seeking to use the procurement process by providing them with information on best practices. Also, they can advise on the purchasing of insurance from organizations such as the Overseas Private Investment Corporation (OPIC, 2019). Some types of political instability, such as riots or war, may be mitigated through political risk insurance. The availability of such insurance is dependent on the circumstances of the political situation.

#### 5.3.1.4 Postcompletion

*5.3.1.4.1 Auditing Capital Projects.* A compliance audit of capital projects could include an examination of the contract procurement to ensure that all laws were in compliance. Audits of capital infrastructure projects could audit the expenditures made as part of the financial audit of the financial statements that contain those expenditures. A performance audit could examine the efficiency and effectiveness with which the capital project and related procurement were carried out (The World Bank and Caribbean Organization of Supreme Audit Institutions, 2018).

### *5.3.2 Public–Private Partnership Financial Risk*

One strategy to reduce the risk of uncertainty in the use of PPP is to have an explicit written policy on the government's use of the private sector to finance and deliver capital infrastructure. If a government does not explicitly express its commitment to include the private sector in capital infrastructure financing and delivery, the uncertainty surrounding the government's commitment to private sector involvement will negatively impact the use of capital infrastructure financing and delivery options such as PPPs and may result in contracts which do not have the express support of the country's political leadership. As a result, private sector involvement in PPP capital infrastructure financing and delivery may not be as active as countries where such support is made explicit.

#### 5.3.2.1 Strategies to Reduce Financial Risk

*5.3.2.1.1 Financial Risk in PPP Contract Negotiation.* Without a sufficient and unified financial policy framework to support the selection of and use of PPPs for financing and capital project delivery, capital improvements planning can become politicized, with minimal attention paid to quantitative assessment of potential capital projects. Because of the lack of sufficient and unified financial policy, capital project selection will not be based on established and written policy for decision support nor a formal project prioritization process. In some cases, large capital projects selection and financing may occur on an ad hoc basis without regular formal review and assessment. Without a sufficient formal unified policy framework, the capital project financing and selection at the Capital Budget stage may become more politicized, based on private partner personal relationships with government officials, without adequate and objective competitive bidding and selection. As a result, the capital infrastructure project at the Capital Budget stage of financing and delivery can potentially become inefficient and lack transparency and be open to the possibility of corruption. Consequently, the result is capital infrastructure projects which may not meet the needs and priorities of the government and the stakeholders. An approach that can help in the capital improvements planning selection early in the financing appraisal process is called Multi-Criteria Decision Analysis (MCDA) (The World Bank, 2016), which reflects the most available information as it relates to the Infrastructure finance Policy.

One strategy to reduce financial risk in capital project selection assessment is using the MCDA process as a method, at the early stage of capital improvements project selection, of systematically structuring financing decisions based on multiple factors related to proposed capital project financing. The proposed capital project financing decision should be based on the Infrastructure Finance Policy. This multi-criteria process can be used when information is limited or not currently available and can be revised to accommodate improved data when it becomes available at a later date. The use of MCDA can be especially useful in the capital infrastructure finance decision-support process in the capital improvements planning process because of the need to work within a tight timeframe, information, and capacity limitations in the process. The use of MCDA provides two important policy choices: (1) the selection of criteria to assess the alternatives and (2) weighing the projects against the selected criteria. It is at the risk assessment stage that outside consultation may be useful to provide objective insight into the criteria selected as well as the process for weighing the criteria. Weighing usually involves expert advice from outside the organization, such as peer governments or professional organizations, that can provide information on best practices or organizations such as the World Bank. MCDA, if used objectively, has the potential to provide a system of micro-level, policy-based capital project selection based on the stated government organizational goals, including the criteria of effectiveness, efficiency, feasibility, adequacy, equity, responsiveness, and appropriateness (The World Bank, 2016).

To reduce financial risk, the process should:

Begin with Infrastructure Finance Policy
Initiate CIP Update
Capital Project Identification based on need

- A preliminary review of proposed Capital Projects
- Capital Project Quantitative and Qualitative Analyses
- Capital Projects Criteria-based selection
- Identify sources of financing capital projects

First Year of CIP becomes Capital Budget
Adjustments to the proposed Capital Budget based on updated information
Capital Budget Appropriated
Capital Budget Implemented
Capital Project Procurement
Capital Project Construction and Delivery
Capital Asset operation and maintenance
Capital Asset Inventory Maintained

The capital infrastructure project selection during the CIP process (step 3) should be based on quantitative and qualitative analysis. The use of tools of analysis such as CBA for evaluation and prioritization of proposed capital projects allows decision-makers to identify projected costs and benefits of the proposed project over its useful life. CBA involves the discounting of future flows to NPV. A CBA provides data used to assess and to rank decision alternatives based on a NPV single indicator. Prioritization is based on the capital project, which has the best positive NPV. The challenge in using a CBA is that many costs and benefits, especially benefits, are challenging to quantify. Since the cost–benefit tool itself can be costly for large capital infrastructure projects, its use can have limited use in some types of capital projects, particularly small and medium-size projects. CBA can be used to evaluate and prioritize large capital infrastructure projects. Many governments have formal written guidance on when to use specific analytical tools. These tools should be used during the CIP process.

Financial risk can be mitigated to a certain degree through the use of insurance as a means for compensating for loss from certain risks. Insurance, however, only provides that if a loss occurs, the insured party's financial risk will be reduced. In other words, financial loss risk is reduced. An insurance company will not underwrite a risk that is reasonably likely to occur, nor will they underwrite a loss arising from a poorly written contract. In the case of PPPs, there may be a syndicate of insurers that provide coverage for some projects.

Canada has implemented a substantial contract phase completion payments system, and it is standard policy for 60% of total projects costs to be paid up to and before substantial completion for all social infrastructure projects and up to 85% of projects costs for all road and transit projects (Cassady, Darraugh, Geddes, Palcic, & Reeves, 2019). This policy change also has reduced the usage of long-term PPP financing payment system arrangements (Cassady et al., 2019).

Canada also requires precommitment of financing before the selection of a preferred bidder. Under this PPP contract financing arrangement, investors can only hold their commitment to debt financing for a limited period. This time limitation creates an incentive to bring the deal to financial closure quickly (Cassady et al., 2019).

*5.3.2.1.2 Demand Risk in Strategies in PPP Contract Negotiation.* One aspect of PPP financing is the demand risk. Demand risk is the chance that there will not be sufficient demand for the good or service to be provided under the PPP contract arrangement with the result that the private partner may not be able to repay its obligations from project revenue. Identifying demand risk is challenging, especially in emerging economies such as Albania. When the private partner assumes demand risk in the PPP contract negotiation, the risk is balanced, depending on the PPP contract, by more financial support such as grants or guarantees to mitigate the demand risk.

Some countries such as Canada have few PPP contracts that transfer demand/revenue risk to the private sector (Boardman, Siemiatycki, & Vining, 2016). The government has an active role in designing project specifications and ensuring public sector asset management because of the availability of the government's technical expertise and citizen skepticism toward the use of PPPs has made demand/revenue risk transfer challenging to achieve (Siemiatycki, 2015). The level of technical expertise and citizen questioning reduces the level of complexity in the Canadian procurement process (Cassady et al., 2019), even while it reduces the possibility of taking advantage of PPP benefits.

*5.3.2.1.3 Legal Risk in PPP Contract Negotiation.* Legal risk management is based on precise PPP contract documentation. Such documentation includes (1) project documentation and (2) the PPP contract. The legal system of the country backs the documentation. It is essential to ensure that PPP contracts are legally enforceable.

As described in Chapter 2, each case country national and subnational government that uses PPPs has a different definition of a PPP, which is not necessarily the country's legal term for such partnership, for example, New York State. Also, some countries and states have stand-alone PPP laws and procurement frameworks, such as Mauritius, while others use their traditional procurement laws and regulatory frameworks, supplemented by PPP policies. Mauritius also has a separate law for concessions as well. In those instances, PPP procurement is governed by broader procurement laws and frameworks. The critical point is that the legal system governing PPP in a specific country is aligned with the specific elements of the PPP policy framework (The World Bank, 2018). Investors will want to have access to their rights under the law of the country, and that relevant provisions of the PPP contract can be enforced. Also, alternative PPP contract dispute resolution, such as arbitration and mediation systems, can be used if there is any weakness in the government's legal system.

*5.3.2.1.4 Environmental Risk in Contract Negotiation.* Environmental risk, especially risk in connection with climate change, is difficult to assess. In the case of climate change as an environmental risk, the best approach is to the extent possible, identify the potential environmental risk from climate change for a given project, and define project design and maintenance factors. The government can assess risk through the use of Climate Change Hazard Models (The World Bank Annual Report 5, 2018). Environmental issues that constitute environmental risk often happen after it is too late in the PPP contract to initiate major contract renegotiation. Project costs and private partner performance are the only two factors that can be adjusted (The World Bank Annual Report 5, 2018) in the short term. It is crucial to identify the potential environmental risks during the procurement process so that they can be proactively managed should they occur once the contract has been signed and the capital project has been initiated. It is critical to proactively identify the risk of potential environmental issues during the procurement process so that they can be managed should they occur after the contract has been signed, and the capital project has been initiated.

*5.3.2.1.5 Expressed Risk Allocation in PPP Contracts.* PPP contracts can balance risk allocation between the public and private partners through Force Majeure and Unforeseen Conditions contract terms. A Force Majeure event is an unforeseen environmental occurrence that is beyond the control of the public and private partners. The result of the occurrence is that it prevents either partner from fulfilling its contractual obligations.

The use of PPPs has made demand/revenue risk transfer challenging to achieve (Siemiatycki, 2015). The government's technical expertise, coupled with citizen involvement, in turn, reduces the level of complexity in the Canadian procurement process (Cassady et al., 2019), even while it reduces the possibility of taking advantage of PPP benefits.

*5.3.2.1.6 Legal Risk in PPP Contract Negotiation.* Precise PPP contract documentation is the basis for legal risk management. Such documentation includes (1) project documentation and (2) the PPP contract. The legal system of the country is the support for the specific PPP contract documentation. These requirements are necessary and essential to ensure that PPP contracts are legally enforceable.

As described in Chapter 2, each case country national and subnational government that uses PPPs may have a different definition of a PPP. Further, that definition may not necessarily coincide with the government's legal term for such a partnership, as happened, for example, in New York State. Also, some national and subnational governments have stand-alone PPP laws and procurement frameworks, such as Mauritius.

In contrast, others use their traditional procurement laws and regulatory frameworks, supplemented by PPP policies. Mauritius also has a separate rule for concessions as well. Broader procurement laws and structures in those instances govern PPP procurement. The critical point is that the legal system governing PPP in a specific country should align with the particular elements of the PPP policy framework (The World Bank, 2018). Investors will be concerned that they have access to their rights under the law of the country and that relevant provisions of the PPP contract can be enforced. Also, alternative PPP contract dispute resolution, such as arbitration and mediation systems, can be used to mitigate weaknesses in a government's legal system.

*5.3.2.1.7 Articulating and Balancing Risk Allocation in PPP Contracts.* Balance in risk allocation between the public and private partners is improved through Force Majeure and Unforeseen Conditions contract terms. A Force Majeure event is an unforeseen environmental occurrence that is beyond the control of the public and private partners. The result of the incident is that it prevents either partner from fulfilling its contract obligations. Examples of events could be high winds, floods, and earthquakes. Both Force Majeure and Unforeseen Conditions cover any potential risk, such as environmentally caused risk, from disruption of construction and operation of a capital infrastructure project. The potential risk from a particular environmental event could be identified and articulated in the PPP contract based on the experience of a specific national or subnational government. However, the risk from frequency or intensity of a particular environmental event would be more difficult to forecast (The World Bank Annual Report 5, 2018).

If there is a potential environmental risk, a Force Majeure contract clause should be monitored. A Force Majeure clause in a PPP contract must achieve the right environmental risk balance between the public and private partners. An Unforeseen Condition is an unanticipated or unexpected circumstance or situation that affects the final contract price and/or that completion time terms of a PPP project. An Unforeseen Environmental Condition may be a weather event that has enough force that could result in the loss of life, significant property damage, and/or business disruption (The World Bank Annual Report 5, 2018).

Unless the potential environmental risk has been explicitly identified and assessed, bidders will be able to adequately provide a proposal that meets the criteria and/or the bid evaluators in the procurement process will be able to evaluate a proposal against the project criteria adequately. In most situations involving potential environmental risk, such as climate risk, the public partner retains all the risk (The World Bank Annual Report 5, 2018). The occurrence of extreme unforeseen environmental events will activate the Emergency Works clause in the contract. The Emergency Works clause permits the private partner to request additional compensation from the lender to cover any damages and loss of service associated with these extreme unforeseeable events.

*5.3.2.1.8 PPP Contract Performance Standards to Reduce Risk.* No significant changes should be made to the performance indicators in the contract if a potential yet foreseeable environmental event occurs. A PPP contract that contains environmental risk should include the specific environmental risk as part of the design specifications in the contract. The public partner would include the assessments for risk of flooding, high winds, hurricanes, excessively high temperatures, etc. in the contract. If the private partner states that they do not meet the specified environmental risk performance indicators, then the agreement will specify that the private partner will be ineligible for Force Majeure compensation (The World Bank Annual Report 5, 2018).

Examples of performance indicators for a flooding event could be the number of feet (depth) of the flood. Standards of operational performance for an excessively high-temperature event could be measured by the number of citizens treated for heat exhaustion (The World Bank Annual Report 5, 2018).

Assessment of capital infrastructure project financing risk associated with environmental events is the result of different investment financing timeframes. Private equity investors in PPP environmental projects expect 3–5 years ROI while expectations of ROI range from 10 to 30 years of development banks. The life expectancy of a transportation infrastructure such as a road is 50–75 years. As a result, investment financing is chronically valued too low for these types of projects because forecasts rely on past events in predicting future such environmental events. A national government that accepts environmental risk can offer increased environmental risk mitigation incentives. A development bank or funding partner that requires a specified loan repayment can reduce interest rates and offer credit rating for secured capital infrastructure project (The World Bank Annual Report 5, 2018).

Investors in PPP contracts (especially those involving the risk of environmental events such as the World Bank) must consider the possibility that their investment may be negatively impacted. The potential negative impact on investment is due to the increased risk of environmental events from climate change (The World Bank Annual Report 5, 2018). The public partner should raise awareness of how increased potential risk from environmental events (such as climate change events) threatens capital improvements financing (which may, in turn, lead to reduced environmental risk mitigation). The public partner should also consider the return on resilience investment through strengthening the government's resilience to environmental hazards and disasters include climate risk in credit ratings (which typically undervalues potential environmental risk exposure). Also, the public partner should prioritize high-risk capital infrastructure (such as those that are exposed to potential immediate environmental threats to investment vs. those infrastructure that face potential environmental threats in the long term), and extend the investment period (such as with shorter contracts) to reduce the increased potential risk of environmental events. Terms of 8 years or less do not provide adequate time to incentivize long-term risk mitigation and adaptation (The World Bank Annual Report 5, 2018).

Frequent environmental events increase maintenance and operation capital infrastructure costs because of the enhanced erosion of the capital infrastructure. There are also increased government personnel costs (depending on the terms of the PPP contract) because of the increased need to repair and/or replace environmental event damage to a capital infrastructure. In the case of any capital infrastructure that are subject to environmental events, the cost of building more resilient capital infrastructure is less than the increased maintenance and operating expenses from the environmental events impacting less resilient capital infrastructure. Identifying and calculating the increased costs from environmental events and the increased personnel costs on a capital infrastructure can result in more accurate forecasts of maintenance costs of capital infrastructure that is subject to potential environmental damage (The World Bank Annual Report 5, 2018). Credit rating agencies require cost analysis to assess potential environmental risk throughout the capital project contract period.

*5.3.2.1.9 PPP Contract Dispute Resolution Methods.* A PPP contract is more difficult for the public partner to write, negotiate, and manage because of the bundling of capital infrastructure project design and delivery phases and the extended length of time required to complete the project. As a result, PPP contracts can be subject to contract disputes. A dispute resolution method can be identified in the PPP contract to help manage a potential PPP contract dispute. Also, in some countries, procurement laws in general and PPP laws, in particular, usually spell out the available options for PPP contract dispute resolution. The ability to efficiently and effectively resolve a contract dispute is key to the long-term viability of the capital project and private sector profit. While there are several methods of determining a contract dispute, there is no one correct dispute resolution method that will fit every situation. In considering which dispute resolution method to use, the most expeditious approach may be needed to prevent cost overruns and construction delays.

*5.3.2.1.10 Examples of PPP Contract Dispute Resolution Methods.* Examples of PPP contract dispute resolution methods include: Contract Dispute Mediation, Contract Dispute Regulatory Administrative Body, Contract Dispute Litigation, and Contract Dispute Arbitration.

*Contract Dispute Mediation.* In PPP contract dispute mediation, a neutral third party is appointed to assist the partners in settling their contract dispute. The mediator helps the contract partners in narrowing the issues where they disagree and finding common ground to resolve the issue. Mediation can assist the partners in closing in on the problems that need resolution. The dispute resolution, when reached, is produced by the contract partners, with the mediator facilitating the resolution (Kerf, Gray, Irwin, Levesque, & Taylor, 1998).

*Regulatory, Administration Resolution.* The PPP contract dispute resolution regulatory, administrative body approach involves the regulatory agency resolving certain contract disputes. This approach is low in cost but may take a longer time to decide, depending on the schedule of the administrative, regulatory staff to resolve the dispute.

*Litigation.* The litigation approach to PPP contract dispute resolution can be expensive and time-consuming because of the steps in the process, such as pretrial procedures, adjudication, appeals process, and strength of the legal system to enforce the judicial ruling. These steps in the litigation process intensify when the PPP partners in the contract dispute are in different countries with different legal systems. When the ruling is made on the case, enforcement of the decision may also be difficult if there is not a treaty between the two countries where the PPP partners (public and the private partner) are each based.

*Arbitration.* The arbitration approach to PPP contract dispute resolution involves the selection of an independent panel of experts who arbitrate the dispute reach either binding or nonbinding. In the case of international arbitration, treaties of the countries involving the PPP contract partners in the conflict typically designate arbitration involving a foreign private contractor and a municipal government. Also, in emerging economies, a PPP financing source may require that any outstanding awards as a result of contract dispute arbitration be resolved as a condition to awarding additional financing for future capital projects.

As governments gain more experience with different types of PPPs' procurement financing and delivery, the transaction costs associated with PPP procurement may decrease (Cassady et al., 2019) depending on the government's political and institution dimensions.

## 5.4 Capital Improvements Planning, Capital Management, and Budgeting and PPPs

This section expands on the relationship between capital improvements planning, the capital budget, and PPPs as the basis for capital infrastructure project financing and delivery decisions and the need to balance efficiency and effectiveness in Infrastructure Finance Policy implementation. The Infrastructure Finance Policy forms the basis for a decision to use a PPP as an option to finance and deliver a capital infrastructure. The CIP is the connection to capital management and budgeting and forms the basis for initial decisions on capital projects financing and delivery options.

As described in the Capital Management and Budgeting Framework, the Capital Improvements Planning process involves many phases: (1) financial planning, (2) potential capital project identification, (3) assessment and selection of potential capital projects, and (4) capital project management, monitoring, and reporting. This section expands on those phases in the CIP and highlights fiduciary and legal requirements where challenges may occur in the process.

### *5.4.1 Capital Improvements Plan and Financial Planning*

The financial plan is the basis for decisions on capital project financing. The micro-level financial plan includes a multiyear forecast of revenue and expenditures. It involves a commitment to the Capital Budget (year one of the CIP) and the remaining CIP years. The plan also identifies explicitly the financial resources available to fund the current project and proposed new projects, determines the impact on the operating budget, and quantifies the operating costs or savings that may result from financing a capital project. Thus, the CIP is the connection not only to the Capital Budget but also to the financial plan. The CIP should also provide estimates of its operating and maintenance costs and its debt service costs, project reserve balances, and project revenue requirements (Westerman, 2004). The debt affordability policies should include off-balance-sheet financing, self-imposed debt limits, and long-term financing (Westerman, 2004).

#### 5.4.1.1 Potential Capital Project Identification

The process should involve identifying all potential capital projects since the last CIP update. By methodically identifying all potential projects, the likelihood that all needed capital projects are recognized before they become an emergency will be reduced.

Operation and maintenance should also be identified, as well as the process of identifying potential capital projects. The condition of capital infrastructure should be monitored, assessed, and included in the CIP (Westerman, 2004). Also, identification of deferred maintenance should be included in the CIP. Deferred maintenance is often not reported and not included in total capital budget costs.

The capital projects should be grouped by type and purpose to more readily identify the broad sources of funding and assist in further refining the potential funding by type and purpose. Capital projects that are not selected should be recorded for possible future consideration, and capital projects that are selected for inclusion in the CIP should be prioritized.

*5.4.1.1.1 Assessment and Selection of Capital Projects.* Conducting a comprehensive project assessment before the selection of projects is critical to determine whether the projects are (1) mandatory, (2) necessary, or (3) would like to do. Mandatory capital projects do not require as much up-front analysis and review because the government is usually mandated by law to complete and deliver the project. Necessary or needed projects are typically essential, and the nature of these type projects are more strategic. These projects usually involve benefits to the government or cost savings. This type of project would generally require a higher level of analysis and review, depending on the scope of the project before making the final decision to include the project in the CIP.

### *5.4.2 Capital Budget Monitoring*

Capital project management takes place following the appropriation of the Capital Budget when the government is authorized to expend the funds for the specified capital project. The key to active capital project management is careful project monitoring of construction progress versus the schedule and ongoing status reports such as percent of project completed, percent of project budget expended, and project milestones.

#### 5.4.2.1 Capital Project Monitoring, Legal Requirements, and Closeout Process

The Government Finance Officers Association (GFOA) recommends that the capital project monitoring process should identify and incorporate legal and fiduciary requirements into the capital project management, monitoring, and reporting process. They support the identification of relevant data for external and internal stakeholder information needs. Further, they recommend systems to collect, store, and analyze project data to report results. GFOA also recommends the design of a monitoring system that will efficiently provide reports and updates. Project Closeout and Evaluation of the Monitoring Process are as follows.

### *5.4.3 Legal and Fiduciary Requirements*

Identify and incorporate relevant laws, such as debt capacity limits, voter authorization, procurement laws, including specific laws, on public procurement.

Describe the relationship between each capital project and the master plan and/or the comprehensive plan and the strategic plan.

Identify bond covenant requirements or other conditions related to long-term debt that are used to finance capital projects.

Identify relevant data for external and internal stakeholder information needs.

Identify critical external and external stakeholders in the capital improvements process such as project engineers, bondholders, rating agencies, citizens.

Establish project milestones, performance measures, and reporting criteria based on legal and fiduciary requirements identified above (1).

Plan and design systems to collect, store, and analyze capital project data.

Determine what system is the primary system for collecting, storing, and analyzing capital project data.

Determine the design process for controlling and managing changes to capital project scope, schedule, cost, financing, and contract requirement data and monitoring cost overruns and delays.
Design a system for data accountability, integrity, and accuracy.
Design a capital project monitoring and reporting system.
Plan and design a system for use in project accounting that allows for flexibility in collecting, storing, and analyzing project data for different types of projects.
Identify the process for controlling and managing changes to the capital project contract renegotiations.
Protocols for identifying and addressing project cost overruns and schedule delays.
Regularly monitor capital projects' financial and activity information and provide status reports. The monitoring of capital projects financial activity should include:

Provide ongoing data analytics for capital project financial transactions to support budget to actual, audit, and assessment.
Provide ongoing data on encumbrances and updates on expenditure forecasts versus actual.
Provide data on project retainages, warranties, or other conditional performance schedules.
Monitor availability and appropriateness of revenue sources appropriated in the capital budget.
Forecast and monitor capital project cash flow versus capital project expenditure requirements.
Compare the timing of financing maturity dates versus capital project expenditures.
Monitor receipt of bond proceeds and grant sources and expenditures.
Establish performance measures and monitor against results.

Albania is an example of a country that has designed a comprehensive PPP monitoring framework. The monitoring framework consists of the requirement that government contracting authorities must submit regular and systematic information on actual PPP performance to the Albanian MoF. The Ministry will use the regular submissions to publish an annual report on Albanian PPP performance, which includes the performance of the most strategic capital infrastructure projects, their service delivery efficiency, and any potential risks.

#### 5.4.3.1 Capital Project Status and Activities Reporting

Capita infrastructure projects require established schedules for status reports which compare results to actual, such as:

- Percent capital project completion
- Performance Milestones
- Contract Status

- Capital Project Revenue and Expenditure budgeted versus actual
- Cash Flow and Financing Maturities
- Encumbrances
- Appropriation Balance
- Significant Changes to project scope, costs, schedule, or funding.

### *5.4.4 Capital Project Closeout*

When the capital project is completed, specific actions to close out the project must be carried out:

Confirm that the contract encumbrances are closed out, and the remaining fund balances are transferred to the appropriate account.

Confirm all closeout and reporting requirements of grantors and bond covenants and other reporting requirements are completed.

Confirm capital project closeout is recorded in a fixed asset schedule and added to the capital infrastructure tracking system.

### *5.4.5 Evaluating Monitoring and Reporting Activities*

A regular review of the capital project monitoring and reporting practices should be in place to ensure that the data are accurate, complete, and that the reporting systems are capturing the right data and in the correct format to provide decision support and which meet legal requirements.

## 5.5 Summary

This chapter describes government's capital infrastructure projects financing as well as the Capital Management and Budget system as an output of its Infrastructure Finance Policy and capital projects financing and PPPs as a policy option. The chapter also describes the unified and comprehensive capital management and budget framework which includes: (1) Capital Management and Budget Policies, (2) Capital Budgeting and Financial Management Process, (3) Centralized Capital Management and Budget Execution and Capital Project Management, (4) Infrastructure Maintenance (Srithongrung, 2016, p. 3). The Infrastructure Finance Policy guides the critical components of a Comprehensive Capital Management and Budgeting Framework.

# Part 4
# Infrastructure Finance Policy Implementation Practices

Chapter 6

# Issues in Infrastructure Finance Policy Implementation

This chapter describes the issues in Infrastructure Finance Policy implementation. Infrastructure Finance Policy as a basis for choosing to use a Public–Private Partnership (PPP) to finance and deliver a capital infrastructure project depends on (1) whether the Infrastructure Finance Policy encourages and supports increased private sector involvement, (2) whether government design of an efficient and effective capital management and budget system, and (3) whether procurement system to support the use of PPPs are effective in doing so. Such systems work most effectively if the private partner believes that the PPP is profitable.

Adapting a strategic perspective on Infrastructure Finance Policy design and implementation, which promotes economic growth and development specific to the country, provides the basis for preserving macroeconomic stability (Rajaram, Kaiser, Le, Kim, & Frank, 2014). A [policy-based] public finance framework guides the process of capital infrastructure project financing and delivery (Rajaram et al., 2014). In general, the opportunity should seek to increase the public financing of needed capital projects. Reallocating resources from lower-efficiency uses to higher-efficiency uses results in more economic growth-enhancing opportunities than raising additional revenue or borrowing to finance the same productive expenditures (Rajaram et al., 2014).

The amount of a government's capacity to finance new capital infrastructure projects depends on the fiscal condition of the government. Additionally, their ability to reallocate resources to finance capital projects through Infrastructure Finance Policy and evaluation of nontraditional financing options, such as PPPs, can significantly improve the efficiency of their public spending. In order to improve such efficiency, the essential elements must be in place to minimize the government's risks, be achievable in a lower-capacity context, while providing an effective systemic process for managing public capital investment (Rajaram et al., 2014).

**Public-Private Partnerships, Capital Infrastructure Project Investments and Infrastructure Finance, 179–193**

**doi:10.1108/978-1-83909-654-920201006**

## 6.1 Role of Revenue Forecasting in Infrastructure Finance Policy Implementation

This section describes the strategic role of forecasting capital projects revenue and discusses the impact that current Infrastructure Finance Policy implementation will have on the design and delivery of capital projects.

Strategic and Comprehensive Plans are developed based on a variety of factors such as forecasts of population growth, and changes in the economic base that will impact the types of capital project financing projects needed. The government's Infrastructure Finance Policy should identify and describe the specific types of capital project financing eligible for inclusion in the capital improvements plan, based on the types of financing that is available to the government. The basis for selecting the types of financing available should be based, in part, on the government's multi-year revenue and expenditure forecasts.

Governments should conduct multi-year revenue and expenditure forecasting based on their financial and debt management policies. Multi-year revenue forecasts are the basis for determining the revenue sources and amounts that will be available for financing long-term and short-term operations, including the financing of capital projects. Net Cash Flow uses multi-year forecasts as a basis (Srithongrung, Yusuf, & Kriz, 2019). This multi-year forecast focus is essential because of the long-term nature of capital improvements planning and substantial capital project expenditures commitments. Multi-year revenue and expenditure forecasts are critical for all Governmental and Proprietary funds. However, such forecasts, in conjunction with debt affordability analysis, are especially crucial for the General Fund. This situation is because tax revenue sources may be uneven, and the General Fund is required to be balanced. Multi-year General Fund forecasts are typically for 5–6 years (Sun, 2014) and should be updated at least annually. The forecasts should be updated more frequently, such as quarterly or monthly, if there are anticipated changes in significant sources of funding such as the General Fund. These forecast updates are crucial to ensuring a balanced budget that revenues will support expenditures and may be useful in showing the impact of any proposed policy changes on current revenue and expenditures. Multi-year forecasting and financial policy and planning are essential tools in long-term fiscal sustainability (Sun, 2014). The accuracy of the forecasts (Step 3 below), the stakeholders involved in the forecasting process, and ongoing monitoring of forecast versus actual and the modifications as needed to the forecasts are the basis for a quality multi-year forecasting system.

The budget and finance offices prepare the multi-year forecasts, modifications, and updates, with input from senior management, departments, and legislators. Most multi-year forecasts include key revenue and expenditure assumptions, expenditure projections, and ending fund balances (Sun, 2014).

The comprehensive steps listed below show where forecasting fits within the overall.

Unified and Comprehensive Steps in Infrastructure Finance Policy Implementation System.

Step 1. The Comprehensive Plan (subnational government)
Step 2. The Strategic Plan
Step 3. The Multi-Year Revenue and Expenditure Forecasts*
Step 4. The Debt Affordability Analysis
Step 5. The Statement of Strategic Objective(s)
Step 6. The Assessment of Capital Needs
Step 7. The Proposed Capital Projects for Inclusion in CIP and Financing
Step 8. The Priority Project Ranking Based on Strategic Objective(s) and Criteria
Step 9. The Identification of Capital Improvement Project by Priority
Step 10. The Forecast of Capital Projects Revenue vis-a-vis Financing Options*
Step 11. The Identification and Selection of Financing Sources for Capital Projects
Step 12. The Capital Improvements Plan Adopted
Step 13. The Capital Budget Appropriated
Step 14. The Capital Budget Implemented
Step 15. The Capital Projects procured
Step 16. The Capital Projects Financed and Constructed
Step 17. The Capital Projects Operated and Maintained
Step 18. The Capital Infrastructure Inventory

## 6.2 Role of Independent Capital Project Financial Analysis

This section describes the use of independent project financial analysis in Infrastructure Finance Policy implementation. Appropriate use of expert consultants may help guide a government to more in-depth, complex project financial analysis and evaluation approaches and proactively identify issues in the PPP negotiations are underway, thereby affording all players time to adjust or change course if necessary.

Many governments do not have the in-house expertise to perform extensive qualitative and quantitative assessments for all proposed capital projects. The challenge is in developing both capital project financing assessment capability and capacity and based on the unique needs of each government. The capital project financial assessment function must be effectively managed and must have a gatekeeping function to screen projects that do not meet the criteria (Rajaram et al., 2014). Also, having a well-structured and transparent evaluation assessment feedback system in place should lead to continuous assessment improvement for future capital project assessments (Rajaram et al., 2014).

Rajaram et al. (2014) have identified the critical features of a long-term approach to building capacity:

Select the project financing option which best supports Infrastructure Finance Policy

Select the project financing and delivery option that is effective and leads to the completion of the project on schedule [and on a budget],
Develop a sufficient and sustainable operation and maintenance system for the capital infrastructure created by public financing,
Develop a process of [continuous feedback] learning to improve future capital project selection, implementation, and operation, and
Select the capital project financing and delivery option with risk allocation that ensures efficient and effective capital project implementation.

In the selection of the project financing option that best supports Infrastructure Finance Policy, the critical point is that the increased use of PPPs to finance and deliver capital projects requires a unified and comprehensive Capital Management and Budgeting system. Such a unified system includes analysis of both traditional procurement and options such as bundled contract PPP arrangements. When the financing and delivery decision is made, based on the recommendation, the contract is negotiated to achieve the projected outcome. Such an analysis will ensure that the financing and delivery option chosen for a project will yield the best value for the money. The options are (1) traditional government financing and delivery of a capital infrastructure project or (2) bundled contract for financing and delivery option through a PPP. The best method for analysis would be to prepare two capital project financing and delivery proposals: (1) traditional contracting and (2) bundled contracting. Both analyses are independently reviewed for the best value-for-the money and risk-sharing arrangement (Rajaram et al., 2014) and with recommendations made based on the independent analysis.

In developing a sufficient and sustainable operation and maintenance system for the capital infrastructure created by public financing, there are four major financial assessments which must be considered in assessing financing and delivery options for proposed capital projects:

*Financial Assessment*: For traditional financing and delivery of proposed capital projects, assessment should consider the adequacy of multi-year revenue forecasts to cover operating, maintenance, and debt service costs. For proposed capital projects that involve user charges, the demand and market risk is assessed as part of the overall financial assessment.

*External Cost of Public Funds Assessment*: If a proposed capital project involves traditional financing and delivery of proposed capital projects, the economic appraisal must identify the external costs of raising additional public funds, including economic efficiency, administrative, and debt management costs of an added unit of revenue.

*Costs of Market Risk Assessment*: If the revenue from a proposed capital project is based on user charges, the risk must be identified and shared with consumers through contract negotiation.

*Productivity or Cost-Efficiency Assessment*: Different contracting arrangements result in different incentives for cost-efficiency in the financing and delivery of the proposed capital project and considered in assessing the proposed projects (Rajaram et al., 2014).

## 6.3 PPP Performance Measurement and Monitoring and Feedback

Capital Project Performance Monitoring and Feedback. This section describes the development of a process of [continuous feedback] learning to improve future capital project selection, its implementation and operation, and the importance of a written PPP performance monitoring system in dictating how project monitoring will be carried out, based on the terms of the contract.

The government specifies the required contract performance output specification that must be met by the private partner in the output standards delineated in the contract. The quality of the PPP performance output is specified, measured, and monitored through a performance management system (Heavisides & Price, 2001). The level of actual output PPP versus the output standards determines future payments by the public partner. If the actual output does not meet the specified output standards, as written in the contract, a possible private partner payment reduction is considered.

During the procurement phase, the PPP technical output specification, which is also called performance-based specification, is the most crucial document in PPP procurement in terms of capital project performance measurement and monitoring. The technical output specification provides (1) the formal statement of the private partner service requirements, (2) there is an evaluation of the basis on which bidders prepare their proposals and bids, and (3) forms the basis against which performance or quality of service delivered by private partners is monitored during operation of the completed PPP project (Oyedele, 2013).

In the Planning and Design Phase of the PPP capital project, performance assessment should focus on (1) the comprehensiveness of the risk analysis, (2) the capital project requirements and identified performance measurement outputs, (3) suitability of the chosen financing option, and (4) capital project arrangement. Measures of assessment are based on criteria identified in the feasibility study since they are identified as a critical success factor for PPPs (Liu, Love, Davis, & Smith, 2013; Quanji, Zhang, & Zhang, 2016). In PPP contracts such as Concessions, the appropriateness of both the private partner and the PPP contract period are essential aspects of contract measurement and monitoring (Liu et al., 2013; Quanji et al., 2016).

PPP technical output specification is different from traditional technical output specification. Traditional technical output specification defines how a capital project is delivered by specifying such input items as materials and labor. PPP technical output specification is concerned with the private partner's actual output performance measurement at different phases (Oyedele, 2013). The PPP technical output specification contained in the contract includes two parts, (1) physical adaptation and (2) technical performance standards (Oyedele, 2013; Robinson & Scott, 2009), depending on the PPP type. The first part, physical adaptation, includes the material aspect of the capital infrastructure expected to meet the requirements of the users. Capital project physical performance standards also include the extent and levels of output required, the weightings of capital delivery each of the phases of the capital project, depending on priority, the performance assessment criteria, the revised contract period if delivery does not meet the criteria and heightened sanctions for repeated or widespread failure to meet criteria. To maximize the potential for PPP success, the current and future private partner should have a clear understanding of the consequences of not meeting technical performance output measurement specifications (Oyedele, 2013).

In a formal PPP performance measurement system, actual performance output is compared with the performance assessment criteria. The performance measurement system includes the process for identifying what to measure (identify key performance output indicators) and how to assess performance (based on a weighing system where each phase is given a weight based on their priority) and when to measure (Oyedele, 2013) as described below. Assessing PPP's actual performance output against the criteria is more challenging than traditional capital project funding and delivery. This challenge stems from the complexity of the PPP contract bundling. Because of the contract bundling complexity, the factors involved, such as contract documentation, financing, taxation, technical details, subagreements, and risks (market, financial, project, environmental) can change over the length of the project (Grimsey & Lewis, 2002; Liu et al., 2013). Any such changes add significant challenges to PPP monitoring and assessment.

There are two stages of performance measurement used at both the project selection stage and the project implementation stage. One stage is ex-ante financial performance measurement, and the other stage is ex-post evaluation. At the project level, ex-ante financial analysis is a preproject study used to analyze financing options, based on the financial feasibility analysis and cost analysis. Ex-post assessment is a comparison between project performance criteria and actual project outcome achievements at each phase of the implemented project and forecasts future work completion based on actual performance output (Liu et al., 2013).

Other contract monitoring performance measures should include the efficiency and effectiveness of financial closure since financial closure (the phase in which the conditions are met before the release of financing) in the PPP procurement phase authorizes the implementation of financing arrangements. There is considerable effort involved in achieving financial closure (Akintoye & Beck, 2009). Such closure is critical to the ultimate success of the capital project and the PPP.

The government should identify a central unit or agency to be responsible and accountable for overseeing the capital project construction, monitoring capital project performance, tracking the use of appropriated funds, and reporting capital project progress. Regular, ongoing government monitoring of a capital project helps to avoid capital project cost overruns. Once the private partner becomes responsible for the management of a capital project, the government can have an administrative team monitor the private partner's performance rather than managing the project's monitoring process itself (Savas, 2000).

Successful capital project implementation (on time and within budget) is achieved if governments [proactively] detect and address problems in capital project execution as early as possible (Srithongrung et al., 2019). Effective project monitoring helps to minimize cost overruns for large and time-consuming capital projects, which increases funding efficiency. The key to effective capital project monitoring is to compare progress versus actual, both construction and budget, and prepare status reports at the agency and central unit levels (Srithongrung et al., 2019).

## 6.4 Flexibility During Capital Project Design in Contract Negotiation

Flexibility is critical during capital project design. This section describes the need for the public partner to maintain flexibility when using a PPP to be able to renegotiate the terms of the contract to respond to unforeseen changes in the external environment.

The difference between the typical capital project design approach and a flexible approach is to identify potential changes proactively and to prepare for the possibility of such adjustments during contract negotiations. A key issue when introducing flexibility into the capital project design is the identification of and readiness for changes at any given stage of the capital project, rather than the traditional capital project design approach that uses rigid traditional standards (Kosmieja & Paslawski, 2016). The introduction of flexibility during capital project design comes at the time of the initial assessment of the capital project design and delivery options. The identification of the need for flexibility during the capital project design phase limits the necessity for contract change and the resulting need to renegotiate the contract (Kosmieja & Paslawski, 2016).

## 6.5 Infrastructure Finance Risk Allocation in Financing and Delivery

It is crucial to select the capital project financing and delivery option with a risk allocation that ensures efficient and effective capital project implementation (Rajaram et al., 2014). This section discusses the potential capital infrastructure project risks in the context of Infrastructure Finance Policy and financial planning and the need to clearly articulate the factors that minimize the risks to both parties during contract negotiation and renegotiation.

### *6.5.1 Minimizing Infrastructure Finance Risk*

A microlevel capital project financial plan is critical to the success of a PPP project (Kwak, Chih, & Ibbs, 2009), based on the macrolevel Infrastructure Finance Policy. The higher evaluation weights assigned to financial criteria reflect the importance of the financial dimension and financial risk. The Hong Kong government, for example, allocates 65% to financial weights, 20% to engineering, and 15% to transport in evaluating bids for BOT tunnel projects (Kwak et al., 2009).

Paying for and delivering large, complex capital projects requires assessing different financing and delivery options on the part of the public partner to match the capital project needs. When the capital project is appropriated, and the capital project is contracted, the final decision is made on the type financing and delivery. A private sector financing practice in many PPP contracts, depending on the type of PPP contract, is to use as much long-term debt as they can afford, in concert with cash flow forecasts, in order to generate an attractive return to shareholders (Levy, 2011). PPP projects are typically financed by the private partner with both equity and debt, and highly leveraged. Equity financing may cover 10%–30% of total project costs, and debt financing covers the remaining 70%–90% (Levy, 2011). The higher debt may provide a higher rate of return to equity investors, but it also can increase the private partner financial risk. The appropriate balance between equity and debt is essential in financing a PPP project (Zhang, 2005). Governments can minimize the costs of capital project financing and delivery by accurately assessing the cost of traditional financing and delivery of a capital project versus the cost of private sector financing and delivery through a PPP.

## 6.6 Risk-minimizing Financing Strategies Under Different Financing Conditions

The Capital Improvement Plan identifies Capital Projects and the primary sources of financing. Capital project financing strategies are dependent, in part, on potential risk conditions (Schaufelberger & Wipadapisut, 2003). Selected financing strategies under different potential risk conditions include

Low Financial Risk Strategies

Apply high debt-to-equity ratio to financing for maximum leverage and maximum return on invested equity
Establish minimum contingency credit facilities to minimize financing costs
Use capital markets to procure debt finance to reduce interest costs
Procure long-term financing early to reduce financing costs

High Financial Risk Strategies

Apply for loans from international lending organizations
Use fixed-rate or standardized-rate debt financing
Express loans and debt in local monetary units
Negotiate and structure revenue increases provision in local monetary units in the PPP contract
Seek government support and guarantees
Establish a contingency credit line to cover unanticipated expenses

High Market Risk

Finance early project construction phases with equity and temporary loans and refinance during operation with lower-cost long-term debt
Structure debt repayment schedule to start low and escalate during the initial years of operation

Negotiate PPP contract terms that allow increases in user fees
Establish a contingency credit facility to cover unanticipated revenue shortfalls
Restructure debt, if necessary, to solve cash flow problems during the concession construction phase of the project.

Adapted from Kwak et al. (2009) and Schaufelberger & Wipadapisut (2003).

## 6.7 Role of Government in Minimizing Capital Project Costs

Transaction Costs. This section discusses the role governments should play in seeking to minimize total capital project costs. At the macrolevel, the government's capital infrastructure financing decisions impact economic growth and efficiency. At the microlevel, the decision whether to build (make) in-house or to purchase (buy) services was introduced by Coase (1937), who distinguished between organizational hierarchy as a governance structure (coordinated through the authority), the hierarchy of the entrepreneur (through the labor/subordination mechanism), and the market mechanism (coordinated by different players through price mechanism). Coase further explained that there is a cost of using the price mechanism (a transaction cost) (Athias & Saussier, 2019). The management of total production costs and transaction costs (introduced in Chapter 1 and discussed in Chapter 5) is needed to achieve what North calls *adaptive efficiency*. That is, the ability of societies to be flexible and adapt in the face of rapid change that effectively alters reality (North, 2005). *Adaptive efficiency* then guides strategic economic policies, such as Infrastructure Finance Policy, in achieving macrolevel economic performance and at the microlevel, strategies such as unified Capital Budgeting and Management systems for gaining more substantial competitive advantage through the market. Governments can minimize the costs of capital project financing and delivery by accurately assessing the cost of traditional financing and delivery of a capital project versus the cost of private sector financing and delivery through a PPP. Part of the assessment should include transaction costs.

## 6.8 The Role of Transaction Cost Theory in Evaluating PPP as Policy Choice

Transaction Cost Theory. This section builds on Chapter 5 in describing transaction cost theory and introduces Public Choice Theory as an approach to evaluate the choice of PPPs to finance and deliver capital projects.

According to Transaction Cost Theory, the market has a productive efficiency advantage because of more substantial incentives related to the private ownership of profit and the competitive pressure that permits penalizing the poor performance of agents. In some cases, the market governance structure may achieve better cost-efficiency through economies of scale generally associated with high fixed cost services (Athias & Saussier, 2019). For example, some private partners may have many other public clients and may be present in many markets. Thus, the private partner can spread high fixed price project costs across a larger area of production. This productive efficiency advantage is not typically possible for a single geographic public partner.

Further, the governance of the market dimension can achieve productive efficiency gains over the public sector when it optimally allocates risks. The market makes it possible for the public partner (depending on the contract) to transfer demand, availability, and construction risks of some capital projects to the private partner, who may be better equipped to manage the risks. The public partner usually retains certain risks, such as political and environmental risks. Retaining political risk is especially an issue in emerging economies such as Albania. Political and policy uncertainty are two of the significant structural causes of the uneven impact of PPPs on economic growth in some emerging countries (Baker, Khater, & Haddad, 2019).

During the PPP contract negotiation phase, political instability may delay contract negotiation, increase contract transaction costs, and compromise government effectiveness in emerging economies such as Albania. This situation is because some contract negotiations are delayed because of change in political leadership and policy design under which the choice of the type of capital project selected, the choice of private partner, the nature of the transaction, and the price of the service may subject to unforeseen change (Baker et al., 2019).

## 6.9 Potential Bond Rating Impact on Use of a PPP

This section discusses the potential Bond Rating impact on government use of a PPP. Standard and Poor Rating Agency (S&P) evaluates the nature of a government's financial obligations under a PPP agreement in its determining whether the obligation is part of a government's tax-supported debt (Standard & Poor's, 2019). A PPP includes some level of private financing, and there is typically a transfer of construction and/or operating risk to the private partner. The private financing typically ranges from about 10% of the total project cost for PPP Concession availability payment type projects to about 30% for volume-based projects (Standard & Poor, 2015). In volume-based contracts, volume (demand) risk is transferred to the private partner. In these types of PPPs, the public partner receives a payment upfront and/or overtime in exchange for allowing the private partner to operate and collect the capital project revenues over the contract term. Funding for this PPP Concession type comes from user fees or tolls, and the private partner assumes most of the operating and volume risk. For availability payment projects, the government transfers construction and operation risks but retains the risk of demand. In that case, the public partner's annual payments are for making the facility available for use, regardless of volume or amount of revenue from the project (Standard & Poor, 2015). S&P may treat the governments PPP obligation as debt, as a contingent liability, or neither based on the revenue source used to pay the PPP obligation and whether S&P consider the public partner's debt obligation as financed by tax-backed revenue (General Fund, appropriations, and Special Revenue Fund). S&P determines the portion of PPP Concession financing that involves public partner debt, and the extent of the debt impact is based on the type of payments (milestone or availability) and the Net Present Value of the payments (S&P). If S&P determines that revenue to be used to repay the obligation is tax-backed, they will include the obligation as tax-backed debt. If the revenue is used to repay the obligations are from an Enterprise Fund, or a nontax-backed revenue source, such as toll revenue or grant anticipation revenue bonds paid from federal funds, the agency does not include the obligation as tax-supported debt or a contingency liability.

A PPP Concession contract with availability payments has features of the contracting arrangement that make the financing debt-like since the public partner enters into a long-term contract to pay. In most cases, the public partner payment obligations are fixed payment commitments, with penalty or termination payments for private partner performance issues. Frequently the public partner makes the payment obligations from the same revenue sources as traditional tax-exempt debt. This financing arrangement is similar to debt, because the payments fund capital improvements and because the public partner owns the infrastructure.

In deciding the amount of debt to include in debt statements, S&P evaluates milestone, and payment obligations independently (Standard & Poor, 2015). Milestone payments are made when a project construction milestone identified in the contract is reached and occurs before the capital infrastructure is available for use. Milestone payments are treated as debt and added to the PPP financial close (Standard & Poor, 2015). Availability payments include a fixed part that represents both the capital part of the project debt issued by the partner and the equity partner's contribution and a variable part that represents life cycle operations and maintenance expenses. Adding the total future annual payments represents a comprehensive forecast of the public partner's total obligation over the project life cycle (Standard & Poor, 2015). Operation and Maintenance expense is separated from the availability payments. S&P adds availability payments as a debt-like obligation on delivery of the infrastructure (Standard & Poor, 2015). S&P discounts future payments to the net present value of the principal component of the PPP payment. Because of such subtle nuances, the PPP project procurement process must be open and transparent.

## 6.10 Role of Communication in Transparency During PPP Procurement Process

### *6.10.1 Public Participation and Disclosure*

This section describes the role of two-way communication in the PPP project procurement process to provide capital projects finance transparency. Transparency is a critical success factor for positive PPP contracting outcomes. Thus, a transparent and efficient PPP project procurement process (Liu et al., 2013; Osei-Kyei & Chan, 2015) is both essential and required as elements needed to ensure a successful outcome. The PPP procurement process is complicated because of bundling the phases of the capital project and the long-term nature of the PPP contract. A transparent, efficient, and accountable procurement system with an open public communication channel helps to provide for capital project transparency (Liu et al., 2013) and is a significant factor in promoting a stable economic environment for the PPP implementation.

In a market testing phase of the procurement process (if market testing is used), the capacity and interests of the market to finance and deliver the PPP is determined. At this point, the communication feedback regarding contract requirements may result in a revision of the bid specifications. The communication feedback may be either formal or informal through pre-bid discussion (Liu et al., 2013). During the pre-award phase, the communication channels should consist of an open, interactive procurement process with continuing dialogue with the relevant participants (Liu et al., 2013). Ongoing communication channels between the private partner and the public partner are critical to ensuring each partner's requirements and needs are understood and met and utilized in proactively identifying and addressing potential problems before they occur (Liu et al., 2013). In this way, the contract is completed efficiently and effectively. Also, ongoing feedback on the adequacy and efficiency of capital project processes, the availability of ex-post evaluation and auditing, and also helps capital project transparency (Liu et al., 2013).

It is essential to have ongoing, open, two-way communication between the public and private partners in order to have successful contract outcomes (on-time and on-budget). This open, two-way communication is especially true that the private sector to have a clear understanding of the government's procurement policies and regulations. However, it is also true that the public sector understands just what the private partner can and cannot deliver in terms of financing and project construction delivery. Ongoing, open, two-way communication is especially important because of the shared authority between the public and private partners in financing and delivering the capital project Thus, it is crucial in the procurement process, and especially in negotiating the PPP contract, that the authority and responsibility of each partner be well-defined and communicated (Cheung, Chang, & Kajewski, 2012). To achieve such a level of understanding, it is wise for each party a Customer Relationship Manager to keep communications channels clear and ensure there are no miscommunications. Compared to traditional procurement, where the procedures and timing for communicating are comparatively clear and structured, the scope and depth for dialogue in PPP procurement differ because of the high level of uncertainty due both the contract bundling and long contract periods.

Another major communication issue is the level of commitment of each partner to the partnership and the project. The level of commitment to the success of the project is directly related to the overall quality of the leadership's clarity and understanding of the PPP. It is also related to the management of the relationship of the partners (via appointed Customer Relationship Manager) and their level of trust. Thus, the level of commitment of the capital project PPP partners impacts the quality of the capital project financing and delivery.

The inclusion of multiple parties leads to a discussion about the contract from different perspectives, which heightens the need for clear and effective communication (Liu et al., 2013).

The level of commitment of each partner is especially important since there is a higher probability that the need for contract renegotiation may arise because of the long length of the PPP contract period. Therefore, there is a greater reliance on well-managed PPP relationships, especially at senior organizational levels, to maintain a robust contractual relationship (Cheung et al., 2012; Zou, Kumaraswamy, Chung, & Wong, 2014). The quality of the management of the relationship of the partners in the PPP partnership is a pivotal contributor to the success of the PPP project (Zou et al., 2014). The strong partnership relationship cannot develop (Zou et al., 2014) without the commitment of the top levels of each partner because they decide the allocation of resources. One way that senior management can communicate their commitment is through the use of a policy statement, such as the case with Mauritius.

In addition to the level of commitment, an essential aspect of communication is feedback on the level of accountability in the PPP procurement process. Not having a system of post-project auditing is an obstacle to closing the communication feedback loop and to the ability to demonstrate accountability to stakeholders (Liu et al., 2013). A challenge in post-auditing is in maintaining a balance between an open, efficient, and effective public procurement process and strict adherence to bureaucratic rules and regulations. A system of continuous self-evaluation, the use of performance standards, coupled with a system of post-auditing, helps to ensure continuous improvement of the procurement process.

In choosing a PPP as a policy option to finance and deliver a capital infrastructure project, the public partner is acting as both a contract partner and as a managing authority (Liu et al., 2013) but in a different way than in a more traditional capital project financing and delivery because of the PPP contract bundling. The public partner's communication skills (unless they are enhanced by way of skilled Customer Relationship Managers by both parties) are directly related to its institutional dimensions, that is, capital management and budget processes and, in particular, its procurement skills and expertise in structuring and implementing the PPP procurement process.

PPPs involve building and managing contract relationships. The relationship relies on cooperation, trust, and teamwork (Olatunji, Olusola, Oluwatosin, & Rufus, 2016). Trust involves confidence in the reliability of a person or system. It entails reliance on the integrity or character of a person or thing (Olatunji et al., 2016). Trust is an essential characteristic of productive organizations and is the basis for commitment to the partnership. This commitment is the basis for administering contracts, extraordinarily complex contracts such as PPPs, and achieving long-term organizational policy goals.

As described in Chapters 1 and 2, Mauritius Economic Agenda for the New Millennium spells out its strategic policy goals. The government's guiding principle is to invest massively in education, training, and information technology, as well as in capital infrastructure and the environment, to transform the county to be fully integrated into the new global economic environment and reduce the budget deficit to a sustainable level (https://finance.gov.Mauritius) Major programs to improve the quality and effectiveness of public expenditures are implemented through the use of the appropriate policy. Mauritius has also developed its institutional and legal framework to encourage the private sector to play a more significant role in procuring and financing capital infrastructure projects and services in the public sector through a well-designed PPP (Mauritius PPP Policy Statement, 2003).

## 6.11 Infrastructure Finance Policy Implementation – the Case of Mauritius

This section uses Mauritius as an example to describe the relationship between the Infrastructure Finance Policy, capital improvements plan, the capital budget, capital project financing, and long-term benefit/risk distribution from PPPs. It discusses the need to have the pieces fit together into a unified framework with successful outcomes that meets the needs of both partners.

The relationship between Infrastructure Finance Policy and its implementation through the capital improvements plan, the capital budget, and to the capital project financing is dependent on the political, institutional, and legal dimensions, described in Chapter 3. The public partner's political commitment, implemented through policies, laws, and regulations (the legal dimension) and the consistent implementation and application of policies (public institution commitment), such as Infrastructure Finance Policy, are critical basis to the efficient and effective use of PPPs as an Infrastructure Finance Policy option. Mauritius' Infrastructure Finance Policy and its implementation is described next and is expanded on in Chapter 8.

### *6.11.1 Mauritius Infrastructure Finance Policy*

In use of the private sector as an option to finance and delivery capital projects, the Mauritius Infrastructure Finance Policy is the basis for awarding Concession PPP. The policy is implemented based on Mauritius articulated principles, that is, the need for the private sector to be significantly involved in the implementation of public services, as described in Chapter 2.

### *6.11.2 Mauritius Capital Improvements Planning Process Example*

The Capital Improvements Planning process in Mauritius involves the use of a Capital Improvements Project Plan Committee to ensure that capital projects submitted by individual agencies and selected for funding are implemented on time and on budget. Mauritius capital improvement plan includes a list of multi-year capital projects in rank order. The criteria for capital projects ranking within the plan includes government priorities, funding availability, and national sector strategies.

### *6.11.3 Mauritius Capital Budget*

The Mauritius Capital Budget describes the process for how the capital projects are prioritized in the Budget Document and the method used for systematic selection. The Capital Projects are listed based on the strategic objectives and priorities.

### *6.11.4 Mauritius Capital Project Financing*

Mauritius uses a Public Sector Investment Program which lays out the Five-Year Capital Infrastructure Investment Plan based on the Strategic Plan.

### *6.11.5 Mauritius Capital Projects Monitoring*

Mauritius monitors capital projects performance through a Project Planning and Monitoring Unit. The Unit manages and monitors capital project implementation.

## 6.12 Summary

This chapter summarizes the issues at different stages in Infrastructure Finance Policy implementation and the need to establish best practices and evaluate the policy throughout the Infrastructure Finance Policy implementation cycle. It discussed the importance of a strategic perspective on Infrastructure Finance Policy design and implementation to promote economic growth and development specific to the country in order to provide the basis for preserving macroeconomic stability (Rajaram et al., 2014). Policy-based financing then guides the process of infrastructure financing and delivery.

This chapter discusses the government's ability to finance new capital infrastructure projects as being dependent on the fiscal condition of the government and its ability to reallocate resources to finance needed capital projects. The evaluation of nontraditional financing options such as PPPs to improve the efficiency of public spending results in more efficient resource allocation. In order to improve *allocative efficiency*, the essential elements must be in place to minimize risks, be achievable in a lower-capacity context, and provide an effective systemic process for managing capital infrastructure financing and delivery (Rajaram et al., 2014).

Chapter 7

# Best Practices in PPP Policy Choice Based on Infrastructure Finance Policy and Implementation

## 7.1 Infrastructure Finance Policy and Implementation Best Practices

This chapter begins with the use of *best practices* in Infrastructure Finance Policy implementation and evaluation when considering whether to utilize PPPs in capital infrastructure projects financing and delivery. The experience and context when choosing PPPs as an infrastructure finance and delivery policy option are different in each country, depending on its political, legal, financial, and institutional dimensions. Also, the prior experience with and the length of time using finance and delivery options other than traditional funding of capital projects have an impact on the country's ability to successfully formulate and implement the use of PPPs as an Infrastructure Finance Policy option. Thus, best practices for one country may be different from another country because of differences in policy options, as well as skills in successfully financing and delivering capital infrastructure through the use of PPPs. However, national and subnational governments can establish Infrastructure Finance Policy implementation benchmarks for comparison; for example, how do their successful PPP financed and delivered capital projects outcomes compare year over year? Furthermore, it is difficult for emerging economies, such as Albania, in the short run, to select and apply benchmarks given their high public debt levels, limited economic diversification, and high exposure to external and internal risks. For emerging economies, it may be more advantageous to (1) select a small number of key performance measures to benchmark, (2) compare year over year, and (3) adjust as necessary before adopting a best practice. In the early stages of PPP in the context of Infrastructure Finance Policy formulation and implementation, it is best to learn from the past experiences of other national and subnational governments, Then, over time, develop relevant key performance measures and practices as the government becomes more experienced in choosing alternative financing and delivery policy options such as PPPs.

**Public-Private Partnerships, Capital Infrastructure Project Investments and Infrastructure Finance, 195–203**

**doi:10.1108/978-1-83909-654-920201008**

The Infrastructure Finance Policy is the government's formal written strategic policy that guides the long-term Infrastructure Finance Policy planning and implementation phase of long-term capital improvements planning. Infrastructure Finance Policy is the basis for identifying potential financing sources such as PPPs (Beckett-Camarata, 2019). Mauritius initiated its Infrastructure Finance Policy in 2002, and its success established PPPs as a positive and viable policy option for private sector involvement in the financing and delivery of capital infrastructure. The policy provided the basis for subsequent PPP legislation and a joint task force to develop the legal and organizational framework for PPP selection as a financing and delivery option.

### *7.1.1 Examples of Infrastructure Finance Policy and Implementation Best Practice*

#### 7.1.1.1 Political Stability as Best Practice

Political stability is an essential factor and precondition in the successful design and implementation of Infrastructure Finance Policy to support the use of PPPs. For politically stable countries, such as Mauritius, the prime minister or his/her equivalent establishes good working relationships with their ministries in designing the government's Infrastructure Finance Policy and strategic priorities.

As part of the process, the Mauritius Ministry of Finance and Economic Development works closely with line ministries in implementing policy, such as Infrastructure Finance Policy. The Procurement Policy Office in the Mauritius Ministry of Finance and Economic Development is responsible for overseeing and managing PPPs in the country.

#### 7.1.1.2 Laws to Support PPP as Best Practice

A country's PPP and procurement legislation establishes the legal framework which supports a PPP as an infrastructure financing and delivery policy option. The legislation provides the legal basis for private sector participation policy in the government's capital project development, financing, and operation. Legislation, as described in Chapter 2, is critical because it spells out (1) the range and type of capital projects that the government supports, (2) the process for PPP contract award, and (3) which agency or agencies (or ministries) have responsibility for implementation of PPP projects.

### *7.1.2 Mauritius PPP Laws as Best Practice to Support PPP*

The Public-Private Partnership Act of 2004 defines PPPs and describes oversight of PPPs through the PPP Act of 2004, as amended in 2008. When an issue arises that is not covered in the Act, the Public Procurement Act of 2006 and the Public Procurement Act of 2008 are referred to the Build-Operate-Transfer (BOT) Projects Bill, 2016 (BOTPB) (applies in cases of PPP that involve new construction).

Mauritius is an example of a country with a unified and Comprehensive Capital Management and Budgeting framework which supports Infrastructure Finance Policy implementation. The framework forms the basis for selecting the best option for financing and delivery of infrastructure capital projects. The system must be based on a clear and consistent political commitment, at the policy level, to private sector involvement in financing and delivery of capital infrastructure in order to have the basis for successful structuring of nontraditional financing and delivery, such as PPPs. This unified and comprehensive system for policy implementation must be supported by an adequate legal framework, appropriate to the specific government, that consists of laws and regulations to support the use of PPP for capital infrastructure project financing and delivery.

As noted in Chapter 2, judges at the national and subnational levels, in Common Law countries such as the United States, play a more active role in contract PPP dispute decisions. Civil law countries such as Albania base their legal decisions on statutes, with little scope for judicial input in settling PPP disputes in these countries. However, regardless of the type of law in a country, a clear, consistent, and stable political and legal framework underpinning PPP as a policy option and choice is still necessary for Public-Private Partnerships to succeed.

## 7.2 Infrastructure Finance Policy and Capital Management and Budgeting Best Practices

As described in Chapter 6, Infrastructure Finance Policy, along with other policies such as Asset Management Policy and Debt Management Policy, plays a vital role as the basis for unified and comprehensive capital management and budgeting system. These policies provide standardization of capital infrastructure financing and delivery options, including the use of PPPs and their selection as a policy option, and serve as a basis for efficient and effective financing decisions. The use of these micro-level financial policies is especially important in shaping the capital planning and budgeting process because of the complexity of the planning and decision-making process and the impact that long-term financing has on current and future resource allocation decisions. With such strategic infrastructure finance policies in place, as in Mauritius, such policies help to provide the system in which to shape unified, comprehensive capital management and budgeting decision support process. This unified, systematic capital management and the budget process will, in turn, have a long-term, positive impact on managing capital costs and the ways that capital costs impact the operating budget.

### *7.2.1 Capital Management and Budgeting System as a Best Practice*

A collaborative decision-making process, as part of unified and systematic capital management and budgeting system, typically involves an extensive formal communication system. At the strategic level, the Mauritius Ministry of Finance and Economic Development or similar office works closely with executive officials of line agencies in identifying potential capital projects that will achieve strategic priorities. The officials typically serve as the Prime Minister, Governor, or similar Chief Executive and participate in setting strategic priorities as described in Political Stability as Best Practice (see Political Stability as Best Practice, p. 184). The Ministry of Finance and Economic Development in Mauritius, for example, reviews the proposed capital projects for technical merit and then meets with chief executives of line agencies to narrow down the requests based on overall strategic priorities, organizational goals, and the government's fiscal condition.

In some national and subnational governments, a packet of Decision or Financing Decision Support materials is prepared as part of the Capital Management and Budget process to support the capital project request. The decision or financing support materials (also can be called Business Case or Project Request) includes documentation and financial analyses to support the capital project request. An example of documentation is a statement of compliance with mandated architectural standards or other similar standards. Also included in Decision Support documentation is a description of the relationship of the proposed capital project to (1) the Infrastructure Finance policy, (2) Strategic Policy Priorities, (3) cost-benefit analysis, and (4) Risk Assessment. An Executive Summary of the Decision Support Package provides data and other pertinent information to those at the Ministry or similar level, who make the final financing and delivery choice.

Separating a Capital Project into various phases and assessing each phase is a way to assist a government in determining which phases will require the most funding and how that information fits into each project funding and finance option decision, as well as identifying potential construction problems. For example, the government can delineate three capital project phases: (1) predesign, (2) design, and (3) construction. To ensure that the capital projects are adequately planned for during predesign and adequately implemented during the design phase, the government can provide analyses of the predesign phase and a design development phase. A Budget Evaluation Team may be used to review the capital project predesign phase and an analysis of the project's value engineering to ensure that overall technical issues and costs are considered and if overall materials and methods considered for the capital project to meet standards of value and quality (Government Accountability Office [GAO], 1998).

The PPP capital project is a bundling of rights, obligations, and risks which are priced and allocated between project partners. The final funding/financing arrangement is related to the specific contract design, construction, operation pricing, and allocation of risks (depending on the type of PPP and contract). In the Mauritius PPP financing structure, for example, the Procurement Policy Office in the Mauritius Ministry of Finance and Economic Development oversees PPP management. The Procurement Policy office reviews and analyzes the proposed projects and then meets with Ministry officials to narrow down the list of requested projects, based on the Infrastructure Finance Policy and strategic priorities. At the meetings, the Ministry reviews the requested projects in light of the government's strategic priorities and financing options based on the government's priorities.

The capital project requests selected are included in the Capital Improvements Plan (CIP). Through the CIP, the government can review and refine a capital project's scope and cost estimates. By refining the scope and cost estimates on an ongoing basis, the government can reduce project cost overruns. While cost estimates beyond the current fiscal year are preliminary, by refining the scope and cost estimates, decision-makers are provided with current capital project cost estimates. As the capital projects move closer to implementation through the Capital Budget, the project scope is refined to more closely reflect the updated project costs. The review and refinement of the project's scope and cost estimates can be conducted annually, at which time the project moves forward from year 5 to year 4, year 3 to year 2, and year 2 to year 1 (Capital Budget).

The capital budget process necessitates that the full estimated cost of a potential capital project be calculated and considered when the decision is made to include the project in the CIP. The estimated cost of the capital project needs to be considered in the financing decision because financing the project will require a commitment of resources, both current and future. The government can determine the budgetary impact of the decision by considering both the full current and future cost of the capital project. In that way, they maintain better control over short-term and long-term capital expenditures; identification of the full cost (short-term and long-term) of a capital project upfront provides added flexibility in selecting the best financing option.

Sound preliminary capital project cost estimates depend on useful data. A predesign application process is used by some governments to develop the cost estimates and the scope of work for a potential capital project before a final decision to commit resources to finance the project. The predesign application process is especially useful for potential capital projects that may have critical political and policy implications for a government. In the predesign application process, (1) the capital project is described, (2) the policy and demographic changes are identified, (3) the operating budget impact is estimated, and (4) a project cost plan including the project scope and schedule is delineated. The predesign application must also describe the relationship of the capital project to the government's strategic plan. Development of sound preliminary cost estimates early in the capital planning process results in minimal project scope and cost changes in later phases of a project, adding further strength to the process.

The establishment of clearly defined roles and responsibilities is a basis for the successful implementation of Infrastructure Finance Policy. The government's strategic planning process specifies the sectors and priorities for capital project selection and their financing and delivery. The use of a strategic planning process is important for the government to assess its internal and external environment, its strengths and weaknesses, and its current and future mandates that impact current and future operations. Based on this assessment, the organization identifies gaps. These gaps are part of the budget discussion process. Mission analysis identifies the resources needed to fulfill the organization's mission, including capital infrastructure. The organization's capital budget process then is guided at the strategic level by requirements. The organization's mission and goals are reviewed when performing the gap analysis. In this way, the analysis can include such alternatives as to the modification of an existing capital infrastructure as a financing and delivery option.

An appropriate level of review and approval, supported by financial, technical, and risk analyses, is a significant factor in making sound infrastructure financing and delivery decisions. A consistent and thorough review and approval framework, which is part of the unified and systematic capital management and budget process, and documented by data analytics, will result in more efficient and effective capital financing and delivery decisions, supported by complete information. The level of assessment in the review process is based on the size, complexity, and cost of the capital project, as well as the organization's prior experience with similar capital projects. Very costly capital projects, span an extended length of time or are fundamental to the organization's strategy or structure, will typically require more analysis, review, and approval levels that capital projects that cost less have shorter time frames or have less organization impact (GAO, 1998).

In selecting and ranking capital projects for inclusion in the CIP, preestablished criteria and ranking of proposed projects are used. For example, the Commonwealth of Virginia screens potential PPP capital infrastructure road projects against specific criteria in the Public-Private Transportation Act. The criteria are used to determine whether a project will (1) benefit from private sector innovation, (2) achieve the appropriate level of risk transfer, (3) determine if it has stakeholder support, and (4) fit well within the Infrastructure Finance Policy (The World Bank, 2013). Governments determine the best mix of capital projects by reviewing all proposed projects together with existing capital infrastructure. The proposed capital projects are ranked according to the specific criteria.

The selected capital projects are recorded in the CIP, which covers a 5, 6, or 10-year period. The CIP is updated annually or biennially. The identified capital projects ranked in priority order based on specific criteria help the organization to manage the organization's resources and its use of debt to finance capital projects. Capital Operation and Maintenance plans should also be considered in the Capital Improvements Planning process because of the need to balance the maintenance of existing capital infrastructure with identification of the need for new capital infrastructure. In this way, the decision-makers have complete information on infrastructure maintenance plans that must be incorporated with long-term CIPs in determining whether and when to construct a new capital infrastructure.

Many governments include all capital projects (those selected and those not selected) in their long-term CIP and align all the project requests with their strategic plan. They align each capital project with the capital infrastructure life cycle and strategic goals and objectives. By developing a long-term CIP, which considers the projects chosen and not chosen, the government can continue to systematically reassess the chosen capital project's scope and costs, which helps to reduce future cost overruns.

### *7.2.2 Mauritius Utility Scale Wind Farm Build-own-operate PPP Best Practice*

The Cure pipe Point Wind Farm is in the municipality of Cure pipe Point in Mauritius which is an example of a Wind Farm Energy Build-Own-Operate (BOO) PPP. The partners in the PPP are Suzlon Group and PAD Green/ Valum Holding Consortium as PPP private partners. The private partners in this PPP formed a Special Purpose Vehicle. The Central Electricity Board, Republic of Mauritius is the Public Partner (Republic of Mauritius Ministry of Renewable Energy and Public Utilities, 2012).

### *7.2.3 Financial Risk Reduction Best Practice*

Based on the Infrastructure Finance Policy, a government should identify capital infrastructure project financing from different sources such as tax and non-tax revenues, potential grants, long-term debt, and alternative financing sources such as PPPs. This identification of financing at a strategic level is essential to be able to specify the aggregated level of potential capital project financing (Srithongrung, 2019; Steiss, 2005).

As described in Chapter 6, innovative methods such as the use of Multi-Criteria Decision Analysis (MCDA), used in the early stage of CIP project selection, involve the systematic structuring of financial decisions based on multiple factors related to financing the capital project. The decision to propose the capital project is based on Infrastructure Finance Policy. The use of MCDA in the Infrastructure Finance Policy implementation decision support process can be useful when operating within a tight time frame. The process involves policy choices based on (1) selection of criteria to assess the policy choices and (2) weighing the capital projects against the criteria. The selection process includes experts both inside and outside the organization who can provide insights into the decision support process. The MCDA process has the potential for providing a micro-level, policy-based capital project selection system based on the government's policy goals (The World Bank, 2016).

### *7.2.4 Stakeholder Involvement as Best Practice*

This section describes the role, key issues, and the significant stakeholders in choosing to use a PPP to finance and deliver a capital project. Primary stakeholders include private partners, lenders, consultants, and citizens. It discusses the importance of having a complete understanding of the needs and requirements of each stakeholder. It discusses the need for reconciliation of stakeholder needs with the necessity to use appropriate and relevant assessment tools in choosing a PPP capital infrastructure financing and delivery option.

The levels of capital project review are based on the political and financial significance of the proposed capital projects as a general rule. Many governments have a Capital Improvements Committee, made up of critical internal and external stakeholders, which meet as needed to provide input into short-term and long-term capital project decisions. This stakeholder input then provides a basis for the selection of capital projects based on criteria and the allocation of funding and financing to the selected Capital Projects. The Minister of Finance and Economic Development or other Chief Executive does not usually become directly involved in the operational details of the capital project financing and delivery decisions unless the capital project is strategically significant or is extremely large and capital intensive.

### *7.2.5 Key Issues Involving the Use of Stakeholders*

Some reasons for including stakeholders in the infrastructure financing and delivery decision process are because of the resources that the private partner has and the potential for opposition by citizens to PPP financing and delivery (Jordan, 1990). The potential for citizen opposition, especially at the local government level, is the main reason why some argue for citizen stakeholder involvement in the financing and delivery process (Nederland & Klijn, 2019).

In some types of PPPs, and some capital budget and management systems, a vital issue is that the process of financing and delivering capital infrastructure does not allow for a great deal of stakeholder involvement (Nederland & Klijn, 2019) beyond input into the CIP project selection. This situation occurs because of the wide variety of government rules and processes, especially in the capital procurement phase, that restricts who is involved in the contracting process. Because PPP as an Infrastructure Finance Policy option is more complicated than traditional funding and delivery of capital infrastructure, the involvement of citizens, for example, may be restricted to capital improvements planning committees. After the capital project selection for financing and delivery, and during the selection phase of the contract procurement process, there is an interaction between the public and potential private partners but only to the extent of contract negotiation. The procurement process leaves little room for other stakeholders, such as citizens (Savas, 2000), to be involved. The nature of government contracts is such that once the contracts are awarded, there is little room for other stakeholder involvement (such as citizens) because of the need to achieve deadlines and performance targets (Nederland & Klijn, 2019). Also, much of the private partner information is proprietary.

Another issue that influences the use and level of stakeholder involvement is related to the government's internal management orientation (Skelcher, 2005; Nederland & Klijn, 2019). One of the critical concerns in the use of external stakeholders is contract flexibility, where the wording of the contract is followed based on the intent of the law rather than the letter of the law (DeVries & Yehoue, 2013). If contract problems arise, a flexible contract provides for smoother contract renegotiation to allow for the long-term viability of the project. In addition, flexible contracts can provide for more significant incentives for adapting the contract to allow for unanticipated events, which can create incentives for cooperative behavior (Athias & Saussier, 2010). A PPP contract that contains many tight performance measures and inflexible time schedules and penalties makes it challenging to include external stakeholders and thus may negatively impact the extent of stakeholder involvement (Nederland & Klijn, 2019).

Another issue that influences the use and level of stakeholder involvement is the relationship that either the public or private partners have with individual project stakeholders. A key part of that relationship is trust. The trust is based on the interaction of the public and private partners over time and into the broader capital project network surrounding the partnership (Klijn & Koppenjan, 2016). Trust is essential as a basis for the commitment of the partners to the successful completion of the project. When the level of trust is high, stakeholders will be more inclined to participate in the project, and the critical public and private stakeholders are more likely to encourage other stakeholder participation (Nederland & Klijn, 2019).

## 7.3 Summary

This section summarizes the establishment of best practices in the use of PPPs and the importance of stakeholder input into the policy implementation stage of the Infrastructure Finance Policy cycle.

While best practices for one country may be different from another country because of differences in those factors, successful financing and delivery of infrastructure through the use of innovative financing mechanisms, such as PPPs, can be achieved through the establishment of Infrastructure Finance Policy and setting implementation benchmarks for comparison. The question that the government needs to ask and to collect data on is: How do their successful PPP-financed and delivered capital projects compare year over year? They can compare significant factors such as (1) partnership trust; (2) project delivery time; (3) efficient execution; and (4) contract monitoring. It is difficult for emerging economies in the short run, such as Albania, to select and apply benchmarks given their high public debt levels, limited economic diversification, and high exposure to external and internal risks. In those cases, it may be more advantageous to select a small number of crucial policy implementation performance measures to benchmark, compare year over year, and adjust as necessary before selecting and adopting an appropriate best practice. In the early stages of PPP Infrastructure Finance Policy formulation and implementation, it is best to learn from the past experiences of other similar national and subnational governments and, over time, to develop key performance measures and practices as the government becomes more experienced when choosing PPP as a policy option.

Chapter 8

# Summary

This section summarizes the use of PPPs in Infrastructure Finance Policy decisions as a policy tool for the twenty-first century. It reiterates how governments can achieve successful capital infrastructure delivery outcomes with an infrastructure finance policy option of using PPPs to finance and deliver capital infrastructure through a robust institutional framework (political, legal, economic, and organization) to implement the policy.

This chapter summarizes the role of Infrastructure Finance Policy in the selection and use of PPPs as infrastructure finance and delivery option and provides examples of financing and delivery systems at the national and subnational levels. The chapter also recommends guidelines for laws and regulations so that policymakers can observe the specificity of those laws and regulations which are most effective in different legal contexts.

## 8.1 PPPs as an Infrastructure Finance Policy Option

Infrastructure Finance Policy is the formal strategic statement that guides capital improvement planning in identifying potential capital infrastructure project financing and delivery options such as PPPs. Integration of Infrastructure Finance Policy and use of PPP as a policy option implemented through a unified Capital Management and Budget system to manage PPP to achieve long-term policy goals. The Infrastructure Finance Policy should be implemented in the context of long-term capital infrastructure financing goals and the need for greater efficiency and effectiveness in financing and delivering public services. Governments can choose to use PPPs as one way to achieve greater efficiency and effectiveness in capital infrastructure financing and delivery. The financing and delivery of capital infrastructure projects are vital because capital infrastructure underpins the essential functions of government.

Governments, and especially small subnational governments and emerging economies, cannot afford to finance their infrastructure gaps solely through tax revenues and grants. The rationale for choosing PPPs as an Infrastructure Finance Policy option is that while governments must provide mandated core activities and services, they may have less specialized nontraditional infrastructure financing and delivery in-house expertise than the private partner, as in the case of New York

**Public-Private Partnerships, Capital Infrastructure Project Investments and Infrastructure Finance, 205–214**

**doi:10.1108/978-1-83909-654-920201009**

State. Choosing the policy option of a PPP for infrastructure finance and delivery requires more complex private sector involvement than traditional capital funding. Governments generally enter into PPP agreements in order to (1) finance and deliver infrastructure for which taxpayer resources may not be currently available, (2) reduce construction or service costs through private sector efficiencies, (3) control timing of expenditures, or (4) a combination of the previous three (DiNapoli, 2014).

The Infrastructure Finance Policy options of choosing a Public-Private Partnership are (1) to structure a more efficient and effective overall capital improvements planning, management, and budgeting system, (2) to deliver capital infrastructure projects on time and within capital budget, (3) to more effectively manage the use of long-term debt, (4) to create a better balance between traditional means of funding capital infrastructure (long-term debt, equity financing, and capital reserves), and (5) to provide the opportunity for more enhanced public value.

Understanding the role of public value is vital to understanding the principles which guide decision-making and to understand how the choice to use a PPP fits into an overall institutional dimension framework. Financing and delivering an infrastructure capital project through the use of a PPP as a policy option is an example of expressing a public value.

The Capital Improvement Plan is one way that public value, expressed through citizens, politicians, and translated by public managers, is articulated. Mauritius has an Infrastructure Finance Policy implemented through a unified and comprehensive capital management and budgeting system. The Capital Improvements Plan Committee ensures that the capital projects are assessed and ranked so that they are implemented on time and within budget. The Ministry of Finance and Economic Development Unit reviews capital projects for potential PPP financing.

In Albania, selected capital infrastructure projects are listed in the Capital Improvements Plan. Only capital infrastructure projects listed in the first year of the Capital Improvements Plan are budgeted. The projects are ranked based on political priorities, funding availability, and national sector strategies. Long-term debt financing, if managed, is an effective tool for paying for infrastructure capital projects because pay-as-you-go is rarely a viable option as the primary means of financing a capital project. A selection of infrastructure financing sources may include (1) general tax revenue; (2) revenue from other specific tax revenue sources; (3) user fees such as toll roads; (4) proceeds from bond sales (debt); (5) designated capital improvement fund; and (6) PPP financing. Another option is the use of long-term debt and the use of reserves. Governments face a delicate balance between long-term borrowing to build and maintain capital infrastructure and affording the debt repayment and debt service payments involved in financing a capital project. The argument for a government incurring long-term debt is that the public investment will lead to increases in government revenue.

## 8.2 Capital Management and Budgeting System

Since PPP is only one financing and delivery option for a capital project, it is crucial to consider the capital management and budget system and the context of the Infrastructure Finance Policy design and implementation. The political, economic, legal, and organization dimensions are shaped by and shape the Infrastructure Finance Policy.

It is essential to consider the context, especially the government's need to maintain economic stability and to balance the budget to be fiscally sustainable. The Infrastructure Finance Policy's implementation is dependent on a unified and comprehensive capital management and budget system and an efficient and effective system for evaluating the best method of financing and delivering a capital project. An economic analysis; a fiscal affordability assessment; an identification and allocation of potential risks; a comparative assessment with traditional procurement; an assessment of the market for potential investors; and an environmental impact assessment will aid in assessing the likelihood of effective decision outcomes based on the Infrastructure Finance Policy.

## 8.3 Choosing Public-Private Partnerships as an Infrastructure Finance Policy Option

Selecting a PPP (depending on the contract) for financing and delivery may result in higher costs than bond financing but may ultimately provide more significant benefit to citizens. However, a PPP chosen based on appropriate and Infrastructure Finance Policy and an optimally structured, unified, and comprehensive capital management and budgeting system may result in lower total infrastructure finance and delivery costs, including operation and maintenance. PPPs benefit citizens when the private partner can manage the capital infrastructure project risks in a manner that allows the projects to be financed and delivered more cost-effectively, thus offsetting any higher cost of private financing as compared to traditional infrastructure financing and delivery. PPP, however, is not always the best policy option for every capital infrastructure project, and a government must have a system and analytical capability in place to provide an assessment of whether PPP or traditional financing and delivery will provide more Value for the Money to citizens such as used in Mauritius. Each national and subnational government is different in terms of making the right policy choice in financing and delivering an infrastructure finance project. Each project differs in terms of the amount of risk transferred to the private partner and the extent of potential efficiency gains by choosing a Public-Private Partnership.

The policy choice to use PPPs as an Infrastructure Finance Policy option (depending on the form and contract) provides the opportunity for a government to pass capital infrastructure financing and delivery roles in capital improvements to the private partner while keeping the government's focus on retaining and improving core government services. Properly implemented, this approach can result in a lower capital outlay for the government and a more efficient and effective service to the citizen (Asian Development Bank, 2012). A government's track record of the soundness and consistency in the use of finance policies (including infrastructure finance policies) creates a standard for attracting private investment (Hammami, Ruhashyankko, & Yehoue, 2006). The sustainability of

PPP contractual relationships depends on the quality of the legal dimension (see Chapter 3), as well as other framework dimensions.

Infrastructure Finance Policy provides the basis for strategic identification of sufficient country-specific infrastructure financing and delivery options, instruments, and vehicles that broaden the financing objectives available for capital infrastructure projects. In turn, these finance and delivery options increase and diversify the investor base, which may lower the cost of capital infrastructure financing (OCED, 2015). The Infrastructure Finance Policy presents available financing options to promote a common understanding of infrastructure financing priorities. Implementation of the Infrastructure Finance Policy will also provide a basis for a risk-based implementation and monitoring framework to support financing and delivery mechanisms such as PPPs (OCED, 2015) (discussed in more detail in Chapter 2).

The extent to which a government organization contributes to efficiency depends to a considerable extent on its policies, such as its Infrastructure Finance Policy. Infrastructure Finance Policy is implemented through well-developed strategic capital infrastructure plans, such as presented in the Mauritius National Plan. Adequate capital infrastructure financing and delivery, environmental protection and economic development, improved standards of living, and increased employment opportunities are the outcomes of sound Infrastructure Finance Policy. Infrastructure Finance Policy implementation works best within a system that integrates it with other policies such as Debt Management Policy and Tax Revenue Policy. For example, governments determine the funds needed to finance infrastructure and how to allocate financing between the public and private sectors, in part, based on their debt policy, debt affordability, their ability to finance new capital infrastructure projects with debt, and their ability to finance capital projects through own-source tax revenue.

In deciding whether to finance and deliver a capital infrastructure project, investors will be ordinarily interested in the government's master plan, its capital improvements plan, its Infrastructure Finance Policy, and its history of involvement with the private sector in financing and delivering capital projects. Each capital infrastructure project and its proposed funding within the capital improvements plan is considered on its own merits. Sound, well-structured, and implemented infrastructure finance policy is critical for achieving a balance between public and private financing and maintaining long-term debt limits.

The Infrastructure Finance Policy guides the implementation of the Capital Improvement Plan and is the basis for choosing and implementing financing options through the Capital Budget. Having private sector involvement in infrastructure financing and delivery requires an articulated and stable government investment environment. It provides the basis for the government's approach to its long-term infrastructure financing and delivery needs through the capital budget. The stability and commitment of political leadership are essential in implementing the Infrastructure Finance Policy. Mauritius' National Development Plan, implemented within a stable political environment, provides the basis for its multi-year capital investment and infrastructures the need for the public sector to be involved.

Based on the Infrastructure Finance Policy, the government can determine the form of financing and delivery, factoring in constraints, risks, policy goals, and unique requirements and characteristics of the government. Different types of risks are involved in the financing and delivery of infrastructure capital projects such as Financial Risk, Commercial Risk, Country Institutional Risk, and Cyber Risk. Financial risk is especially significant because it involves potential increased capital infrastructure project costs. The government should identify the total risks and balance the risk and cost between the government and the private partner in contract negotiations. An example of an appropriate risk balance appears in Table 1.1 by (1) the type of risk nature of the risk and (2) party bearing the risk.

Financial risk management and mitigation for PPPs is different from other capital infrastructure project financing and delivery financial risk management methods because of the increased complexity introduced by the PPP private partner's broader scope and involvement in all phases of the capital infrastructure project as compared to traditional government financing methods. Equally important is the fact that the government should identify potential risks during the pre-award phase of the PPP contract to ensure that they consider the most cost-effective measures in the contract negotiations before the contract award.

## 8.4 Institutional Framework for PPP

Infrastructure Finance Policy is an instrument to achieve long-term national and subnational objectives. There is a range of institutional systems in place to implement the policy. Governments need a clear delineation of institutional boundaries. This delineation of institutional boundaries is important because analysis of the optimum financing and delivery option requires attention to the rules of the game governing organizational boundaries for transactions such as infrastructure financing and delivery through public and private partnerships.

The institutional framework, e.g., the political, legal, economic, and organization, must be taken into consideration and incorporated into a cohesive whole, especially considering the magnitude of the additional coordination costs they generate (Baker, 2016). Creating and maintaining the quality, capability, and capacity of leadership of these institutional dimensions is key to government efficiency and control over transaction costs (Baker, 2016). Institutional framework quality impacts the level of private investment in PPP (Wang, Liu, Xiong, & Zhou, 2018) and affects PPP transaction cost.

The political, legal, economic, and organizational dimensions shape public value. Specifically, (1) the political dimension shapes a government's macro-policies through voting, representation, and political responsiveness; (2) the legal dimension upholds individual rights, procedural due process, and fairness; and (3) the organizational dimension values administrative efficiency. This dimension values technical rationality and belief in technological progress. The economic dimension emphasizes the most efficient or cost-effective means of achieving an end, without attention to the value of the end. New York State, for example, communicates its public value primarily through its laws and in the State's

Executive Budget, specifically in articulating the use of PPP Design-Build financing and delivery to achieve projects delivered on a guaranteed or accelerated schedule. The State has limited debt capacity.

The political, economic, legal, and organization dimensions influence Infrastructure Finance Policy implementation. The political dimension is important because it influences the stability of a government and its policies, and subsequently, the level of private sector interest such as the involvement of the private sector in government production and distribution, both important to sound, effective Infrastructure Finance Policy design. An example is Albania, where the transaction costs are high due to noninclusive policy making by the political leadership. The economic dimension is essential because it can influence PPP use due to high outstanding debt, as we see in many countries such as Albania, Mauritius, and New York State. The legal dimension is essential because respect for the rule of law (contract management) is an essential foundation for the success of PPPs. The law dimension is the basis for confidence in and abiding in the rules and norms of society. The quality of contract enforcement and the courts define this dimension. The judicial system in Albania has limited accountability, a backlog of cases, and widespread corruption, all of which negatively impact investor confidence in investing in PPP. The legal dimensions in other governments such as Mauritius and the States of New York and Indiana articulate a healthy and transparent legal environment that supports PPP laws. There are stable government organizational dimensions in New York State, Indiana, and Mauritius and improving organizational effectiveness in Albania's strategic planning and budgeting systems within its administrative dimension.

Transaction costs in connection with coordinating the relationships between the policy actors in each dimension and policy outcomes in a market exchange, such as the use of a PPP, involve bounded rationality in understanding Infrastructure Finance Policy options. Furthermore, asymmetric information may hinder the implementation of rules of the game in complex capital infrastructure financing and delivery. Coordinating the different policies and policy actors' policy interpretations are challenges in determining and managing the resulting transaction costs and in evaluating the efficiency and effectiveness of policy alternatives and the government's ultimate policy choice. An ineffective dimension framework may weaken the policy option to use PPPs because the interests of the private sector are not protected, such as the case of Albania, and a robust, useful institutional framework encourages inclusive contractual arrangements despite environmental risk and uncertainty, such as the case with Mauritius. Issues involving PPP contract uncertainty and risk and their impact on transaction costs are challenging to identify. For example, one of the partners can influence the exchange transaction after an unforeseen event, such as a natural disaster was in the case of Albania. Another excellent example of the effective management of contract risk and uncertainty is the use of a flexible contract in the Cure Pipe Wind Farm PPP contract because of a lack of wind data availability. The contract used tariff-based bidding based on normative wind speed with adjustment for wind speed, adjusted after 2 years based on average wind speed during that time.

The transaction costs of a PPP capital infrastructure project ultimately impact the cost of financing and delivery of the capital infrastructure project. The transaction cost depends on the capability and capacity of the PPP partners. Transaction cost also includes the level of risk and complexity of the PPP. Economic efficiency is depending on an institution's policy and implementation capacity and capability, especially as it pertains to PPP contract expertise. This situation is especially true concerning assessing the costs and benefits of financing a capital project which provides a decision rule for choosing a policy alternative. Table 2.2 provides an example of a Wind Farm Feasibility analysis using cost-benefit analysis.

## 8.5 Benefits of PPPs as an Infrastructure Finance Policy Option

Benefits from the use of PPPs infrastructure finance and delivery option based on the Infrastructure Finance Policy are the overall quality of infrastructure financing and delivery outcomes and their creation of positive public value. While the government may not have complete information on all the costs in a PPP, it also does not necessarily know all financial liabilities in a traditional capital project arrangement because traditional capital project arrangements procured in phases. In a PPP, a government has a more definite sense of its financial responsibility because the private partner bundles the phases, and the costs generally fixed. If additional financing is required to complete construction, the private partner is typically required to make up the shortfall, depending on the contract.

At the time a capital infrastructure project is selected for financing, regular monitoring of the capital and operating budgets is critical in ensuring that the projects are implemented as appropriated through the budget process. Several issues must be considered, such as Hard Operating Budget Constraints: External Balanced Budget Rules and Changes in International Accounting Standards impacting the recording of contingent liabilities. Also, public managers face conflicting priorities. Under a hard budget constraint, some governments may have an increased incentive to use some types of PPP financing and delivery arrangement. Debt levels also play an essential role in the decision to use PPP for financing and delivering a capital project. Because PPPs obligate the government to pay future costs in connection with the timing of financing capital projects, the assessment of contingent liabilities is vital in the decision to finance and delivery of a capital infrastructure project. The PPP risk is the contingent financial risk arising from the PPP contract.

The government's capacity to finance new capital infrastructure projects depends on the financial condition of the government. Part of that process involves the ability to assess nontraditional financing options; however, the essential elements must be in place to minimize the government's total risk. As part of the process of reducing risk, the government should conduct multi-year revenue and expenditure forecasting based on their financial and debt management policies. The multi-year revenue forecasts are the basis for determining the amounts available for financing long-term and short-term operations. Such forecasts, in conjunction with debt affordability analysis, are critical for analyzing all governmental and proprietary funds. Multi-year forecasting and Infrastructure Finance Policy are essential tools in long-term fiscal sustainability.

Flexibility in Infrastructure Project Design in Contract Negotiation is crucial, as we see from the Cure Pipe Wind Farm PPP. It is also essential to have ongoing, open, and two-way communication between the public and private partners to have successful contract outcomes. The communication and level of commitment and quality level of the management of the PPP relationship is a pivotal contributor to the success of the project. Also, feedback on the level of accountability in the PPP procurement process is critical.

Examples of Infrastructure Finance Policy implementation at the national government level. This section provides examples of the implementation of innovative capital infrastructure projects PPPs, using examples of systems such as the National Government of Mauritius and Subnational New York State government.

## 8.6 Infrastructure Finance Policy Implementation—The Case of Mauritius

### *8.6.1 Example of Infrastructure Finance Policy Best Practice*

The Infrastructure Finance Policy is the government's formal written strategic policy that guides the Infrastructure Finance Policy planning and implementation phase of long-term capital improvements planning. Infrastructure Finance Policy is the basis for identifying potential financing sources such as PPPs (Beckett-Camarata, 2019). The Mauritius Infrastructure Finance Policy established PPPs as an option for private sector involvement in the financing and delivery of infrastructure and other capital infrastructures. The policy provided the basis for subsequent PPP legislation and a joint task force to develop the legal and organizational framework.

The relationship between the Infrastructure Finance Policy and its implementation through the capital improvements plan, the capital budget, and the capital project financing are dependent on the political, institutional, and legal dimensions. Mauritius, in the example case, has demonstrated its commitment to its Infrastructure Finance Policy through its political, legal, economic, and organizational dimensions and implemented through comprehensive and unified capital management and budget systems. The Mauritius Infrastructure Finance Policy is the basis for awarding Concession PPPs. An Investment Program supports the Infrastructure Finance Policy and lays out the 5-Year Infrastructure Investment Plan based on the strategic plan. The projects are managed and monitored through the Project Planning and Monitoring Unit.

Mauritius has a system of laws that support PPPs. The laws are relevant because they spell out the range and type of capital projects that the government supports, the process for the PPP contract award, and the agencies that have responsibility for implementing PPP projects. At the strategic level, the

Mauritius Ministry of Finance and Economic Development works closely with executive officials in line agencies in identifying potential capital projects that will achieve strategic priorities. The Ministry reviews the proposed capital projects for technical merit and then meets with the executives of the line agencies to narrow down the requests based on the overall strategic priorities, organizational goals, and the government's financial condition. Mauritius Utility-Scale Wind Farm Build-Own-Operate PPP is an excellent example of a capable PPP that created an innovative approach to identifying and assigning risk.

Political stability is an essential factor and precondition in the successful design and implementation of an Infrastructure Finance Policy that supports PPPs as a policy option. For politically stable countries, such as Mauritius, the prime minister or his/her equivalent establishes good working relationships with their ministries in designing the government's infrastructure Finance Policy and strategic priorities. As part of the process, the Ministry of Finance and Economic Development works closely with line ministries in implementing policy, such as Infrastructure Finance Policy. The Mauritius Procurement Policy Office in the Ministry of Finance and Economic Development is responsible for overseeing and managing PPPs in the country.

### *8.6.2 Examples of Laws which Support PPPs*

It is also vital that laws be clear, transparent, and enforced to ensure private investment stability, and government institutions align with the existing law. PPPs may be especially appropriate for (1) high-risk infrastructure with large, (2) long-term revenue streams that are difficult for governments to fund, where there are issues with government capital workforces, or (3) where the need for upfront financing is not immediately available to the government.

Laws have been enacted in countries to provide specific legislation that stipulates the legal basis for PPP contracts. New York State has authorized certain state agencies to enter into the Design-Build PPP contracts for physical capital infrastructure. Mauritius uses the legal term Concession and has a stand-alone PPP law. Mauritius also has two sets of systems for PPP laws and has an extensive framework designing and implementing Infrastructure Finance Policy. Indiana law defines PPP as a BOT agreement, and the Indiana Department of Transportation (INDOT) and the Indiana Financing Authority (IFA) have legislative authority to procure projects. New York State, Indiana, and Mauritius have a stable political, economic, legal, and organization dimension framework. Albania lacks a coherent dimension framework that translates Infrastructure Finance Policy into unified and comprehensive capital management and budgeting system for financing and delivering capital infrastructure.

A country's legal system is an essential foundation of PPP. Countries follow either a common law or civil law system. Common law systems include constitution or codified laws written and unwritten, and judicial decisions are binding but decisions can be overturned, and there is extensive freedom of contract with few provisions implied in the contract by law. Everything is allowed that is not expressly prohibited by law—examples of common law: New York State.

Civil law systems follow a codified system of law that includes a written constitution based on specific codes; only legislative enactments are considered binding; writings of legal scholars can influence the courts; and courts have specific jurisdiction regarding codes and their interpretation, for example, the Albania legal system. Mauritius has a hybrid legal system. Relying on laws alone in civil law countries can be difficult because rules are often ambiguous, and it is not always clear what specific terms mean. In civil law countries, the contract is generally enforced by the administrative courts. The United States and other common law countries have greater flexibility in granting different types of security over infrastructures, which is a basis for funding arrangements through BOTs, for example.

# Chapter 9

# Infrastructure Finance Policy Design and Implementation Strengths and Limitations

This section will review Infrastructure Finance Policy Design and Implementation gaps and reasons for the mismatch. It will identify and describe dimensions that can cause Infrastructure Finance Policy gaps between policy design and implementation, such as inadequate institutional dimensions (political, legal, organizational) (Cuttaree, 2008).

A government policy objective in implementing Infrastructure Finance Policy is that a portion of its infrastructure financing should come from the use of Public-Private Partnerships as we see to varying degrees in Albania and Mauritius.

## 9.1 Infrastructure Finance Policy Design and Implementation—The Case of Albania

This section uses Albania as an example to describe the gap between the Infrastructure Finance Policy design and its capital improvements plan, the capital budget, capital project financing, and long-term benefit/risk distribution from PPPs. It discusses the need to have the policy design and implementation fit together to support successful policy outcomes that meet the needs of both partners.

The relationship between Infrastructure finance policy design and its implementation through the capital improvements plan, the capital budget, and to the capital project financing is dependent on the political and legal dimensions, described in Chapter 3. The public partner's political commitment, implemented through policies, laws, and the consistent implementation and application of policies (organizational capacity and capability), such as Infrastructure Finance Policy, is critical to the efficient and effective adoption of PPPs as an infrastructure finance policy option. Albania's Infrastructure Finance Policy design and its implementation follow.

### *9.1.1 Albanian Infrastructure Finance Policy*

In Albania's use of the private sector as an option to finance and delivery capital projects, the Infrastructure Finance Policy as the basis for awarding PPP

**Public-Private Partnerships, Capital Infrastructure Project Investments and Infrastructure Finance, 215–223**

**doi:10.1108/978-1-83909-654-920201011**

Concession is implemented based on Albania's articulated principles of transparency, nondiscrimination, proportionality, efficiency, equal treatment, mutual recognition, and legal certainty, as described in Chapter 2.

In Albania, the government's Infrastructure Finance Policy is implemented primarily through the political system. There is still limited government legal and organizational capacity and capability and, as a result of the imbalance, undue political influence in implementing public policy (UN, 3/17). One example of the political pressure is that the government has produced overly optimistic revenue forecasts to support planned spending increases that have, in turn, negatively impacted capital financing (MoF, 2014; as cited in Beckett-Camarata, 2019). Political demands to justify and maintain growth in spending in the Operating Budget have negatively impacted financing capital infrastructure.

The guiding principles in Albania for Infrastructure Finance Policy implementation through PPPs (especially Service Concession contracts), (1) transparency, (2) nondiscrimination, (3) proportionality, (4) efficiency, (5) equal treatment, (6) mutual recognition, and (7) legal certainty, are clear. The evolving political values dimension and its undue influence in administrative decisions have hampered the ability of Infrastructure Finance Policy to guide capital management and budgeting and Albania's appropriate use of PPP for financing and constructing capital projects.

### *9.1.2 Political Dimension*

For emerging economies, such as Albania, political risk is especially an issue in Infrastructure Finance Policy implementation. As noted in Chapter 1, political and policy uncertainty are two of the main reasons for the uneven impact of the policy choice of PPPs on economic growth in some emerging economies (Baker, Khater, & Haddad, 2019).

In Albania, the government communicates Infrastructure Finance Policy as a Public Value primarily through the political values dimension. There is still limited government legal and organizational capacity and capability and, as a result of the imbalance, undue political influence (UN, 3/17). One example of the overemphasis on the political values dimension in articulating public values is that the government has produced overly optimistic revenue forecasts to support spending increases that have, in turn, negatively impacted capital financing (MoF, 2014; as cited in Beckett-Camarata, 2019). Political pressure to justify and maintain growth in spending in the Operating Budget has negatively impacted financing capital infrastructure. The Guiding Principles for implementing PPPs in Albania (especially Service Concession contracts) are that transparency, nondiscrimination, proportionality, efficiency, equal treatment, mutual recognition, and legal are clear. The evolving political values dimension and its undue influence in organizational decisions have hampered the ability of Infrastructure Finance Policy to guide capital management and budgeting and Albania's appropriate use of PPP for financing and constructing capital projects.

### *9.1.3 Inadequate Legal System for Enforcing Laws*

Albanian PPP law covers Concessions and is defined as a Private-Public Partnership agreement between the Contracting Authority and the economic operator. Albania's legal system is based on Civil Law. Albanian PPP law clearly defines the boundaries and scope of application of the concession legal framework. Under Civil Law, only legislative enactments are binding, and there is little opportunity for judicial law in civil, criminal, and commercial courts. The legislation defines PPPs, the sectors covered, responsible authorities, and private sector eligibility. The legislation limits the risk of a challenge to the validity of PPP contracts.

Civil law is the basis for Albania's legal system. The first Albanian Law on Concessions was adopted in 1995 and repealed with the adoption of the Concession Law of 2013. The strength of the Albanian PPP legislation and legal framework is that the law spells out the specific PPP law. There is a clear definition of the boundaries and scope of application of the concession legal framework. Under civil law, only legislative enactments are binding, and there is little opportunity for judge-made law in civil, criminal, and commercial courts. The legislation defines PPPs, the sectors covered, responsible authorities, and private sector eligibility. The legislation limits the risk of a challenge to the validity of PPP contracts.

The legal system in Albania has limited accountability, poor interinstitutional cooperation, a backlog of cases, and widespread corruption. Access to the legal system is held up by procedural obstacles such as low court capacity, high court fees, and long length of judicial procedures (Beckett-Camarata, 2018). There are inconsistent application and uneven enforcement of laws, which still present significant challenges to the quality of and adherence to the rule of law. Though judges' training and career management have improved, assessment of the judicial system reveals corruption, undue interference by the executive branch, limited transparency, and a growing backlog of cases.

### *9.1.4 Organization Dimension*

The Concession Treatment Unit is the PPP Unit established in the Ministry of Economic Development, Financial Services, and Corporate Affairs, in collaboration with the Central Tender Board (World Bank PPP Country Profile Mauritius). Division of Power between Different Public Authorities involved in PPP is clear and coordinated. The Central Tender Board has procurement responsibility, with formal PPP Contract approval from the Cabinet (Article 11, PPPA). Division of Power between Different Public Authorities involved in PPP is clear, coordinated, and spelled out in the Law (EBRD Legal Assessment ppp-ebrd.com, 2017).

### *9.1.5 Organization Capacity and Capability*

External evaluators such as the World Bank have noted that, while there have been improvements in policy implementation in Albania, such improvements in government effectiveness have been limited and even undermined by continuing weaknesses in the quality and integrity of public procurement processes and regulations and the inadequate use of merit-based hiring of qualified public administrators (Beckett-Camarata, 2018). This weakness, in turn, has impacted Albania's organizational capacity and capability and, in turn, the efficient and effective use of PPPs in Albania.

### *9.1.6 Monitoring*

There is also a need for increased capacity and capability in both the organization and legislative institutional dimensions to establish and systematically monitor the implementation of government policies, including Infrastructure Finance Policy, and consistently track progress toward meeting government objectives (SIGMA, 2001), including a cohesive capital planning and management.

## 9.2 Albanian Capital Improvements Planning Process Example—Strengths and Limitations

The Capital Improvements Planning process in Albania involves preparation of capital project requests by individual agencies and submission of the requests to the Ministry of Finance (MoF) (Beckett-Camarata, 2019). Albania's capital improvement plan includes a list of multi-year capital projects in rank order. The criteria for capital projects ranking within the plan include political priorities (the major priority), funding availability, and national sector strategies. As a result of excessive political involvement in the capital improvements planning process, however, the process is not consistently followed.

### *9.2.1 Albanian Capital Improvements Planning and Project Financing*

Before 2008, Albania's capital financing strategies involve sustained high rates of economic growth, averaging about 6.2% (World Bank, 2015), but the global financial crisis beginning in 2008 and the Eurozone crisis resulted in capital project financing using Commercial Loans (World Bank, 2015), which has resulted in unsustainably high levels of debt and has impaired its access to affordable financing. The Albanian Capital Improvements Plan includes both publicly funded projects and foreign-financed projects.

### *9.2.2 Albanian Capital Budget*

Revenue forecasting has been a challenge for implementing Albania's capital budget. Operating Budget cuts in Albania have negatively impacted the Operating Budget and required expenditures adjustments because of over-forecasted revenue. This, in turn, limited capital project financing options. Based on Albania's experience with capital project financing, capital expenditure targets are overly optimistic levels, despite a history of poor performance (Beckett-Camarata, 2019; PEFA, 2012). Capital expenditures are separated in the capital budget and it is clear that capital expenditures are inadequate for building and maintaining the country's infrastructure.

### *9.2.3 Albanian Capital Projects Monitoring*

Albania has recognized the importance of systematically monitoring capital projects and has implemented a new policy where contracting authorities are required to submit project performance data to the MoF and Economy. This new reporting policy should result in the availability of timely PPP project performance and updated data on performance risks.

### *9.2.4 Summary*

In emerging economies such as Albania, civil society is still growing. There is still limited government organizational capacity and capability and judicial independence and, as a result of the imbalance, undue political influence (unicef.org, 2017). Labor unions are powerless; both the authorities and private companies are typically hostile to organizing and collective bargaining efforts. Civil society outside Tirana is especially underdeveloped and is a critical issue in the ongoing EU in the integration process. The Albanian government has acknowledged the need to establish more inclusive policy making (United Nations and Government of Albania, 2017).

There is a lack of consistency in Albanian PPP policies that translate PPP laws into a unified capital budget financing system. Until the national government has such a unified system in place, government effectiveness can be assessed using broadly defined objectives and outcomes in various sectors of government PPP activity, such as periodic external evaluations, using benchmarks (Beckett-Camarata, 2018).

The Infrastructure Finance Policy should identify which types of capital projects are eligible to be included, for example, reconstruction of existing facilities, new facilities, and the acquisition of land. The policy also should state which budget the capital project expenses come from, i.e., operating or capital budget. The policy should state the available funding options that the government intends to use, including any operating surplus and fee revenue. The policy should also briefly spell out the debt limits and provide a reference to the broader government Debt Policy.

This section will review and discuss specific cases of Infrastructure Finance Policy design and implementation successes and the reasons for their success. It will identify factors that contribute to successful PPPs (such as organizational capacity and capability, appropriate PPP laws and legal system, planning and feasibility study, transparent and competitive procurement, consistent monitoring, and flexibility toward unpredicted events) (Cutaree, 2008).

## 9.3 Infrastructure Finance Policy Design and Implementation—The Case of Mauritius

In the case of Mauritius Infrastructure finance policy design and implementation, there is present a robust cohesive political, economic, legal, and government organization framework, primarily executive and legislative institutions, to systematically monitor government policies, including its Infrastructure Finance policy. Mauritius has an efficient and transparent legal environment that supports economic development and PPPs (The World Bank, 2019).

### *9.3.1 Mauritius Infrastructure Finance Policy*

The Mauritius Infrastructure Finance Policy is the basis for awarding Concession PPP. The policy is designed and implemented based on Mauritius articulated principles, that is, the need for the private sector to be significantly involved in the implementation of public services, as described in Chapter 2. In identifying the need for the private sector to be substantially involved in the implementation of public services, Mauritius is articulating a public value.

The government's Infrastructure Finance Policy is communicated as a Public Value primarily through both the economic (market) value dimension and the legal value dimensions. Because of Governmental budgetary constraints, the need for the private sector to be substantially involved in the implementation of public services (e.g., roads, public transport, hospitals, schools) is recognized as crucial to ensuring the delivery of better facilities faster and generally cheaper over the long term through risk-adjusted and whole life costs of a particular service (Mauritius NDP, 2004).

### *9.3.2 Political Dimension*

Mauritius is politically stable. The government is a stable, multiparty, parliamentary democracy. The government has shifting coalitions, which are a feature of its politics. The President is head of state, and the Prime Minister has full executive powers and heads the government (Indiapost.com, 2019). The Alliance Lepep won legislative elections held in December 2014, a coalition comprising the Militant Socialist Movement (MSM), the Mauritian Social Democrat Party (PMSD), and the Liberation Movement. The coalition secured a parliamentary majority (Indiapost, 2019).

### *9.3.3 Legal Dimension*

Mauritius defines PPP as an agreement between a contracting authority and a private party. Under the agreement, the private party performs a function on behalf of the contracting authority. The private partner receives a benefit for performing the function in the form of revenue or fees or some combination. The

Act does not apply to PPPs that include a construction phase. The BOT Act applies in that case.

Mauritius has a cohesive system of PPP laws and uses the legal term Concessions and, in the legal sense, has a stand-alone PPP law. Mauritius also has two sets of systems for PPP laws and Concessions independent of whether they regulate PPPs as a stand-alone system or whether in the broader context of their procurement law. Mauritius PPP legislative and legal framework consists of the Public-Private Partnership Policy Statement, 2003, and the Guidance Manual, which clearly explain specific PPP law. The legal framework consists of the Public-Private Partnership Act, 2004; the Build-Operate-Transfer Projects Bill, 2016; the Public Procurement Act, 2006; and PPP regulations, 2008.

### *9.3.4 Mauritius Capital Management and Budgeting Process*

#### 9.3.4.1 Capital Improvements Planning

Capital improvements planning, capital budgeting, and financial management in Mauritius are based on the Mauritius National Development Program. For example, the plan provides the basis for multi-year capital investment plans. In Section 14.4 of the Program, one of the critical planning objectives is to provide strategic guidance and context in the improvement and provision of new capital infrastructure to enable the planned capital infrastructure to be achieved and provide guidance for strengthening the institutional and legal framework (NDP, 2004, p. 4).

#### 9.3.4.2 Capital Management and Budgeting

A significant component of the Mauritius Infrastructure Finance Policy implementation is the use of Public-Private Partnerships at the capital improvements planning stage to bring forward projects for early implementation (Mauritius NDP, 2004). Legislation supports the strategy. In the National Development Program, Section 19.3.5 on Public-Private Partnerships further articulates the Infrastructure Finance Policy. Mauritius note that because of governmental budgetary constraints, the need for the private sector to be substantially involved in public services (e.g., roads, public hospitals, schools) is critical to ensuring delivery of better facilities, faster and generally cheaper over the long term through risk-adjusted and whole life costs of a particular service. The PPP option is an intimate element in all infrastructure project financing and delivery considerations.

A PPP Secretariat Unit in the Mauritius Ministry of Finance and Economic Development reviews projects for potential PPP financing based on its Infrastructure Finance Policy. PPP can be a useful mechanism for implementing land use planning projects contained in local plans or Action Area Plans and through MTEP, other ministries, and agencies scheme (Mauritius NDP, 2004).

The Capital Improvements Project Plan Committee, under the Finance and Audit Act, was initiated to ensure that capital projects are designed and delivered, risks adequately assessed, and projects are implemented on time and within budget. The Project implementation unit is in five ministries and departments. There is a multidisciplinary project unit made up of technical officers and consultants in engineering, economics/finance, and project management.

An Asset Register has been developed in the Accountant-General Department to improve the recording of capital infrastructure and help in the determination of capital infrastructure's value and in budgeting for capital infrastructure, including acquisition, upgrading maintenance, and disposal. An Asset Replacement Program (buildings, vehicles, equipment) has been developed and implemented through line ministries.

Mauritius has identified government borrowing on the domestic market as a primary source for financing capital infrastructure. As part of the Investment Implementation Plan, the government overhauled its Public Investment Management Framework to speed implementation, transparency in procurement, and obtain Value-for-the-Money. It also set up an alternative method for procurement through Build Operate and Transfer (BOT) for line Ministries for implementation of capital projects. The BOT Act (see Chapter 3) provides for private sector participation in capital infrastructure financing and delivery. The Act provides a legal framework for a simple and effective process for facilitating the expeditious implementation of BOT projects and ensures value for money, transparency, and accountability (Mauritius Investment Guide, 2015).

In implementing its Infrastructure Finance Policy, Mauritius uses a Public Sector Investment Program document that lays out the Infrastructure Finance Plans for 5 years based on its Strategic Plan. The plan is updated when the Budget is presented. The capital projects listed in the document reflect the priorities and values articulated in the needs, objectives, and priorities and laid out in the Medium-Term Expenditure Plan. The capital projects list in the document describes the objectives, project benefits, and community priorities, which are prioritized in the Budget document. The Mauritius Budget describes how capital projects are prioritized in the budget and the method used for systematic project selection. The Infrastructure Finance Policy design, as in the case of Mauritius, is implemented through the capital improvements plan. The capital projects selected as potential PPPs are specific and quantifiable and tied to the infrastructure finance policy. The capital project preparation process includes mechanisms to solicit expert advice internally and externally.

Mauritius is an example of a country which has a well-designed Infrastructure Finance Policy. As a result, the use of Public-Private Partnerships, which are supported by strong institutional dimensions, the policy is implemented successfully. Albania is an example of an emerging economy which has a well-designed Infrastructure Finance Policy and uses Public-Private Partnerships but has fragmented and weak institutional dimensions with which to implement their policy.

A government's Infrastructure Finance Policy design provides a Public-Private Partnership option in order to (1) have a more efficient and effective overall capital planning, management, and budgeting program, (2) provide capital improvements on time and within capital budget, (3) more effectively manage the use of long-term debt and provide for more enhanced public value, and (4) provide a better balance between traditional means of funding government capital improvements (long-term debt, equity financing, and capital reserves) and private financing.

While there are capital infrastructure private partnership investment opportunities available on a global level, private investors in government capital infrastructure often do not fully take advantage of these opportunities, usually because of weak government Infrastructure Finance Policy (Klepsvik, Emery, Finn, & Bernhard, 2014). Capital infrastructure investment can pose specific risks to private investors, even under normal circumstances. The choice of using of one single private partner through a PPP arrangement with government under an Infrastructure Finance Policy is a relatively recent basis for capital infrastructure financing and delivery in many countries. Some countries do not yet have either the necessary basic capital infrastructure in-house contacting expertise for choosing a PPP or experience and capacity to manage the inherent risks involved in complex PPPs. In that case they need to include training in PPP contract negotiation and implementation as part of their PPP policy implementation. A well-developed policy (such as Infrastructure Finance Policy design and implementation) can provide a basis to appropriately increase the quality and quantity of private investment in (and delivery of) infrastructure (Klepsvik et al., 2014) because it spells out the government infrastructure finance policy priorities. The resulting efficient and effective use of both public and private resources to finance and deliver infrastructure ensures quality infrastructure which delivers public value to its citizens.

# References


Abdel-Aziz, A. (2007). Successful delivery of public-private partnerships in infrastructure development. *Journal of Construction Engineering and Management*, *133*(12), 918–931.

Adarkwa, O., Smadi, O., & Alhasan, A. (2017). Lessons to be learned from bankruptcy filings in public-private partnership (PPP) filings in the United States. Iowa Center for Transportation Research and Education. *MOJ Civil Engineering*, *2*, 66–70.

African Development Bank (AfDB). (2018). Transforming Africa's transport sector through PPPs. Retrieved from www.AfDB.org. Accessed on May 15, 2019.

African Development Bank. (2019). Evaluation of AfDB's use of PPPs report. Retrieved from www.AfDB.org. Accessed on September 30, 2019.

Akintoye, A., & Beck, M. (2009). *Policy, finance and management for public-private partnerships*. West Sussex: Wiley-Blackwell.

Albania Mof. (2014). Retrieved from http://www.financa.gov.al/. Accessed on May 10, 2019.

Albanian Law of 2013. (2013). Albanian Law of 2013, Article 8 (5) of Law No 125/2013. Retrieved from albanianlawblogspot.com. Accessed on June 19, 2019.

Alesina, A., & Perotti, R. (1996). Income distribution, political instability and investment. *European Economic Review*, *40*(6), 1203–1228.

Alford, J., & Hughes, O. (2008). Public value pragmatism as the next phase of public management. *The American Review of Public Administration*, *38*(2), 130–148.

Alford, J., & O'Flynn, J. (2009). Making sense of public value: Concepts, critiques and emergent meanings. *International Journal of Public Administration*, *32*(3–4), 171–191, 626–639.

Ammar, S., Duncombe, W., & Wright, R. (2001). Evaluating capital management: A new approach. *Public Budgeting & Finance*, *21*(4), 47–69.

Amsler, L., & O'Leary, R. (2017). Collaborative public management and systems thinking. *International Journal of Public Sector Management*, *30*, 6–7.

Ansar, A., Flyvberg, B., Budzier, A., & Lunn, D. (2001). Should we build more large dams? The actual cost of hydrapower development. *Energy Policy*, *69*, 43–56.

Aoki, M. (2001). *Toward a comparative institutional analysis* (pp. 1–457). Cambridge, MA: MIT Press.

Aoki, M. (2007). Wither Japan's corporate governance? In M. Aoki, G. Jackson, & H. Meyajima (Eds.), *Corporate governance in Japan: Institutions, change and organizational diversity*. New York, NY: Oxford University Press.

APEC/OCED. (2019). *Financing infrastructure in APEC economies: APEC/OCED report on selected effective approaches*. Paris: Asian Development Bank. Land Policy. Retrieved from www.adb.org. Accessed on May 16, 2019.

Aronson, J. R., & Schwartz, E. (2004). *Management policies in local government finance* (5th ed.). Washington, DC: ICMA.

Asian Development Bank. (2012). *Public-Private Partnership Operational Plan 2012–2020*. Retrieved from www.adb.org. Accessed on May 7, 2019.

Asian Development Bank. (2019). *How PPPs advisory services can narrow Asia's infrastructure gap*. Retrieved from www.adb.org. Accessed on May 9, 2019.

Asongu, S., & Kodila-Tedika, O. (2016). Tribalism and government effectiveness. MPR Working Paper No. 78142. *Economics Bulletin*, *37*(1), 1–16. Retrieved from https://mpra.ub.uni-muenchen.de/78142/1/MPRA_paper_78142.pdf

Athias, L., & Saussier, S. (2010). Contractual flexibility or rigidity for public-private partnerships? *Theory and evidence from infrastructure concession contracts*. doi: 10.2139/ssrn.828944. Retrieved from https://www.researchgate.net/publication/24112198. Accessed on January 3, 2020.

Bajari, P., Houghton, S., & Tadelis, S. (2014). Bidding for incomplete contracts: An empirical analysis of adaptation costs. *The American Economic Review*, *104*(4), 1288–1319.

Baker, N. B. (2016). Transaction costs in public–private partnerships: The weight of institutional quality in developing countries revisited. *Public Performance and Management Review*, *40*(2), 431–455.

Baker, N. B., Khater, M., & Haddad, C. (2019). Political stability and the contribution of investment commitments in infrastructure to GDP: An institutional perspective. *Public Performance and Management Review*, *42*(4), 808–835.

Balasubramanian, P., Jovanovic, B., & Kirk, J. (2010). *Feasibility study of the arenal volcano wind project* (pp. 1–218). Unpublished Master's thesis, Worcester Polytechnic Institute, Worcester, MA.

Beckett-Camarata, J. (1998). *An empirical investigation of strategic planning and its effect on financial performance*. Unpublished Ph.D. Dissertation, Virginia Commonwealth University.

Beckett-Camarata, J. (2003). An Examination of the relationship between the municipal strategic plan and the capital budget and its effect on financial performance. *Journal of Public Budgeting*, *15*(1), 23–40.

Beckett-Camarata, J. (2018). Public Choice and Financing Local Government Reform in Albania. In H. Levine & K. Moreno (Eds), *Positioning governments and markets in public management* (pp. 186-197). Hershey, PA: IGI Global.

Beckett-Camarata, J. (2019). Capital management and budgeting processes in Albania. In A. Srithongrung, N. B. Ermasova, & J.-E. Yusuf (Eds.), *Capital management and budgeting in the public sector* (pp. 157–177). Hershey, PA: IGI Global.

Benington, J., & Moore, M. H. (2011). *Public value: Theory and practice*. New York: McMillan International Higher Education.

Bergstahler, D., Hail, L., & Leuz, C. (2006). The importance of reporting incentives: Earnings management in European public and private firms. *The Accounting Review*, *81*(5), 983–1016.

Bhatia, S. (2019). Public sector finances as determinants of private investment in PPP projects: Experiences from select countries. *Journal of Economics, Management and Trade*, *23*(6), 1–17.

Bilodeau, B., Laurin, C., & Vining, A. (2007). Choice of organizational form makes a real difference: The impact of corporatization on government agencies in Canada. *Journal of Public Administration Research and Theory*, *17*(1), 119–147.

Biondi, Y., & Sierra, M. (2016). Accounting for Pension Obligations in the European Union: A Case Study for EPSAS and Transnational Budgetary Supervision (May 27, 2016). 14th International Conference on Pension, Insurance and Savings, University of Paris Dauphine and University of Berkeley, Paris, 9 and 10 May, 2016, 83rd International Atlantic Economic Conference (IAES), Berlin, 22–25 March 2017, SSRN. Retrieved from https://ssrn.com/abstract=2785725. Accessed on October 10, 2019.

Blanc-Brude, F., Goldsmith, H., & Valila, T. (2009). A comparison of construction contract prices for traditionally procured roads and public-private partnerships. *Review of Industrial Organization*, *35*(1–2), 19–40.

Bland, R., & Rubin, I. (1997). *Budgeting: A guide for local government*. Washington, DC: International City/County Management Association.

Boardman, A. E., & Vining, A. (2012). The political economy of public-private partnerships and analysis of their social value. *Annals of Public and Cooperative Economics*, *83*, 117–141.

Boardman, Anthony E., Siemiatycki, M., & Vining, A, (2016). The Theory and evidence concerning public-private partnerships in Canada and elsewhere (March 1, 2016). SPP Research Paper 9(12). SSRN. Retrieved from https://ssrn.com/abstract=2804683. Accessed on February 20, 2020.

Bosworth, B., & Miluseva, S. (2016). Innovations in infrastructure financing. Retrieved from www.brookings.edu. Accessed on October 5, 2019.

Boyer, E. J., & Scheller, D. S. (2008). An examination of state-level public-private partnership adoption: Analyzing economic, political and demand related determinants of PPPs. *Public Works Management and Policy*, *23*(1), 5–33.

Boyle, M. (2009). Two kinds of self-knowledge. *Philosophy and Phenomenological Research*, *78*(1), 133–164.

Brousseau, E., & Glachant, J. (2002). The economics of contracts and the renewal of economics. In E. Brousseau & J. Glachant (Eds.), *The economics of contracts: Theories and applications* (pp. 3–30). Cambridge; New York, NY: Cambridge University Press.

Brown, T. L., Patoski, M., & Van Slyke, D. M. (2018). Complex contracting: Management challenges and solutions. *Public Administration Review*, *78*(5), 739–747.

Bryson, J. M., Crosby, B. C., & Bloomberg, L. (2014). *Public value and public administration*. Washington, DC: Georgetown University Press.

Buckberg, E., Kearney, O., & Stolleman, N. (2015). *Expanding the market for infrastructure public-private partnerships: Alternative risk and profit-sharing approaches to align sponsor and investor interests* (pp. 1–29). U.S. Treasury. Retrieved from USTreasury.gov. Accessed on July, 2019.

Bunch, B. (2013). Capital planning and budgeting. In J. R. Bartle, W. B. Hildreth, & J. Marlowe (Eds.), *Management policies in local government finance* (6th ed., pp. 253–278). Washington, DC: International City/County Management Association.

Buso, M., Marty, F., & Tra, T. P. (2014). *Public private partnerships from budget constraints: Looking for debt hiding?* Hal.id 01275217. Retrieved from https://halshs.archives-ouvertes.fr/halshs-01275217/document. Accessed on December 12, 2019.

C40 Cities Facility. (2017). The C40 cities finance facility supports cities to support and deliver climate change projects. Retrieved from www.c40cff.org. Accessed on September 19, 2019.

Caribbean Development Bank. (2017). Caribbean PPP Toolkit (2017). Retrieved from www.sustainableids.org. Accessed on August 10, 2019.

Caribbean PPP Toolkit. (2017). Retrieved from www.sustainableids.org. Accessed on August 10, 2019.

Cassady, C., Darraugh, F., Geddes, R. R., Palcic, D., & Reeves, E. (2019). Understanding PPP tendering periods in Canada: A duration analysis. *Public Performance and Management Review*, *42*(6), 1259–1278.

CDC Group.uk. (2019). Our investments. Retrieved from www.cdcgroup.com. Accessed on July 10, 2019.

Center on Budget and Policy Priorities. (2019). Che-Ching Huang. Policy basics: Tax expenditure. Retrieved from https://www.cbpp.org/research/federal-tax/policy-basics-federal-tax-expenditures. Accessed on June 5, 2019.

Chan, A. P., Lam, P. T. I., Chan, D. W. M., Cheung, E., & Ke, Y. (2010). Critical success factors in PPPs in infrastructure developments: Chinese perspective. *Journal of Construction Engineering and Management*, *5*(136). 484–494.

Cheung, E., Chan, A., & Kajewski, S. (2012). Factors contributing to successful public private partnership projects: Comparing Hong Kong with Australia and the United Kingdom. *Journal of Facilities Management*, *10*, 45–58. doi:10.1108/14725961211200397

Chicago Federal Reserve Board. (2019). Chicago fed letter. Retrieved from www.chicagofed.org/publications/chicago-fed-letter. Accessed on November 2019.

Chohan, U. (2019). *Public value theory and budgeting: International perspectives*. London: Routledge.

Chohan, U., & Jacobs, U. (2017). Public value in politics: A legislative budget office approach. *International Journal of Public Administration*, *40*, 1–11.

Civil Code of the Republic of Albania. (2012). Albania's constitution of 1998 with amendments through 2012 Retrieved from https://www.constituteproject.org/constitution/Albania_2012.pdf?lang=en. Accessed on August 13, 2019.

Clark, R. M., & Hakin, S. (2019). *Public-private partnerships*. Cham: Springer.

Coase, R. (1937). The nature of the firm. *Econometrica*, *4*, 386–405.

Coase, R. (1984). The new institutional economics: A symposium. *Journal of Institutional and Theoretical Economics*, *140*(1), 229–231. Retrieved from https://chicagounbound.uchicago.edu/journal_articles/2966/. Accessed on February 5, 2020.

Congressional Budget Office. (2012). *Using public-private partnerships to carry out highway projects* (pp. 1–31). Retrieved from www.cbo.gov. Accessed on May 7, 2019.

Crocker, K. J., & Masten, S. (1996). Regulation and revisited contracts revisited: Lessons for transaction cost economics for public utility regulation. *Journal of Regulatory Economics*, *9*(1), 5–39.

Crocker, K. J., & Reynolds, K. J. (1993). The efficiency of incomplete contracts: An empirical analysis of air force engine procurement. *The RAND Journal of Economics*, *24*(1), 126–146.

Crus, C. O., & Marques, R. C. (2013). Exogenous determinants for renegotiating public infrastructure concessions: Evidence from Portugal. *Journal of Construction Engineering and Management, 139*(9), 1–37.

Cuttaree, V. (2008). Successes and Failures of PPP Projects. Paper presented at Seminar on Legal, Economic and Implementation Issues in Public-Private Partnership (PPP) Projects. Warsaw, June 27, 2008. Retrieved from http://siteresources.worldbank.org 12/18. Accessed on February 1, 2019.

DeVries, P., & Yehoue, E.B. (2013). *The Routledge companion to public-private partnerships* (pp. 9–38). Abingdon: Routledge.

DiNapoli, T. P. (2014). *Planning and financing New York State's capital investments* (pp. 1–25). Albany, NY: Office of New York State Comptroller. Retrieved from www.osc.state.ny.us/reports/capital_report. Accessed on May 14, 2019.

DiNapoli, T. P. (2016). Capital assets. Retrieved from https://www.osc.state.ny.us/localgov/pubs/listacctg.htm#capital. Accessed on October 2019.

DiNapoli, T. P. (2018). *First half of 2018: Highest growth in New York State sales tax in almost eight years* (pp. 1–10). Albany, NY: Office of the New York State Comptroller. Retrieved from www.osc.state.ny.us/reports. Accessed on July 15, 2019.

Donohue, N. (2019). Commonwealth of Virginia SmartScale Project. Presented at Federal Reserve of Chicago. April 5, 2019. Retrieved from https://www.civicfed.org/sites/default/files/unlocking_the_box-pagano.pdf. Accessed on November 10, 2019.

Dosi, C., & Moretto, M. (2013). Procurement with unenforceable contract time and law of liquidated damages. *Journal of Law, Economics, and Organization, 31*(1), 160–186.

Dudkin, G., & Valila, T. (2005). Transaction costs in public-private partnerships: A first look at the evidence. *Competition and Regulation in Network Industries, 1*, 1–47.

Dumez, H., & Jeunemaitre, A. (2010). The management of organizational boundaries: A case study. *Dans Management, 113*, 152–171.

Ebdon, C. (2004). Capital management practices in U.S. counties. *Public Works Management and Policy, 8*(3), 192–202.

Eckerd, A., & Heidelberg, R. L. (2015). Public incentives, market motivations, and contaminated properties: New public management and brownfield liability reform. *Public Administration Review, 75*(10), 252–261.

Eggertsson, T. (2005). *Imperfect institutions: Possibilities and limits of reform*. Ann Arbor, MI: University of Michigan Press.

EPEC. (2011). The European PPP expertise center. *2011 Activities*. Retrieved from https://ec.europa.eu/economy_finance/events/2011/2011-11-08_ec-epec/pdf/barret_thadden_8_nov_2011_brussels_en.pdf. Accessed on August 1, 2019.

Epstein, D., & O'Halloran, S. (1999). *Delegating powers: A transaction cost politics approach to policy making under separate powers*. Cambridge; New York, NY: Cambridge University Press.

European Bank for Reconstruction and Development (EBRD). (2011). European bank finances the Tirana Airport PPP for reconstruction and development. Retrieved from www.ebrd.com. Accessed on July 20, 2019.

European Bank for Reconstruction and Development (EBRD). (2017). Legal assessment PPP-cbrd. Retrieved from https://ppp-ebrd.com/. Accessed on May 17, 2019.

European Bank for Reconstruction and Development (EBRD). (2019). Municipal public-private partnership framework. Retrieved from www.ebrd.com. Accessed on May 30, 2019.

European Court of Auditors (ECA) Special Report. (2018). PPPs in the EU: Widespread shortcomings and limited benefits. Retrieved from https://www.eca.europa.eu/en/Pages/DocItem.aspx?did=45153. Accessed on May 30, 2019.

European Investment Bank (EIB). (2019). Investment resources. Retrieved from www.FranklinTempleton.com. Accessed on May 9, 2019.

Fishbein, J., & Morrell, C. (2009). Capital program considerations in challenging times. *Government Finance Review*, *15*(3), 15–23.

Fisher, R. C. (2016). *State and local public finance*. New York, NY: Routledge.

Franklin, Templeton. (2019). European Investment Bank. Retrieved from https://www.franklintempleton.com/?gclid=EAIaIQobChMIk9KF6gIVaQilCR0jDAUGEAAYASAAEgL1NPD_Bwe&gclsrc-aw.ds. Accessed on May, 2019.

Frieden, J. A. (2014). *Currency politics: The political economy of exchange rate policy*. Princeton, NJ: Princeton University Press.

G-20 Infrastructure Action Plan. (2019). G-20 infrastructure outcomes. Retrieved from www.ghub.org. Accessed on October 23, 2019.

Ghobadian, A., O'Regan, N., Gallear, D., & Viney, H. (2004). *Public-Private Partnerships: Policy and experience*. Basingstoke: Palgrave McMillan.

Giannakis, G. A., & McCue, C. P. (1999). *Local government budgeting: A managerial approach*. Westport, CT: Quorum Books.

Government Accountability Office (GAO). (1998). Leadings practices in capital decision-making (pp. 1–80). Retrieved from www.gao.gov. Accessed on January 9, 2020.

Government Finance Officers Association (GFOA). (2019). *Tax exempt financing: A primer*, 1–32. Retrieved from https://www.gfoa.org/sites/default/files/Tax-Exempt Financing_APrimer.pdf. Accessed on November 23, 2019.

Government Finance Officers Association (GFOA) Board. (2007). Capital-project monitoring and reporting (2007). Retrieved from www.gfoa.org. Accessed on October 23, 2019.

Government Finance Officers Association (GFOA) Board. (2019). Debt management policy. Retrieved from www.gfoa.org. Accessed on May 20, 2019.

Government Performance Project. (2005). Grading the states 2005: A look inside. Retrieved from www.results.gpponline.org/States. Accessed on May 20, 2019.

Governmental Accounting Standards Board (GASB). (2019). Capital assets. Retrieved from https://www.gasb.org/jsp/GASB/GASBContent_C/ProjectPage&cid=1176173270952

Grief, A., & Laitin, D. D. (2004). A theory of endogenous institutional change. *American Political Science Review*, *98*(4), 633–652.

Grimsey, D., & Lewis, M. K. (2002). Evaluating the risks for public private partnerships for infrastructure projects. *International Journal of Project Management*, *20*, 107–118.

Gross, J. (2018). To P3 or not to P3. *Government Finance Review*, *28*(3), 1–6.

Guasch, J. L. (2004). *Granting and renegotiating infrastructure concessions doing it right* (pp. 1–191). Washington, DC: The World Bank Institute.

Guzman, T., & Moldogaziev, T. (2012). Which bonds are more expensive? The cost differentials by debt issue purpose and the method of sale: An empirical analysis. *Public Budgeting and Finance*, *32*, 79–101.

Hammami, M., Ruhashyankko, J.-F., & Yehoue, E. B. (2006). *Determinants of public-private partnerships in infrastructure* (pp. 3–35). International Monetary Fund Institute. Working Paper. Washington, DC. Retrieved from www.imf.org. Accessed on December 9, 2019.

Hart, O. (2003). Incomplete contracts and public ownership: Remarks and an application to public-private partnerships. *The Economic Journal*, *13*(486), 69–76. Retrieved from https://onlinelibrary.wiley.com/doi/abs/10.1111/1468-0297.00119. Accessed on January 5, 2020.

Hart, O., & Moore, J. (1994). *Debt and seniority: An* analysis *of the* role *of hard* claims *in constraining management*. National Bureau of Economic Research Working Paper No. 4886. Cambridge, MA: NBER.

Hayo, B., & Voigt, S. (2007). Explaining de facto judicial independence. *International Review of Law and Economics*, *27*(3), 269–290.

Heavisides, B., & Price, I. (2001). Input versus output performance-based measurement in the NHS: The current system. *Facilities*, *19*(10), 344–356. Emerald Insight. Retrieved from researchgate.net. Accessed on January 20, 2010.

Helm, D., Wardlaw, J., & Caldeco, B. (2009). *Delivering a 21st century infrastructure for Britain*. London: Policy Exchange.

Hildreth, W. B. (2009). The financial logistics of disaster: The case of hurricane Katrina. *Public Performance and Management Review*, *32*(3), 400–436.

Ho, S. P. (2006). Model for financial renegotiation in public-private partnership projects and its policy implications: A game theoretic view. *Journal of Construction Engineering and Management*, *132*(7), 1–40. Retrieved from https://gpc.stanford.edu/sites/g/files/sbiybj8226/f/ping2011.pdf

Hodge, G. A. (2014). The risky business of public-private partnerships. *Australian Journal of Public Administration*, *63*(4), 37–49.

Hodge, G. A., & Greve, C. (2016). On public-private partnership: A contemporary review. *Public Works Management & Policy*, *22*(1), 1–14.

Holzrichter, M. (2019). Unlocking the box: Best practices for financing Illinois infrastructure. Retrieved from www.MayerBrown.com. Accessed on May 20, 2019.

Hou, X. C., Xu, Y. L., & Wang, Y. X. (2009). Analysis of critical risk factors in PPP sewage treatment projects based on a sewage treatment project in Quanzhou. *Construction Economy*, *4*, 40–43.

Huge, D., & Jones, W. (2015). Connecting P3s, bond ratings and debt calculation. *Government Finance Review*, *31*(6), 1–5.

Huizinga, H., Laeven, L., & Nicodeme, G. (2006). Capital structure and international debt shifting in Europe. *ETPF Research Paper*, *263*, 1–42.

Indiana Court of Appeals. (2019). C.J. Bradford, Chief Judge. Retrieved from www.in.gov/judiciary/appeals. Accessed on June 20, 2019.

Indiana Judiciary. (2019). C.J., Bradford, Chief Judge. Retrieved from www.in.gov/judiciary. Accessed on June 20, 2019.

Indiana PPP Code. (2016). Indiana Code 5-23-3-2. Retrieved from https://codes.findlaw.com/in/title-5-state-and-local-administration/in-code-sect-5-23-3-2.html. Accessed on June 20, 2019.

Indiana PPP Code. (2017). Indiana Code 5-23-1-1 to 5-23-7-2; 8-15-7. Retrieved from https://law.justia.com/codes/indiana/2017/title-5/article-23/chapter-1/section-5-231-1/. Accessed on June 20, 2019.

Indiana State Code Files. (2016). Indiana PPP code 815, 5-6-2. Retrieved from https://statecodesfiles.justia.com/Indiana/2016. Accessed on June 20, 2019.

Indiapost.com. (2019). The Economy of Mauritius (2019). Retrieved from www.indiapost.com. Accessed on August 12, 2019.

INDOT. (2016). Public-Private Partnerships. Retrieved from https://www.in.gov/indot/3186.htm. Accessed on June 20, 2019.

Infragov.com. (2015). State information. www.infragov.com. Retrieved from www.irmi.com/articles/expert-commentary. Accessed on February 15, 2020.

Interamerican Development Bank Group (IDB). (2019). Overview. Retrieved from www.imf.org. Accessed on May 10, 2019.

International Monetary Fund (IMF). (2019). Albania staff report. No. 19/207. Retrieved from www.sustainableids.org. Accessed on December 10, 2019.

Jamali, D. (2004). Success and failure mechanisms in public-private partnerships in developing countries: The Lebanese context. *International Journal of Public Sector Management*, *17*(5), 414–430.

Jordan, G. (1990). Sub-governments, policy communities and networks: Refilling the old bottles? *Journal of Theoretical Politics*, *2*, 319–338. Retrieved from https://journals.sagepub.com/doi/10.1177/0951692890002003004. Accessed on November 12, 2019.

Joskow, P. L. (1991). The role of transaction cost economics in antitrust and utility regulatory policies. *Journal of Law, Economics, and Organization*, *7*(Special Issue), 53–83.

Kaganova, O. (2011). Guidebook on capital investment planning for local governments. Urban development series; knowledge papers no. 13. Washington, DC: World Bank. Retrieved from https://openknowledge.worldbank.org/handle/10986/17394. Accessed on September 10, 2019.

Kerf, M., Gray, R. D., Irwin, T., Levesque, C., & Taylor, R. R. (1998). *Concession for infrastructure* (pp. 1–189). The World Bank/Inter-American Bank. World Bank Technical Papers No. 399. Washington, DC: The World Bank. Retrieved from https://documents.worldbank.org/en/publication/documents-reports/documentdetail/413031468766780427/undefined. Accessed on November 19, 2019.

Kettl, D. (2015). *The politics of the administrative process* (6th ed.). Thousand Oaks, CA: SAGE Publications.

Khmel, V., & Zhao, S. (2015). Arrangement of financing for highway infrastructure under the conditions of public-private partnerships. *International Association of Traffic and Safety Sciences*, *39*, 1–8.

Khoury, E. R. (2019). Governor Mario M. Cuomo bridge. Retrieved from www.HDRINC.com. Accessed on May 5, 2019.

King, J. R. (1995). Debt and equity financing. In S. Parthasarathi (Ed.), *Tax policy handbook* (pp. 158–160). Washington, DC: International Monetary Fund.

Klepsvik, K., Emery, R., Finn, B., & Bernhard, R. (2014). Budgeting in Albania. *OCED Journal on Budgeting*, *32*(2), 1–70. Retrieved from www.oced.org. Accessed on May 15, 2019.

Klijn, E. H., & Koppenjan, J. M. F. (2016). *Governance networks in public sector*. London: Routledge.

Koppenjan, J. F. M., & Enserink, B. (2009). Public-private partnerships in urban infrastructures: Reconciling private sector participation and sustainability. *Public Administration Review*, *69*, 284–296.

Kosmieja, M., & Paslawski, J. (2016). Flexible designing of large sports complex. *Archives of Civil Engineering*, *LXII*(2). 77–88. Retrieved from https://www.semanticscholar.org/paper/Flexible-Designing-of-Large-Sports-Complex-Ko%C5%9Bmieja-Paslawski/6af3eb2670000a8959fd0841145945c55a06127e. Accessed on February 10, 2020.

KPMG-mu. (2019). KPMG in Mauritius. Finance Act 2019. Retrieved from https://assets.kpmg/content/dam/kpmg/mu/pdf/2019/mu-Tax-Alert-Finance-Act-2019.pdf. Accessed on August 10, 2019.

Krane, D., Rigos, P. N., & Hill, N. B. (2001). *Home rule in America: A fifty-state handbook*. Washington, DC: CQ Press.

Kumari, A. & Sharma, A. K. (2017). Physical and Social Infrastructure in India and its relationship with economic development. *World Development Perspectives*, *5*, 30–33.

Kumari, A., & Sharma, A. K. (2018). Causal relationships among electricity consumption, foreign direct investment and and economic growth in India. *The Electricity Journal*, *31*(7), 33–38.

Kwak, Y. H., Chih, Y. Y., & Ebbs, C. W. (2009). Toward a comprehensive understanding of public-private partnerships for infrastructure development. *California Management Review*, *51*(2), 51–78.

Levy, S. M. (2011). *Public-Private Partnerships. Case studies on infrastructure development*. Reston, VA: American Society of Civil Engineers Press.

Liu, H. J., Love, P. E. D., Davis, P., & Smith, J. (2013). Performance measurement framework in PPP projects. Conference paper presented at International Conference on PPP Body of Knowledge at University of Central Lancashire, Preston, UK.

Lynn, L. E. (2009). Restoring the rule of law to public administration: What Frank Goodnow got right and Leonard White didn't. *Public Administration Review*, *69*(5): 803–813.

Marlowe, J. (2012). Capital budgeting and spending. In R. D. Ebel & J. E. Petersen (Eds.), *The Oxford handbook of state and local government finance*. New York, NY; Oxford: Oxford University Press.

Marlowe, J., Rivenbark, W. C., & Vogt, A. J. (2009). *Capital budgeting and finance: A guide for local governments*. Washington, DC: International City/County Management Association.

Mauritius 2015 Budget. (2015). At the Crossroads. Retrieved from http://budget.mof.govmu.org/budget2015/BudgetSpeech.pdf. Accessed on August, 2019.

Mauritius 2019/20 Budget Speech. (2019). Embracing a brighter future together as a nation. *Pravind Jugnauth*. Retrieved from www.pmo.govmu.org/Budget2018. Accessed on August 10, 2019.

Mauritius Cure Pipe Wind Farm Report. (2012). Mauritius action plan for wind technology. *Crisi*, 1–21. Retrieved from cdc-n.org. Accessed on June 22, 2019.

Mauritius Investment Guide. (2015). Retrieved from https://www.africalegalnetwork.com/russian/wp-content/uploads/2015/12/Mauritius-Investment-Guide-2015.pdf. Accessed on August 15, 2019.

Mauritius Ministry of Finance and Economic Development. (2019). Public Procurement Act (2006). Retrieved from http://publicprocurement.govmu.org/Pages/default.aspx. Accessed on June 13, 2019.

Mauritius Ministry of Renewable Energy and Public Utilities. (2012). Cure pipe wind farm report. Crisi Infrastructure Advisory. Retrieved from http://poublicutilities.govmu.org/English/Pages/default.aspx. Accessed on June 22, 2020.

Mauritius National Development Program (NDP). (2004). *Government of Mauritius national strategy* (Vol. 2). Retrieved from https//:search?q=Mauritius+National+Development+Plan+2004&oq=Mauritius+National+Development+Plan+2004. Accessed on May 18, 2019.

Mauritius PPP policy statement. (2003). Ministry of finance, financial services and corporate affairs. Retrieved from http://bot.govmu.org/English/Policy%20Statement/Pages/default.aspx. Accessed on June 18, 2019.

Mauritius PPP Regulations. (2008). Retrieved from http://mof.govmu.org/English/Documents/financial%20management%20kit/PubproReg2008UpdatedVersion140912.pdf. Accessed on June 18, 2019.

Mauritius Public Procurement Act. (2006). Ministry of Finance, Financial Services and Corporate Affairs. Retrieved from www.publicprocudement.govmu.org. Accessed on June 18, 2019.

Mauritius Strategic Plan. (2019). Pravind Jugnauth. Retrieved from http://budget.mof.govmu.org/ budget2018-19/2018_193-YearPlan.pdf. Accessed on June 9, 2019.

McQuaid, R. W., & Scherrer, W. (2010). Changing reasons for public-private partnerships (PPPs). *Public Money & Management*, *30*(1), 27–34.

Mikesell, J. L. (2014). *Fiscal administration: Analysis and applications for the public sector* (6th ed., pp. 1–625). Boston, MA: Cengage.

Melesi-Ferretti, G. M., & Moriyama, K. (2006). *Fiscal adjustment in EU countries: A balance sheet approach* (pp. 1–23). IMF Working Paper No. 04/143. Washington, DC: International Monetary Fund (IMF).

Millar, A. (1988). Selecting capital projects for local governments. *Public Budgeting and Finance*, *8*(3), 63–77.

Mintz, J., & Smart, M. (2006). *Incentives for public investment under fiscal rules*. World Bank Policy Research Working Paper 3860. Washington, DC: The World Bank. Retrieved from www.worldbank.com. Accessed on January 20, 2020.

Mooi, E. (2015). *Transaction cost analysis* (Vol. 9). Wiley Encyclopedia of Management. Hoboken, NJ: John Wiley & Sons.

Moore, M. (1995). *Creating public value: Strategic management in government*. Cambridge, MA: Harvard University Press.

Moynihan, D. P. (2009). Our useable past: An historical contextual approach to administrative values. *Public Administration Review*, *69*(5), 813–822.

Mujica, R. F. (2019). New York State budget (pp. 1 –1353). Albany, NY: Office of the New York State Governor. Retrieved from www.budget.ny.gov. Accessed on July 11, 2019.

Municipal Securities Rulemaking Board (MSRB). (2019). Denver Colorado airport terminal remodeling delays. Retrieved from www.msrb.org. Accessed on June 9, 2019.

Murphy, M. (2017). Strategies for managing state debt. Retrieved from www.PewTrusts.org. Accessed on September 19, 2019.

Musgrave, R. A. (1959). *The theory of public finance: A study in political economy*. New York, NY: McGraw-Hill.

Nabatchi, T. (2018). Public values frames in administration and governance. *Perspectives on Public Management and Governance*, *1*(1), 59–72.

National Association of State Budget Officers. (1999). Capital budgeting in the states-paths to success: A comparative analysis of capital budgeting practices in the states. Retrieved from www.NASBO.org. Accessed on January 15, 2020.

National Association of State Budget Officers (NASBO). (2014). Capital budgeting in the states. Retrieved from www.NASBO.org. Accessed on January 15, 2020.

Nederland, J, & Klijn, E. H. (2019). Stakeholder involvement in PPPs: Its influence on the innovative character of projects and project performance. *Administration & society*, *51*(8), 1200–1226.

Newman, J., & Perl, A. (2014). Partners in clime: Public-Private Partnerships and British Columbia's capacity to pursue climate policy objectives. *Canadian Public Administration*, *57*(2), 217–233.

New York Courts. (2019). Structure of the courts. Retrieved from www.courts.gov. Accessed on June 2019.

New York in-Depth. (2019). Appellate divisions of the New York state supreme court. Retrieved from www.guides.ll.georgetown.edu. Accessed on June, 2019.

New York State Assembly. (2015). PPP Act of State of New York, Chapter 56 of 2011 (p. 24). Retrieved from www.nyassembly.gov/leg. Accessed on September 9, 2019.

New York State Budget. (2000). New York State Executive Budget 2020. Retrieved from www.budget.ny.gov/pubs/archive/fy20. Accessed on September 19, 2019.

New York State Finance Law. (2012). Amended by Part HH of Chapter 58, 2012 Article 5-E, F. Retrieved from nysosc9.state.ny.us. Accessed on July 25, 2019.

New York State Finance Law. (2012b). Retrieved from www.farrelfritz.com/ny-state-finance-law-137

New York State Senate. (2011). Part F, Chapter 56 of the Laws of 2011. This Act cannot be found in New York State Consolidated Law since it only exists as part of the 2011 New York State budget language bill.

North, D.C. (2005). *Understanding the process of economic change*. Princeton, NJ: Princeton University Press.

New York State Senate. (2015). Retrieved from https:/www.nysenate.gov/legislation/bills/2015. Accessed on September 23, 2019.

New York State Unified Court. (2019). Retrieved from www.nycourts.gov/courts; www.moderncourts.org/wp-content. Accessed on June 19, 2019.

North, D. C. (1990). *Institutions, institutional change and economic performance*. Cambridge: Cambridge University Press.

North, D.C. (2005). *Understanding the process of economic change*. Princeton, NJ: Princeton University Press.

NYSFY2020 enacted capital program. (1999). NYSFY2020 capital program and financing plan. Retrieved from www.budget.nys.gov/pubs/archive/. Accessed on June 17, 2019.

OCED. (2008). Annual report on sustainable development work (pp. 1–44). Retrieved from https://www.oecd.org/greengrowth/sustainabledevelopmentkeyreports.htm. Accessed on June 2, 2019.

OCED. (2009). Private sector engagement in development co-operation.

OCED. (2015). Infrastructure financing investments and incentives (pp. 1–67). Retrieved from http://www.oecd.org/finance/private-pensions/Infrastructure-Financing-Instruments-and-Incentives.pdf. Accessed on May 2019.

OECD. (2017). International cooperation in corruption cases. Retrieved from https://www.oecd.org/corruption/acn/OECD-International-Cooperation-in-Corruption-Cases-2017.pdf. Accessed on June 19, 2019.

Olatunji, S., Olasula, O., Oluwatosin, T., & Rufus, D. (2016). Demystifying Issues Regarding Public Private Partnerships (PPP). *Journal of Economics and Sustainable Development*, *7*(1), 21–33. Retrieved from https://www.iiste.org/Journals/index.php/JEDS/article/view/31227. Accessed on February 12, 2019.

Osborne, S. (2002). *Public-private partnerships: Theory and practice in an international perspective*. Milton Park, Abingdon: Taylor & Francis.

Osei-Kyei, R., & Chan, A. (2015). Review of studies on the critical success factors for public–private partnership (PPP) projects from 1990 to 2013. *International Journal of Project Management*, *33*, 1–12. doi:10.1016/j.ijproman.2015.02.008

Ouchi, W. G. (1980). Markets, bureaucracies and clans. *Administrative Science Quarterly*, *25*(1), 129–141.

Overseas Private Investment Corporation. (2019). Now U.S. international finance development corporation. Retrieved from https://www.dfc.gov/. Accessed on May 2019.

Oyedele, L. O. (2013). Avoiding performance failure payment deductions in PFI/PPP projects: Model of critical success factors. *Journal of Performance of Constructed Facilities*, *27*(3), 283–294.

Pagano, M. (2002). Municipal capital spending during the boom. *Public Budgeting & Finance*, *22*(2), 1–20.

Pagano, M. (2019). Funding and investing in infrastructure. Paper presented at Federal Reserve of Chicago. April 5, 2019. Retrieved from https://www.civicfed.org/sites/default/files/unlocking_the_box-pagano.pdf. Accessed on November 10, 2019.

Paslawski, J., & Rozdzynska, M. (2013). Flexible approach in infrastructure design buffer parking case study. *Procedia Engineering*, *57*, 882–888.

PEFA. (2012). Public expenditure and financial accountability report, 2012. Albania (pp. 1-38). Retrieved from https://www.pefa.org/resources. Accessed on June, 2019.

Petersen, O. H. (2019). Evaluating the costs, quality and value for money of infrastructure public-private partnerships: A systematic literature review. *Special Issue: The Performance and Potential of Public-Private Partnerships*, *90*, 227–244.

Pongsiri, N. (2001). Regulation and Public-Private Partnerships. *International Journal of Public Sector Management*, *15*(6), 487–495.

PriceWaterhouseCoopers. (2010). Capital project and infrastructure spending outlook to 2025 (pp. 1–24). Retrieved from www.pWc.com. Accessed on February 5, 2020.

Prud'homme, P., & Bocajero, J. P. (2005). The London congestion charge: A tentative economic appraisal. *Transport Policy*, *12*(3), 279–287.

Puentes, R. (2014). The Indiana toll road: How did a good deal go bad? Forbes. Opinion. Curated by Avik Roy, Opinion Editor. Retrieved from www.Forbes.com/sites/realspin/2014/10/03/the-indiana-toll-road-how-did-a-good-deal-go-bad/#4cb8baac2087. Accessed on December 23, 2019.

Quanji, Z., Zhang, S., & Wang, Y. (2017). Contractual governance effects on cooperation in construction projects: A multi-functional approach. *Journal of Professional Issues in Engineering Education and Practice*, *143*(3), 1–11. Retrieved from https://ascelibrary.org/doi/abs/10.1061/(ASCE)EI.1943-5541.0000320. Accessed on February 1, 2020.

Rajaram, A., Kaiser, K., Le, T. M. Kim, J. H., & Frank, J. (2014). *The power of public investment management: Transforming resources into assets for growth*. Washington, DC: World Bank Group. Retrieved from Elibrary.worldbank.org

Ramboutsous, A. (2019). Tirana international airport concession. Retrieved from www.benefit4transport.eu. Accessed on May 2019.

Ramlugan, A. S. (2014). *Public-private partnership for road development in Mauritius: The case of Small Island Development States (SIDS)* (pp. 1–69). Unpublished MPhil, Stellenbosch University.

Republic of Albania. (2012). Albanian Civil Law (2012). Retrieved from albanianlawblogspot.com. Accessed on June 19, 2019.

Republic of Albania. (2013). Law of 2013 on Concessions and Public-Private Partnerships. Article 8 (5) of Law No. 125/2013. Retrieved from albanianlawblogspot.com. Accessed on June 19, 2019.

Republic of Mauritius Ministry of Renewable Energy and Public Utilities. (2012). Mauritius action plan for wind technology. Retrieved from publicutilities.govmu.org. Accessed on May 10, 2019.

Reynaers, A. M., & Grimmelikhuijsen, S. (2015). Transparency in public–private partnerships: Not so bad after all? *Public Administration Review*, *93*(3), 609–626.

Robinson, R. (1993). Costs and cost minimization analysis. *Economic Evaluation and Health Care*, *307*, 726–728. Retrieved from https://www.ncbi.nlm.nih.gov/pmc/articles/PMC1678700/pdf/bmj00039-0038.pdf. Accessed on December 2, 2019.

Robinson, H. S., & Scott, J. (2009). Service delivery and performance monitoring in PFI/PPP projects. *Construction Management & Economics*, *27*(2), 181–197.

Roehrich, J. K., Lewis, M., & Michael, G. (2014). Are public-private partnerships a healthy option? A systematic literature review. *Social Science & Medicine, 113*, 110–119.

Rosen, H. S., & Gayer, T. (2014). *Public finance* (10th ed.). Maidenhead: McGraw-Hill.

Rosenbloom, D. (1983). Public administration theory and the separation of powers. *Public Administration Review*, *43*(3), 219–227.

Rosenbloom, D. (2013). Conceptual Map for a Complex Field. *Public Administration Review*, *73*(2), 376–378.

Sachs, T., Tiong, R. L. K., & Wang, S. Q. (2007). Analysis of political risks and opportunities in public-private partnerships in China and selected countries. *Chinese Management Studies*, *1*(2), 126–148.

Salim, M., Shijaku, J., & Guxho, A. (2019). Albania economic reform programme report , 2019–2021 (pp. 1–160). Retrieved from https://financa.gov.al/wp-content/uploads/2019/02/Economic-Reform-Programme-2019-2021.pdf

Savas, E. S. (2000). *Privatization and public-private partnerships* (2nd ed.)New York, NY: CQ Press.

Scharle, P. (2002). Public-private partnerships as a social game. *Innovation: The European Journal of Social Science Research, 15*(3), 227–252.

Schaufelberger, J. E., & Wipadapisut, I. (2003). Alternative financing strategies for build-operate-transfer projects. *Journal of Construction Engineering and Management, 129*(2), 205–213.

Sfakianakis, E., & van de Laar, M. M. (2012). *Assessing contingent liabilities in public-private partnerships*. Working Papers No. 030. Maastricht Economic and Social Research Center, UNU-MERIT, Maastricht.

Siemiatycki, M. (2015). Public-private partnerships in Canada: Reflections on 20 years of practice. *Canadian Public Administration, 58*(3), 343–362.

SIGMA. (2001). SIGMA Policy Brief No. 31, EU Directives. Retrieved from http://www.sigmaweb.org/publications/35645551.pdf. Accessed on October 10, 2019.

Simon, H. (1979). Rational decision making in business organizations. *American Economic Review, 69*(4), 493–513.

Simon, H. (1982). *Models of bounded rationality*. Cambridge, MA: MIT Press.

Singhvi, S. (1996). Using an Affordability Analysis to Budget Capital Expenditures. *Healthcare Financial Management, 50*(6), 70–75.

Skelcher, C. (2005). Public-private partnerships and hybridity. In Ferlie, E., Lynn, L., & Pollitt, C. (Eds.), *The Oxford handbook of public management* (pp. 347–370). Oxford: Oxford University Press.

Smith, N., delaPena, P., Kussy, E., Sethi, S., Wheeler, P., Gifford, J., & Ybarra, S. (2019). *Public-private partnership procurement: A guide for public owners* (pp. 1–150). Washington, DC: U.S. Department of Transportation, Federal Highway Administration.

Smith, R. F. I. (2004). Focusing on public value: Something new and something old. *Australian Journal of Public Administration, 63*(4), 68–79.

Son, S. (2012). Legal analysis on public-private partnership regarding Model PPP rules. Retrieved from https://pdfs.semanticscholar.org/5e69/b1ecb658a70bccf2b8aef421d98b10c5f686.pdf. Accessed on July 10, 2019.

Srithongrung, A. (2006). The impact of state capital budget and management programs on state capital budget decisions and economic performance. Unpublished doctoral dissertation. University of Illinois, Springfield.

Srithongrung, A. (2016). Public finance and monetary policies as economic stabilizer: Unique or universal across countries? *Noesis Instituto de Ciencias Sociales y Administración, 25*, 13–46, 49.

Srithongrung, A. (2017). Capital budgeting and management practices: Smoothing out rough spots in capital outlays. *Public Budgeting and Finance, 38*(1), 47–71.

Srithongrung, A. (2019). Testing public capital budgeting and management theory using panel data analysis methods. In A. Srithongrung, N. Ermasova, & J. Yusuf (Eds.), *Sage research methods cases. Part 2*. Thousand Oaks, CA: SAGE Publications. Retrieved from https://www.uis.edu/iipf/research/academic-papers-and-presentations/. Accessed on February 17, 2020.

Srithongrung, Y., Yusuf, J.-E., & Kriz, K. A. (2019). A systematic public capital management and budgeting process. In Y. Srithongrung, J.-E. Yusuf, & N. B. Ermasova (Eds.), *Capital management and budgeting in the public sector*. Hershey, PA: IGI Global.

Standard and Poor's. (2019). How standard and poor standard and poor's treats PPP in US State and local government debt analysis. *Ratings Direct*. Retrieved from www.standardandpoor.com/ratingsdirect. Accessed on December 9, 2019.

Steiss, A. W. (2005). *Strategic facilities planning: Capital budgeting and debt administration*. Lanham, MD: Lexington Books.

Stiller, S., & Meirjerink, S. (2016). Leadership within regional climate change adaptation networks: The case of climate change officers in Northern Hesse, Germany. *Regional Environmental Change*, *16*, 1543–1555.

Sun, H. (2014). Improving the effectiveness of multi-year financial planning. *Government Finance Review*. Government Finance Officers Association, *20*(3), , 44–50.

Tax Expenditure Policy. (2019). Chye-Ching Huang. Center on Budget and Policy Priorities Retrieved from https://www.cbpp.org/. Accessed on June 8, 2019.

Tax Foundation. (2019). Sources of government revenue in the OCED, 2019. Retrieved from TaxFoundation.org. Accessed on May 10, 2019.

Thai, K. (2001). Public procurement reexamined. *Journal of Public Procurement*, *1*(1), 9–50.

The World Bank. PPP Country Profile; Mauritius PPA, Section 2. Retrieved from ppp.worldbank.org/

The World Bank. (2006).*Independent Evaluation Group. 2006. Hazards of Nature, Risks to Development : An IEG Evaluation of World Bank Assistance for Natural Disasters*. Washington, DC: World Bank. Retrieved from https://openknowledge.worldbank.org/handle/10986/7001. Accessed on August 11, 2019.

The World Bank. (2011a). Tirana international airport concession. Retrieved from www.ppp.worldbank.org. Accessed on August 11, 2019.

The World Bank. (2011b). Annual Report. Retrieved from siteresources.worldbank.org. Accessed on January 9, 2020.

The World Bank. (2013). Policy briefs. Albania. Retrieved from www.worldbank.org. Accessed on August 11, 2019.

The World Bank. (2014). World Bank to support Albania financial sector modernization. A Retrieved from siteresources.worldbank.org. Accessed on January 9, 2020.

The World Bank. (2014). World Bank to support Albania financial sector modernization. Retrieved from www.worldbank.org. Accessed on August 10, 2019.

The World Bank. (2015). The World Bank in Albania. Retrieved from https://www.worldbank.org/en/country/albania. Accessed on April 5, 2019.

The World Bank/International Bank for Reconstruction and Development. (2018). *Procuring infrastructure public-private partnership report* (pp. 1–234). Washington, DC: The World Bank Group.

The World Bank LRC. (2018). Public-Private Partnerships overview. Retrieved from https://ppp.worldbank.org/public-private-partnership/overview/insights-analysis. Accessed on June 22, 2020.

The World Bank PPPLRC. (2018a). Land policy. Public-private partnership legal resource center. Retrieved from www.worldbank.org. Accessed on July 23, 2019.

The World Bank PPPLRC. (2018b). Legal basis for evaluating PPPs. Retrieved from www.worldbank.org. Accessed on June 18, 2019.

Thomassen, K., Vassbo, S., Solheim-Kile, E., & Lohne, J. (2016). Public-private partnership: Transaction cost of tendering. *Procedia Computer Science*, *100*, 818–825.

Thomson Reuters. (2019). Project finance international. Retrieved from www.refinitiv.com. Accessed on September 10, 2019.

Tirana International Airport Study. Retrieved from www.Benefit4transport.eu. Accessed on May 5, 2019.

Toudas, K., Poutos, E., & Balios, D. (2013). Concept, regulations and institutional issues of IPSAS: A critical review. *European Journal of Business and Social Sciences*, *2*(1), 43–54.

Trenkner, T. (2011). The Indiana toll road: A model for privatization? Governing. Retrieved from https://www.governing.com/topics/mgmt/indiana-toll-road-model-privatization.html. Accessed on September 16, 2019.

Uddin, M., & Zack, J. (2016). Public-private partnership projects-what, why and how is risk allocated? *Navigant Construction*, *4*(1), , 1–28.

Unicef.org. (2017). United Nations and Government of Albania. Programme of cooperation for sustainable development 2017–2021 (pp. 1–57). Retrieved from www.unicef.org. Accessed on July 10, 2019.

United States Department of Transportation. (2019). U.S. Highway Administration. P3s. Retrieved from https://www.fhwa.dot.gov/ipd/p3/. Accessed on August 10, 2019.

Vining, A., & Boardman, A. (1992). Ownership versus competition: Efficiency in public enterprise. *Public Choice*, *73*(2), 205–239.

Vining, A., & Boardman, A. (2005). Public-private partnerships in the United States and Canada: There are no free lunches. *Journal of Comparative Policy Analysis: Research and Practice*, *7*(3), 199–220.

Vining, A., & Boardman, A. E. (2008). Public private partnerships: Eight rules for governments. *Public Works Management and Policy*, *13*(2), 149–161.

Vissier, F. G., Martin-Sisteron, H., & Seniuta, A. (2015). France. In B. Wernick, & M Saadi (Eds.), *The Public-Private Partnership law review* (pp. 74–90, Chapter 7). Hull: University of Hull.

Vining, A., & Boardman, A. E. (2008). Public private partnerships: Eight rules for governments. *Public Works Management and Policy*, *13*(2), 149–161.

Vogt, A. J. (2004). *Capital budgeting: A guide for local governments* (pp. 1–408). Washington, DC: International City/County Management Association.

Voltaic, J. (2019). How the army is strengthening cyber cities. Retrieved from www.Fifthdomain.com/dod/cities. Accessed on February 2, 2020.

Wang, H., Chen, B., Xiong, B., & Guangdong, W. (2018). Commercial investment in public-private partnerships. The impact of contract characteristics. *Policy & Politics*, *46*(4), 589–606.

Wang, H., Liu, Y., Xiong, W., & Zhou, D. (2018). Government support programs and private investments in PPP markets. *International Public Management Journal*, *22*(3), 499–523.

Warner, M. E., & Hafetz, A. (2012). Insourcing and outsourcing: The dynamics of privitazation in U.S. municipalities 2002–2007. *Journal of the American Planning Association*, *78*(3), 313–327.

Weimer, D. L., & Vining, A. R. (2017). *Policy analysis: Concepts and practice* (6th ed.). Milton Park, Abington, Oxfordshire: Routledge.

Weeklysift.com (9/14). Indiana Toll Road. Retrieved from http://weeklysift.com/ Accessed on June 22, 2019.

Westerman, N. (2004). Managing the capital budgeting cycle: Best practice examples of effective capital program maagement. *Government Finance Review*, *20*(3), 26–31.

Wettenhall, R. (2003). The rhetoric and reality of public-private partnerships. *Public Organization Review*, *3*(1), 77–107.

Windpower Engineering.com. (2014). Mauritius Utility Scale Wind Farm. Retrieved from https://www.windpowerengineering.com/. Accessed on May 10, 2019.

Williamson, O. E. (1975). Transaction cost economics: The governance of contractual relations. *The Journal of Law and Economics*, *22*(2), 233–261.

Williamson, O. E. (1981). The economics of organization: The transaction cost approach. *American Journal of Sociology*, *87*(3), 548–577.

Williamson, O. E. (1987). Transaction cost economics: The comparative contracting perspective. *Journal of Economic Behavior & Organization*, *8*(4), 617–625.

Williamson, O. E. (1999). Public and private bureaucracies: A transaction cost economics perspective. *Journal of Law, Economics, and Organization*, *15*(1), 306–342.

World Economic Forum. (2017). Sovereign wealth funds. Retrieved from www.weforum.org. Accessed on May 2019.

Xiong, W., Zhao, X., & Wang, H. (2018). Information asymmetry in renegotiation of public-private partnership. *Journal of Computing in Civil Engineering*, *32*(4), 1–11.

Zhang, X. Q. (2005). Critical success factors in public-private partnerships in infrastructure development. *Journal of Construction Engineering and Management*, *131*, 3–14.

Zou, W., Kumaraswamy, M., Chung, J., & Wong, J. (2014). Identifying the critical success factors for relationship management in PPP projects. *International Journal of Project Management*, *32*(2), 265–174.

# Index

Printed and bound by CPI Group (UK) Ltd, Croydon, CR0 4YY

13/09/2026

14961028-0004